More Praise for Chet Holmes and *The Ultimate Sales Machine*

"Chet Holmes is one of the best marketers on the planet. This book proves it. It's a landmark work that you could read and reread forever and just keep getting more and more out of it."

—Hale Dwoskin, *New York Times* bestselling author of *The Sedona Method*

"We all sell for a living—some of us know this and the rest of us don't yet. Either way you have to read this book. Chet Holmes is a consummate professional with sales and marketing know-how that even Homer Simpson could implement without a brain transplant. . . . Applying the success systems in this book will transform your business and your life."

—Stewart Emery, bestselling coauthor of *Success Built to Last*

"Nobody knows more about how to create the ultimate sales machine than Chet Holmes. Read this book and supercharge your business."

—Mark Thompson, bestselling coauthor of *Success Built to Last*

"I built my first company to become the fifty-ninth fastest growing private company in America, and my second one to $85 million in just twenty-one months. We used Chet's concepts at both companies and there is just no one that has such powerful yet practical ways to grow companies. And I love the idea that to be great you only need to know twelve things, not four thousand. That's proven to be so true in my life."

—Scott Hallman, CEO, Business Growth Dynamics, Inc.

"Rarely does a CEO have the opportunity to work with someone as talented as Chet Holmes. In growing my own company, Chet was instrumental in causing a quantum leap in the growth of our sales. . . . Profound changes in your organization are possible by applying the simple yet powerful truths Chet explains in what may be the best business book ever written. As an adviser to CEOs and organizations of every size, I draw on Chet's techniques in every engagement."

—Mitch Russo, founder and former CEO, Timeslips Corporation

"This is by far the best sales book I have ever read and I have read hundreds. As someone who runs [more than] fifteen companies and employs more than six hundred people, I can honestly say this is a book I will refer to for decades to come."   —A. Harrison Barnes, CEO, Juriscape

"Chet's material on 'setting the buying criteria in your favor' is a market breakthrough concept that can propel any company forward if they are wise enough to create it. That one idea, fully embraced can take any company to an entirely new level, enabling them to crush competitors and start a landslide in their favor. I used all of Chet's concepts at Pac Bell and in all my endeavors since the days I discovered them."

—Marc X. Pearl, vice president of sales and marketing, Pacific Bell

"Chiropractors are quintessential small business owners who function more like practitioners than business owners. Chet's material has helped rejuvenate many a chiropractic office as well as helping them really run an excellent business that is highly profitable. More than 3,000 of our chiropractor members have participated in Chet's Mega Marketing program and the endorsements are outstanding."

—Steve Seater, executive director,
Foundation for Chiropractic Education & Research

"This book will be a classic for as long as businesses seek to improve their profits, their sales and their futures."

—Jay Conrad Levinson, author of the Guerrilla Marketing series
(from the note to the reader)

"Chet not only knows more and better ways to grow sales than probably anyone, but even more important, he has the systems that make his concepts realistic and easy to implement. Most of the books I've read on business growth are interesting. But this man's material is out-of-the-park great."

—Loral Langemeier, author of *The Millionaire Maker's Guide to Creating a Cash Machine for Life*

"Far more than just another sales book."   —*Entrepreneur Magazine*

"A holistic sales and marketing campaign that works."   —*Booklist*

"A powerful, entertaining guidebook to mastering the fundamentals that drive thriving sales."   —*Kirkus Reviews*

ABOUT THE AUTHOR

Chet Holmes is an acclaimed corporate trainer, strategic mastermind, business growth expert, and lecturer. His nearly one thousand clients have included major companies like Pacific Bell, NBC, Citibank, Warner Bros., GNC, Wells Fargo, Estée Lauder, Merrill Lynch, and W. R. Grace, as well as small businesses of every kind. Holmes has also designed hundreds of advertising campaigns and sales systems for hundreds of industries. He lives in Los Angeles, California.

Turn your business into the Ultimate Sales Machine today!
Visit www.chetholmes.com/book

The Ultimate Sales Machine

Turbocharge Your Business with Relentless Focus on 12 Key Strategies

CHET HOLMES

PORTFOLIO

PORTFOLIO
Published by the Penguin Group
Penguin Group (USA) Inc., 375 Hudson Street, New York, New York 10014, U.S.A.
Penguin Group (Canada), 90 Eglinton Avenue East, Suite 700, Toronto, Ontario,
Canada M4P 2Y3 (a division of Pearson Penguin Canada Inc.)
Penguin Books Ltd, 80 Strand, London WC2R 0RL, England
Penguin Ireland, 25 St Stephen's Green, Dublin 2, Ireland
(a division of Penguin Books Ltd)
Penguin Group (Australia), 250 Camberwell Road, Camberwell, Victoria 3124,
Australia (a division of Pearson Australia Group Pty Ltd)
Penguin Books India Pvt Ltd, 11 Community Centre, Panchsheel Park,
New Delhi – 110 017, India
Penguin Group (NZ), 67 Apollo Drive, Rosedale, North Shore 0632, New Zealand
(a division of Pearson New Zealand Ltd)
Penguin Books (South Africa) (Pty) Ltd, 24 Sturdee Avenue,
Rosebank, Johannesburg 2196, South Africa

Penguin Books Ltd, Registered Offices: 80 Strand, London WC2R 0RL, England

First published in the United States of America by Portfolio,
a member of Penguin Group (USA) Inc. 2007
This paperback edition published 2008

13 15 17 19 20 18 16 14

THE LIBRARY OF CONGRESS HAS CATALOGED THE HARDCOVER EDITION AS FOLLOWS:
Holmes, Chet.
The ultimate sales machine : turbocharge your business with relentless focus on 12 key
strategies / by Chet Holmes.
p. cm.
Includes bibliographical references and index.
ISBN 978-1-59184-160-9 (hc.)
ISBN 978-1-59184-215-6 (pbk.)
1. Sales management. 2. Organizational effectiveness. I. Title.
HF5438. 4. H63 2007
658.8'1—dc22   2007003251

Printed in the United States of America
Designed by Helene Berinsky

This book is dedicated to the best person
I've ever known my entire life.
And I got to marry her.
The "salt of the earth" never tasted so sweet.

To my Vickey, the lady fantastic

Acknowledgments

On the business side, I'd like to thank Jay Abraham for being a great partner and teaching me so much about growing companies, Jay Levinson for encouraging me to write this book (only took 10 years, Jay, but I did it), Napoleon Hill for inspiring me to want to rise above the trials of a misspent youth, and Howard Linker for handing me that book that changed my life. Thank you to every major trainer out there as I have been like a sponge my entire life, learning from everyone—Tony Robbins, Michael Gerber, Tom Hopkins, Wayne Dyer, Brian Tracy, Denis Waitley, and so on. Thank you, Charlie Munger, for providing me with the first place I ever worked where I had the freedom to prove my theories. Thank you, Dick Harrington, for being my first client when I started my own companies and for teaching me how to make things happen in large-scale organizations. You were a powerful influence and teacher to me and I'm very grateful.

I'd surely like to thank my agent, Lorin Rees, for helping me create a razor-sharp book outline. I'd like to thank my editor, Adrienne Schultz, who helped to sharpen every sentence and chapter. The reinforcement provided by Bruce Sylvester was amazing. He is the most detailed person I've ever known. The entire team at Portfolio—including Adrian Zackheim, smart as a whip, and Will Weisser, devoted to spreading the word—has been a pleasure to work with.

I'd also like to thank Kimberly Delaney, the backbone of the project, who helped me assemble all this material and turn it into a well-organized book.

On the personal side, I'd like to thank my father for teaching me about courage and my mother for giving me so many gifts, from art to music to, most important, the belief in myself that I could accomplish anything. Thanks to my second mom, June, who is the epitome of sophistication and grace under pressure. You helped sculpt me as a young adult and gave me a brother and three more sisters, whom I adore. Thank you to my wife, Vickey, who has been like the calm in my storm, and my children, Jordan and Amanda, who are my greatest source of hope and joy. Okay, Baby, too.

Thanks also go to my friends who taught me things that helped shape my life for the better—especially to Tom Shepard (the Sundance to my Butch Cassidy), Mitch, Scott, Marc, Kit, Paul, and Ralph. You are the only true friends in this long life. I am privileged to know you. To my spiritual genius friend, Hale Dworskin, a special thank you.

I also thank my brother Tim for his hidden beauty that I see so clearly, my sister Vicki for her indomitable spirit, Martin (who I hope will live up to his enormous potential), and, lastly, Stephen M. Ryder. I will forever acknowledge how you took me from the life I was headed for and set me on a path of learning. You set my soul on fire with your great writing. You awakened my ambition at every level, and you sculpted the early founda-tions of my telephone skills that have helped me get to just about anyone on Earth. I'll always remember the good times, like rehearsing Kings in Bloomfield. I never laughed so hard. I want you to know (to quote your own great writing), "Wherever you are, if you think of me and smile—at that very moment—wherever I am, I'll be smiling too."

Contents

A Note to the Reader

I've heard Chet Holmes speak on many occasions, and I've had the privilege of working with him on many others. He is so accomplished and wise in a broad array of topics that I began to encourage him to write a book. It took a lot of pigheaded discipline and determination on my part to finally get him to do it.

Now that I've read *The Ultimate Sales Machine*, I'm even more proud of my accomplishment in getting Chet to finally put it all into writing. All along, I thought that he would select one of his many areas of expertise as the topic for the book. I had no idea that he would include all the areas in one masterful book. I knew that Chet was a brilliant speaker. And I also knew that he was a talented scriptwriter. But I never dreamt that he was as good a writer as he demonstrates in this book or that he could bring to business nonfiction the same level of drop-dead ability that he brings to general audience movie scripts.

As the author of 56 books myself, it has always been my hope that motivated and success-bound business people would read a lot of books. But after reading this book, I realize that in truth, it's all a business person needs to read. Every important aspect of business is covered by Chet in these pages—and they're covered with information that many of you have never heard before. You'll never be able to accuse Chet of being shallow. There are profound insights in this book, crucial details and personal experiences that separate it from every other book on the shelves of your library or bookstore.

Although Chet is a karate master, he pulls no punches in these pages. Learning from him is like learning from a world-class teacher, which comes as no surprise because Chet is truly a world-class teacher. This book will be a classic for as long as businesses seek to improve their profits, their sales, and their futures. Thank you, Chet, for proving that my pigheaded discipline and determination were richly rewarded.

> —Jay Conrad Levinson,
> the father of guerrilla marketing and
> author of the *Guerrilla Marketing* series.
> More than 14 million sold;
> now in 43 languages.

Foreword: When Words Are Never Enough

When Chet Holmes called to tell me he was coming out with a book and would I take a look at it, I thought to myself, Oh, Chet, not another book on sales.

Don't misunderstand me; Chet is a barn burner when it comes to sales.

Chet is a master at what he does.

Chet knows stuff about the selling cycle; the selling system; the positioning of products, services, and companies; and the people who build them and sell them that very few of us in the business of business have ever learned.

But still, my heart hung heavy and my shoulders, too, when Chet called to ask me if I would simply take a look at a few chapters of this new book and perhaps say something nice about what I saw.

But given that Chet is a friend and a master, too, I gritted my teeth and said simply that I would, knowing in my heart that no matter how much a master of sales Chet is, there are very very few folks who can turn that skill into a book that people read, and then read again because the words and the way they are arranged capture the imagination as all great stories do.

I was afraid that when I began to read his book, I would have to tell him the truth: books are hard to do, Chet, but what the hell, you did a good job, and there are so many other things you're good at, you'll never even remember this after a few years go by and the pain of harsh critics goes away, and you discover a brand-new day.

That's what I thought I would have to say to Chet once I took a look at what he sent my way.

But, Chet, I have to say it: you are now a master of books, too!

And that's what I find myself saying to you, dear reader. That Chet Holmes is not only a master of the subject within the covers of this book, but of something much more profound, something much deeper than the subject of sales seems: Chet knows how the world of words works. He knows how stories are told. He knows why the world needs great storytellers, and why companies who are deprived of great storytellers are companies that can't hope to capture the imagination of their customers, their employees, or the people who invest in them, each of whom are suckers for a great story, who love to hear the Once Upon a Time we were all put to bed with at night all those many years ago. Chet teaches you between the covers of this book how to tell stories. And he does that in the best way of all: he tells you a story, and then another, and then yet another, and then still another until you feel like he has got to run out, and then he tells you even another story better than the ones before. And each story works to make *The Ultimate Sales Machine* a book that puts it all together to help you dramatically increase your sales if you are wise enough to follow its advice.

So, Chet, what can I say? You are a master. And this book is about mastery. And you kicked this sucker in the head. Yes, when you read a really neat book, there are very few words left to be said. Other than, great job, Chet. Thanks for the opportunity to tell it like it is.

—Michael E. Gerber,
    bestselling author of *E-Myth*, *E-Myth Mastery*,
    and *E-Myth Revisited*

Preface

Here's a snapshot of the current climate for doing business:

- A corporation fails every 3 minutes.
- A directorship changes every 32 seconds.
- A company changes control every 15 minutes.[1]
- 96 percent of all companies fail within 10 years.
- 26,000 new products and brands are introduced every year.
- 16 percent to 30 percent of consumers change brand loyalty in one evening of watching commercials.
- 74 percent of consumers buy outside their favorite brands.
- 29 percent of consumers do not read a newspaper.[2]

In the past 15 years of working with thousands of entrepreneurial companies and more than 60 of the Fortune 500, I've seen the average cost of getting in front of a client virtually triple. If it cost you $100 to get in front of a client 15 years ago, today it's costing you $300. The rates have increased for every major advertising medium, including television, radio, and newspaper, while the penetration of every one of those vehicles has decreased. With more TV and radio choices than ever, the large audience you used to be able to reach in one place is now scattered among hundreds of media channels. New technologies like satellite radio and TiVo have made it possible for consumers to avoid commercials completely. All this means that it's getting harder and harder to reach the consumer, and the market that you're in has become fiercely and viciously competitive. Does anyone think it's going to get easier?

When I teach seminars in front of thousands of business owners, I begin by saying that I can absolutely help each one of them transform their business into the Ultimate Sales Machine. You can even expect this to be fast. I've doubled the sales of many companies in 12 months flat. I will go on to say: "You're going to understand all the principles I share with you here today, as there's nothing but logical information here. You're going to agree with them. You're going to *know* that I am right and that these principles will work in your business. . . . And then you will still *not do them*." That always gets a laugh. I continue: "I call this the reverse psychology portion of my lecture where I'm goading you into applying a powerful force for creating success from what you're going to learn here today. And that force, my friends, is 'pigheaded discipline and determination.'"

As a speaker who has been out there speaking for 15 years now, I've had the pleasure of many business owners and executives coming up to me and saying: "You know, Chet, your stuff has really helped me. But I gotta tell you, the *most* important lesson I learned from you was what you said about pigheaded discipline and determination." If you apply the learning curve in this book to your business with pigheaded discipline and determination, you, too, will come up to me at a seminar one day and thank me for the fact that your business now slaughters your competitors at every turn, runs without you, and is highly profitable. In short, you will have mastered your business so that it runs like a finely tuned sales-making machine.

How do you become a master of anything? How do you help others become masters? The key lesson I've learned again and again, ever since I was a kid studying karate, is that mastery is not about being special or more gifted than anyone else. Mastery is a direct result of pigheaded discipline and determination. The promise of this book is that you will learn how to create mastery in your business resulting in the finest, most profitable, and best-run business you can have. You will get the tools to become a master of three crucial areas: marketing, management, and sales. Mastery in each of these areas is necessary to make your business run like a machine.

Machine Beginnings

When I was 15 years old, I tried a new method for increasing my karate skills. I had a high vaulted ceiling in my bedroom. I screwed a cowhide rope into the peak of the ceiling and attached a softball to the other end, at chest level. My intent was to kick and chop the ball and then to be able to deflect it, block it, kick it, or chop the ball again when it came bouncing back.

With my first karate chop at the ball with my hand, the ball bounced out to the edge of the rope and back fast, smacking me in the head. This wasn't going to be as easy as I thought. I tried all kinds of kicks—hook kick, front kick, back kick, side kick—but again and again the ball flew to the end of the rope and then bounced back, hitting me in the head, elbow, shoulders, or chest.

I worked on this for several weeks and made very little progress. After a month, there were a couple of times when I could actually block the ball from hitting me. After three months of doing this every single day, I could hit the ball with any one of the body's weapons—my hands, my feet, my elbows, and my knees. I could even do a spinning back kick and hit it again, then block it expertly as it flew at me from a different angle.

After six months, the ball never touched me. I could spin artfully in the air, flawlessly blocking the ball at every angle. It was amazing. I could literally catch, kick, or swat that ball with every move any time I liked and faster than I would've ever thought possible. My body was operating like a machine, responding to the ball as if preprogrammed to anticipate every possible move the ball could make.

Imagine my skill level when that ball would ricochet around the room with lightning speed and my reflexes were even faster. It was thrilling. I felt such power. I realized that becoming a master of karate was not about learning 4,000 moves but about doing just a handful of moves 4,000 times. This repetition trained my body to run like a machine—and that's what constant and focused repetition will do for your business. No matter what comes up, your responses are automatic because you've prepared for and developed the skills to deal with every possible scenario. More important, by focusing like a laser beam on the 12 strategies in this book you will outsell, outmarket, and outmanage your competition at every turn.

It is the same with any business; there are basics that you can do over and over again until every aspect runs like a machine. In the near future you can have every person in every department know how to handle any circumstance that arises. Where other companies have one or two approaches for getting appointments with clients, your salespeople will have 10 different approaches and they will perform each one expertly. Your salespeople will have answers and perfect follow-up letters for every possible situation. Your customer service people will know how to respond to any complaint or special order or return situation that comes their way without having to consult their manager. Stress levels will be lower because every employee will have the information, training, and tools to do their jobs confidently and effectively. What will it take to get you there? One thing: pigheaded discipline and determination.

Look at any area in your life where you have a great achievement—you know you worked at it. Perhaps you are a great golfer. Perhaps you're good at tennis. Perhaps you play piano. Any area of achievement in your life required you to stick with the basics until you became great. And yet so many businesses don't do that. Being great at sales, for example, requires you to be good at only seven things. Yet, my sales audits of hundreds of companies reveal that few, if any, have outlined this process in the kind of detail that creates greatness.

Is your company or department growing at the rate you desire? In almost every company that I've helped to grow, everyone is working very hard, from the CEO to the salespeople, right down the line. But if you don't have the tools necessary to master each area of the business, you are working harder, not smarter. This book offers the tools. Not only does it supply you with the pigheaded mind-set, but it also provides you with complete how-to instructions to create the Ultimate Sales Machine.

Introduction

The owner of one of the largest carpet cleaning companies in the country—Rug Renovating, which covers the tri-state metro area of New York, New Jersey, and Connecticut—came to me for help. Here's a company with 30,000 clients that was finding that efforts to get new clients were becoming less and less effective over the years. Any business owner reading this has probably noticed the same problem. Although he came to me looking to gain more clients, my first reaction was to find out whether he had maximized the clients he already had. I asked him how often his current clients buy. He answered: "They buy about once every three years. We send coupons and discounts frequently, but the numbers don't change." I asked, "How would you like it if we could get your clients buying twice a year instead of once every three years?" He was very excited at the idea, but no previous approach had worked.

Like nearly every company in the world that sells carpet cleaning, this company was using product data in its sales process. Product data is straightforward and has very little strategic value. This is product data: "We clean X square feet of carpeting for Y dollars." But adding market data can make the product data much more powerful. As you will learn in Chapter Six, every company can dramatically strengthen its sales and marketing materials by adding market data.

Here's what we found for this carpet cleaning company:

FACT: Your carpets act like a giant health filter, capturing dust, dirt, bacteria, pollen, dust mites, their waste, and the bacteria that feed on it.

Government studies have shown that when you remove carpets from buildings, people get sick four times more often. But, like any filter, your carpets become saturated and ineffective over time—creating a need for professional quality cleaning. And even vacuuming every day does not kill bacteria embedded in the carpet.

The EPA found that professional carpet cleaning actually gets carpets 1,500 percent cleaner than even vacuuming every day. The steaming hot water used by professionals kills germs and bacteria that build up in your home.

This is an example of how market data can motivate purchasing when people might not even feel they need the product. Product data like "We sell carpet cleaning" only appeals to people who think they need their carpets cleaned right now. The goal of most people when they get their carpets cleaned is to get them to look better. Little do people realize that it makes their home healthier. This puts cleaning your carpets on the same level of importance as taking the kids for their yearly checkup.

Here's a company that has actually gone beyond product data to study every aspect of carpet cleaning, right down to the government studies about the cleanliness of your air quality within the home. From the EPA's research, we created a concept called the Gold Service. The goal was to get customers on a schedule to have their carpets cleaned every six months.

The company owner was very excited about this concept. So was I. We could both do the math and understand how much this would mean for him if it worked. Here I was hired to find the big breakthrough, and I felt I had delivered! Victory was mine. Using the market data, I created a script for their top producer to test for a week. The following week I met with the entire staff over the telephone with the CEO listening. The dialogue went as follows:

CHET: So how did it go?
SALES REP: It didn't work.
CHET: It didn't work?

SALES REP: No. It didn't work.

CHET: Well, how many people did you offer it to?

SALES REP: I offered it to 10 people.

CHET: And nobody bought it?

SALES REP: No, two people bought it.

To the sales rep, the perception was that eight no's out of 10 pitches made the concept a failure. But do the math: if you have 30,000 clients buying once every three years, that's about 10,000 sales per year. Now imagine an extra 6,000 of them (a mere 20 percent) buying *twice* per year. What does that do for this business? It's an enormous increase in volume.

But if it were up to that sales rep, the idea would have died right then and there. This is where pigheaded discipline and determination make the difference between mediocrity and greatness. In fact, it took six months of pigheaded discipline and determination to get every salesperson offering that service to every prospect, every time. This is where most executives fail. Building a sales machine is not going to be about doing 4,000 things; it's going to be about doing 12 things 4,000 times each.

Just one hour a week changed this CEO's life. He made a commitment to spend this hour every week improving and integrating the Gold Service concept. It wasn't easy—it took six disciplined months to integrate this into the fabric and fiber of the business. But, remember, it was six months of *only one hour per week*. Every Monday night at five o'clock without fail the whole company would gather and talk about how this concept could be made more effective, how we could make it easier for the salespeople to use, what ideas the salespeople had to make this more effective, and so on. The whole focus of that hour was to integrate this one concept fully and completely into every aspect of the business.

Not only did the implementation of the Gold Service improve sales, it also stabilized the business. Where the owner used to hope every month that customers would respond to his fliers, he now knows, going into each month, how many people are signed up for the Gold Service cleaning. It made the business more stable in every way and it transformed sales performance.

When I started working with the staff, the lowest sales rep was doing $13,000 a month and the average sales rep was doing $35,000. When I finished working with them, the lowest sales rep was doing $49,000 a month and the highest sales rep was doing $100,000 a month. Sales performance doubled. Initially, the sales staff fought me all the way . . . even though they were on commission.

This company refined its sales process to near perfection within the mentioned six months. Everyone reading this will be able to do the same. But sales is just one piece of the pie. In order to be the Ultimate Sales Machine, you actually have to be great at leading, managing, and marketing. This book lays it out in straightforward language with practical examples spelled out from every angle. And the best part is that you're not going to work harder; you're only going to work smarter.

You can profoundly improve your company or department if you absolutely commit to one hour per week in which you do nothing else but work on making the business much more effective. In the course of this book, you will learn exactly how to spend that hour.

It's not going to be hard to apply the strategies in this book or to transform your business into the Ultimate Sales Machine. The key is learning and practicing the pigheaded discipline and determination you need to constantly address and readdress the 12 areas I'll outline. In order to make this process easy, I've broken this book down into 12 chapters, each focusing on one of the 12 strategies with examples and exercises that will make your business great and grow your sales and profits like mad.

One of my clients is a great learner and is always buying the latest book or program. He heard my presentation at a seminar, liked what I had to say, and retained me to do an audit of his business. When I interviewed his employees, they were practically laughing at me. To them, I was just the latest flash in the pan. They told me that their boss had used 100 different training programs but never made any of them stick.

The missing ingredient for this client and nearly all of the 1,000-plus clients I have worked with directly to improve their businesses is pigheaded discipline and determination. We all get good ideas at seminars and from books, radio talk shows, and business-building gurus. The problem is that most companies do not know how to identify and adapt the best ideas to their businesses. Implementation, not ideas, is the key to real success.

This book is packed with excellent ideas developed on the front lines of capitalism, but more important, this book helps you learn the ways to see these ideas manifest throughout your organization, especially in your bottom line. Once you begin working on the strategies in each chapter, you will see that it's not just about implementing the ideas in *this* book. Your ability to implement any idea you learn anywhere will benefit dramatically from the learning curve presented here.

For example, in Chapter One you'll learn how to maximize productivity through time management at every level of your organization. How well you manage your time and the level of productivity and performance you require from your staff are specific competencies that few businesses ever fully capitalize upon. Let's say you take a great time management course today. You go back to your office and apply the principles and see that they actually work. But when we check back with you three months later, we find you using very little, if any, of the information you learned from taking that one-time course. This is called "event training." You go to an event. You get some training. You come back to your office. You may even try some of the concepts. You may even see them work, but you quickly abandon them because you are missing the pigheaded discipline and determination that make a truly great company or department.

Working Smarter, Not Harder

At seminars and lectures, I've asked my audience, "How many people in this room would like to grow their company or department 10 times larger than it is right now?" Typically, 99 percent of the audience raises their hands. Then I say, "Leave your hands up if you can work 10 times more hours or 10 times harder than you're working now." All the hands go down. The point is that there are companies and departments that are 10 times bigger than yours, and you know they aren't working 10 times harder than you are. They're just working smarter.

The Ultimate Sales Machine is all about working smarter, not harder. Doesn't it seem smarter to take 12 proven strategies and perfect them, than to scramble about using hundreds of different ideas without any real traction on any of them? This book is for executives; CEOs; entrepreneurs; and professionals such as doctors, dentists, and lawyers. It's for middle managers, salespeople, and customer service representatives. In short, it's for everyone who plays a role in operating, marketing, selling, and running a company or department. It offers the kind of information and strategies that are essential for everyone in the trenches doing battle to grow and strengthen their business or department.

Backed by countless success stories of companies just like the carpet cleaner, the Ultimate Sales Machine mind-set is the culmination of my experiences in the trenches. I've run magazines, newspapers, and trade shows for billionaire Charlie Munger and have owned 14 businesses. I've studied karate and owned a karate school on Times Square. I've also personally sold my services to more than 60 Fortune 500 companies and nearly 1,000 other clients. Finally, I've taught millions of business owners and employees through seminars, articles, and my 65 training products, which now sell in more than 20 countries.

IMPORTANT: I set up this book the way you should set up your business. I begin by discussing how to structure your company to maximize everyone's time. Then I move into training and its critical role in any organization from one-person armies to the world's largest companies. As an author, I could have started with sexier and more potent material. But I believe that the right thing to do and the best way to serve you is to begin with the building blocks you *must* have if your company is going to be set up to succeed long term.

Meetings: another building block. I had a client that had terrible meetings, so they stopped having them altogether. No meetings, ever. Wow. Talk about throwing the baby out with the bath water. Where do you learn how to hold a great meeting? Nowhere. So here it is in this book. Meetings are great if you know how to have them, and in Chapter Three I show you how to become a meeting master. I give details on how to run dazzling meetings that will have a profound impact on your company.

After these three chapters, you've got your building blocks. Now you are ready to become a world-class strategist. Chapter Four will change your life. I would love to *start* with this as it's the single strongest lesson any businessperson can learn, but I set the book up as your business should be set up. Get your building blocks in place and *then* erect your skyscraper.

From there the book takes off, teaching all the nuts and bolts of better selling, marketing, and hiring that you will find in 99.9 percent of businesses. The strategies, tips, and insights that I've used to help turn mediocre or ailing companies into bulletproof success stories are right here in this book. Let this be your guide to transforming your business into the Ultimate Sales Machine.

Time Management Secrets of Billionaires

How to Maximize Your Productivity and Help Your People Do the Same

I developed this time management system while I was running nine divisions for billionaire Charlie Munger. I always try to hire bright, aggressive, creative people, so naturally these people were constantly coming to me with new ideas, issues, and concerns. I later learned that no one should have more than six direct reports, but at the time I had something like 22. So I was constantly reacting to my staff's needs for attention. Basically, I was in a reactive mode all the time. I worked seven days a week—10 to 12 hours per day at the office, dealing with interruptions, and then I'd go home and do all the creative work to keep everything going.

I realized that I had to learn how to effectively manage my time, so I took a time management course. In the first 20 minutes, the trainer handed out a work sheet instructing us to track our time over the next three months. At the end of the three months, we were supposed to identify where we were wasting our time. As a person running nine divisions, I rolled my eyes and thought to myself, "If I had the time to track my time for three months, I would not need a time management course." I got up and left the seminar.

Over the years I have broken time management down to six simple steps that take five minutes to complete. Why? Because good time management shouldn't take a lot of time. That's also why this is the shortest chapter in the book.

This chapter will present six simple steps for time management. It will be very logical and you will understand it completely. You will agree with all of the principles and you will know that they will absolutely improve your productivity. But do you have the pigheaded discipline to spend the five minutes every day to take control of your time and then the even more pigheaded discipline to stick with the plan throughout the day? If you have a staff, do you have the pigheaded discipline to police these six simple steps throughout your entire staff? If you do, the payoff will be huge.

Let's get into it: do you function mostly in a reactive or a proactive mode? In my experience, most businesspeople don't take the time to plan and take action because all of their time is consumed by reacting to the business they've already built. To build your business into the Ultimate Sales Machine, you need to be in a primarily proactive mode. Time management is crucial.

Imagine what it would be like if you were suddenly thrust into managing or running a $50 billion company. Do CEOs of giant corporations have more hours in the day than you do? Of course not. But they do need to be masters of this crucial competency: time management. They need to be absolute experts in managing their own time and have the systems in place to make sure that everyone in their organization is skilled in time management as well. Once you understand the time management secrets of running a multibillion-dollar company, you'll have no trouble managing your sales activities, if you're in sales, or getting your company or department to function at its maximum productivity.

My Time Management Epiphany

You've heard of the "one-minute manager." Well, I was the "got-a-minute manager." All day long, every day, various folks on my team would come to me and ask me if I had a minute to talk, and a "got-a-minute meeting" would break out right then and there. In fact, the entire company was run by got-a-minutes. Anyone could go to anyone else any time and a got-a-minute meeting would break out. My employees were in a reactive mode all day long. Although I had successfully grown each of my divisions by at least 100 percent within 12 to 15 months of taking them over, I was out of control and reacting 100 percent of the time. Even on vacation in Hawaii, I was receiving 15 faxes per day (this was before email became the newest time burner).

In contrast, when I had a meeting with Charlie Munger, I had to call his secretary and make an appointment. I had to have a strict agenda. I had to be on time and organized. Every meeting was highly productive and to the point. Then suddenly it clicked that I needed to take control of my time and my staff. So after a few years of working 12-hour days, every single day including weekends, I realized that in order to more successfully run and manage the divisions under my control, I had to get more organized and less reactive. I put out a memo effectively ending my "got-a-minute" management style. Here's what it said:

To: Staff
From: Chet
Do not come to my door and ask if I have a minute. The answer will be no. Unless urgent, hold all thoughts, ideas, issues, or (nonurgent) concerns until the weekly division meeting. Below is a list of when these meetings will be held. Otherwise, I will post two times per day when I will take "got-a-minute" meetings. If your needs can't wait for the weekly meeting, write your name in the got-a-minute times allocated and I will take quick 10-minute meetings.

We broke the company down into nine "impact areas" and held weekly one-hour meetings in each area. An impact area is any part of your company that has a direct impact on the bottom line. Your impact areas may include sales, customer service, product development, and marketing, for example. In order to improve and perfect each of these areas you need to give them a dedicated one hour per week when everyone involved can focus exclusively on *improving* that area.

Once I established weekly impact area meetings, my team learned to hold their ideas until the appropriate meeting instead of coming to my office to share their ideas as they got them. I even put out a pad that had the words "With Chet" on the top of the pad. My staff was then to write down on the pad the things they'd normally interrupt me with and keep that pad in their desk drawer until the weekly meeting.

The memo went out on Thursday, and I recall distinctly that on Friday no one came to my door. It was the first time in years that that had happened, and I did not know what to do with all this uninterrupted time. I could actually concentrate at the office, and I didn't need to bring home the normal mounds of work to be done at nights and on weekends. I had a whole new learning curve headed my way.

No one came to my door on Friday, but, by Monday, the madness started all over. I had to have the pigheaded determination and discipline to train my staff to follow these rules. When someone comes to your door with a "got-a-minute" meeting, you stop them cold and say, "Is this something that can't wait until the weekly meeting?" They will still try to get you to focus on it right then and there. And if you lack pigheaded discipline, you'll cave and jump right into it. So I had to discipline myself and the staff to hold almost everything until the weekly meetings.

And the best part? I went from reacting to the business 70 to 80 hours per week to proactively running and more effectively managing and growing the business in only *nine* hours per week because I broke down my responsibilities into nine major impact areas. The meetings were way more productive than the got-a-minute meetings because these meetings were more formal, structured, and results-oriented. The key staff for each impact area attended their meeting together, so major progress could be made and everyone was there who then needed to take the next step or learn our latest breakthrough. I kept nine pads (one for each impact area), and on each pad I would keep notes of what we had worked on and who had promised to do what before the next weekly meeting.

Yes—to-do's, tasks, and deadlines must be assigned after every meeting. But the key is not to ask for too much to be completed. Make the gains small but constant. If you are having the meeting every week and you are making small incremental gains each and every week, think of the profound transformation you're going to have in 52 weeks. A year from now your company, division, or department can be massively improved. More on this later.

If you run a large company, you will have more impact areas. I helped one executive break down his company into the main impact areas and initiatives he was working on, and he ended up with 17—which means 17 one-hour meetings per week. That might sound crazy to a small-company owner or executive, but it is *the* way to take your company to the next level if you've got a lot going on. This particular executive was working 70 hours per week and getting less done than when I made him break down the company into 17 hours of meetings. Each meeting moved each impact area forward.

Decisions were made weekly. Everything of importance got addressed every week. Everyone was happier. The employees in each area felt more important. Prior to this program, some of them had to chase the boss for weeks to get questions answered or issues addressed. So break it down.

Exercise

Figure out what the impact areas are in your business. Typically if you are running a department, your department is the impact area. But if you're a CEO or general manager of a medium or large company, you may have many impact areas. To make identifying them easier, here is a list of 15 impact areas from another CEO I worked with:

1. Outside sales
2. Inside telemarketing team
3. Marketing activities
4. Customer service
5. CRM (customer relationship management)
6. Purchasing and suppliers
7. Shipping and receiving
8. Inventory control
9. Accounts receivable
10. Personnel
11. Technology
12. Partner relations/vendors
13. Partner relations/affiliates
14. Export sales
15. California initiative

This last initiative was to attack a new market. What initiatives do you or should you have? Now list *your* areas of impact.

The Six Steps to Great Time Management

There are six fundamental steps to great time management. Put these six steps into daily practice, and you won't believe how much you and your staff can accomplish in a regular workday.

Step 1: Touch It Once

Tell me if this sounds familiar. You come into your office, and there on your desk sit three folders and two letters that you must respond to. You look at the first letter and read a few sentences. Dealing with it is clearly going to take more time than you have right now. You put it aside. In one of your folders is another task. You handle that task and your phone rings. You answer the phone and get pulled in a new direction for 10 to 15 minutes. Then you go back to the folder, but, just as you do, an email comes in. You stop to read the email, which contains a task that must be dealt with but requires more time than you have right now.

If you spend just 15 minutes per day to revisit, readdress, or reread documents or emails, you will waste 97 hours per year where no action is taken. Many on your staff will waste an hour per day (scattered throughout the day) revisiting things on which no meaningful action is taken. That equates to *six weeks* of wasted time per year. Want to add six more weeks of productivity to every year? This simple touch-it-once rule and the infrastructure to support this rule within your company can dramatically enhance the productivity of every person working for you.

If you touch it, take action. That's the first step to great time management. Don't open that email or letter until you're ready to deal with it. As you put this rule into practice, you will find that the more files you have for work in progress and the more organized you can be in that process, the more productive you will be. So, for example, suppose I open my email from my PR firm that requires me to approve a press release. I have a PR folder. On my to-do list I write, "Approve press release. See PR folder." That's how organized you need to be today.

The touch-it-once rule is crucial for managing email files. Email is a tremendous asset, but it can also kill your time management if you let it control you. The key to great email management is to institute a company policy that insists on very descriptive subject lines for all emails. Another rule I absolutely insist on at my company is that when the subject of the email changes, the subject line on the email also changes. This is critical.

Say you send someone an email with the subject line "Upcoming Chet Holmes training event" and she writes back something that looks like this:

To: Sherry
From: Marcia
Subject: Upcoming Chet Holmes training event
Yes I'm going. I already reserved my spot. And by the way, did you talk to Dave about the budget item I mentioned to you?

The email goes back and forth again about the problem with Dave, but it still has "Upcoming Chet Holmes training event" in the subject line.

A week or two later, someone asks you what happened with Dave? *One* of these seven emails covers that important issue, but you have to open all seven to find that data point. So change the subject line as you change the content of the email. Every client and employee of mine has to adhere to this rule in order to interact with me. This way, everyone in the company can glance at an incoming email and make the decision, "Can I deal with this now if I open it now?" If you do open something that can't be dealt with right then and there, you file it in an appropriate folder and move the task to your to-do list (more on to-do lists coming up next).

This can't be overstated: email can be the death of good time management. Companies that have new-email alerts constantly sounding keep every person in a reactive mode all day long. If your computer signals when you have an email, DO NOT go directly to read it and answer it at the moment it comes in. Email is there for your convenience. If it's not convenient, don't answer it.

Concentration is like a muscle and it strengthens as you concentrate more. If you stop concentrating every time an email comes in or the phone rings, you actually lessen your ability to concentrate and you become less effective in any situation that requires concentration.

Note: As you go through these six things, don't think about whether you've heard them before. Think about whether you're applying the discipline to implement them.

Step 2: Make Lists

Many people make lists as a way to keep organized. If you don't keep a list, you are most likely a very reactive person. Lists help you stay focused on high priorities and highly productive matters. Keeping a list will double your productivity right away.

When I conduct a seminar on the topic, I go around the room and ask how many people keep lists. Then I ask, "How many items do you usually keep on your list?" There are always a few people in the room who have to-do lists of 25 items or more.

The key to being productive is to stick to the *six* most important things you need to get done that day. You'll find that when you have a long list, it becomes the management tool for your time. When you want to feel productive, you go to your list and just pick something and do it. It feels good. When you have a long list, you generally do the easier, less productive tasks just to trim down the list. At the end of the day, you find that the most important things on the list didn't get completed because they are either the hardest, the most time-consuming, or both.

Long lists also mean that you will never finish your list. There is a negative psychological impact to not finishing your list. But there is an enormous psychological boost to crossing off that sixth item on your list, especially when all six of them were the most important things you needed to do that day.

So here's the rule: list the six most important things you need to do and, by hook or by crook, get those six things completed *each day*. That doesn't mean you don't keep a side list of running items that need to be done. When you plan each day (coming up in a moment), you can go to your long list and use that as a menu of items from which to build your list of the six most important things for that day.

⚙ Exercise

Do this exercise now and we'll build on it as you read the rest of this chapter. Take a clean sheet of paper and write down the six most important things you need to get done tomorrow. Your list might look something like mine:

1. Work on client proposal.
2. Fax contract.
3. Schedule meetings.
4. Conference call with Heidi.
5. Review this month's marketing plan.
6. Work on direct mail letter.

Step 3: Plan How Much Time You Will Allocate to Each Task

Do not think about *when* you will do each task yet. Just determine the amount of time you will realistically dedicate to each task. This is an important step to make sure that the six items on your list can actually be accomplished in a day. If one or more of the items on your list is too big to accomplish in one day, then write down how much time during that day you will dedicate to it. You will take care of bigger projects in manageable chunks of time. This book is a great example. I've been getting book offers for more than 10 years. But I looked at the book as a huge undertaking. Once I made the commitment, I put an hour a week on my calendar to address the book. Within three months, I had a solid book proposal that got me this book deal. What have you been putting off for years? Or what important initiatives are you just not getting to because they take too much time? Do them in small chunks of time.

⚙️ **Exercise**

Next to each item on your list, write how much time you will realistically spend on it tomorrow. Now your list might look like this:

1. Work on client proposal—.5 hour.
2. Revise and fax contract—1.5 hours.
3. Schedule meetings—.5 hour.
4. Conference call—1 hour.
5. Work on marketing plan—1 hour.
6. Work on direct mail letter—2 hours.

Add up the total amount of hours for your "productive tasks." Here it comes to 6.5 hours. I've done this exercise in many seminars, and there are always a few people who add up their hours and get 11 hours' worth of stuff. Not realistic at all when you now must work these six things into the rest of your day. A good guide to go by is that your six most important things should take about six hours. I'll explain why later.

Step 4: Plan the Day

Now that you have allocated amounts of time for each task, you need to plan your day. This is not a general guide to how your day might unfold. It must be specific and have a time slot for absolutely everything. This includes each of the six items on your list as well as time to check email and open mail. Remember, if you are following the first rule and only touching these items once, then you need to have a dedicated period of time each day when you can deal with them.

Note in this fully planned day below that there are two periods of time for miscellaneous and got-a-minute meetings. These miscellaneous periods are absolutely essential because we all know that your day might be interrupted. There are some things you will have to react to that will throw you off your schedule. If you have planned at least two half-hour slots of reactive time, then when you get off track, you've actually built in buffers so that you can get back to your schedule. But, most important, *stick to that schedule no matter what*. Note in the plan below that this is actually a 10-hour day, but only 6.5 of the hours are for your six most important things:

8–8:30:	Send client proposal and check email.
8:30–9:00:	Review employees' time management lists.
9–10:30:	Review, revise, and fax contract.
10:30–11:00:	Miscellaneous meetings (scheduled got-a-minutes), check email.
11–12:00:	Review marketing plan.
12–1:00:	Lunch with client.
1:30–2:00:	Conference call.
2–3:00:	Got-a-minutes, miscellaneous, check e-mail.
3–5:00:	Direct mail letter.
5–6:00:	Check and respond to email.

⚙ Exercise

Write a plan for your day tomorrow that would give you enough time to cross off all six items on your to-do list and stay on top of your email and other tasks.

Step 5: Prioritize

Now that you've done this exercise, look at your day tomorrow and see where you put the most difficult tasks. In seminars, I often see people put the most important task last because it typically takes the most concentration or is the most difficult. But, by the end of the day, there is rarely time or energy to take on this chore. Put the most important task first. This simple step will give you a tremendous sense of control and accomplishment.

We've heard it again and again: only 20 percent of your effort brings 80 percent of your results. Many people drown in busywork that produces few results. They're so busy that they've lost their ability to prioritize and concentrate. I call them "busypeople." I've had a lot of them working for me over the years—dedicated, devoted, even appearing like they are really busy. But when you look at their actual productivity, it's very low. For these people this whole technique becomes critical. And you have to police it like a ninja master to get them to stop all the busywork and focus on productivity.

What would happen if 80 percent of your effort was focused on high-results-producing activities? If you started spending 80 percent of your time on results-oriented work and only 20 percent on everything else, you could conceivably get a fourfold increase in productivity! All it takes is pigheaded discipline and determination.

Tips for Salespeople and One-Person Armies

Every salesperson should have at least 2.5 hours a day of brand-new prospecting. And that's for salespeople who have a full load of current clients. Salespeople who are not managing a large list of current clients need to do at least four hours per day of pure cold calling. I have a client who has software that tracks sales activity, but he never used the software. To our shock, when we actually used the software we found that not one person on the staff was doing more than an hour's worth of cold calling in a single day. When surveyed, the reps thought they were making 40 to 60 cold calls per day. The reality: about 11 to 28 cold calls per day. For new salespeople, their entire day should be spent prospecting.

If you are a one-person army or a very small company and you, as the entrepreneur, are the main person responsible for growing the company, then you personally *must* spend at least 2.5 hours per day growing your company.

What to Do If Your Job Is Designed to Be Reactive

Say you are a salesperson who has to take inbound calls from clients on a regular basis. Say you are a customer service representative whose entire job is to react to customer service calls. What if you're a reception-ist who answers phones or an assistant who has to react to your boss's needs all day. Even people in reactive positions should still plan realisti-cally for some proactive tasks that can get done each day. You should have some proactive tasks that you do each day that move things for-ward or improve the company or your job. Plan time to improve skills, performance, work flow, and organization for you and your department or company. People in more reactive positions will simply have far less time dedicated to proactive tasks—but still have some proactive tasks in every day.

If you are a receptionist and your main job is to answer phones, can you also be productive making lists of prospects for the sales team? It makes me crazy when I go into a company and the receptionist is reading a book because the calls are slow. Can this person be doing some research on the Internet about your industry? Or doing mailings? These questions also apply if you're in customer service. In your weekly meetings (full design in Chapter Three), make it a point to address this issue and put reactive people to work in their down time or slow time.

People REspect What You INspect

· If you want to get your people productive, you should examine how they're prioritizing and planning their day *every day*. Before the advent of the Internet, I would go around the office and check how people were planning their day. I did that for months until every person in the com-pany was doing their plan every day. It took me six months of pigheaded discipline and determination and constant inspection before my employ-ees followed the six steps religiously. I am so intent on having great time management among my key executives, and they from their staff, that I even built an Internet program where employees log in and plan their day. The boss gets an automatic email alert each time an employee com-pletes his or her day's plan. (See "The Ultimate Time Management Tool" on www.chettime.com.)

With or without a program like this, instituting this kind of inspec-tion on how employees are planning and prioritizing will increase their respect for time management and dramatically increase their productivity.

⚙ Exercise

Look at your plan.

- How much of your day is proactive and how much is reactive?
- Where did you put the most important task for the day? At the beginning? In the middle? At the end?
- Rewrite your plan so that you complete the most important task on your list first thing in the morning.
- Group together all of your reactive work, including answering emails and returning phone calls.
- Make sure most of your day is focused on proactive work such as prospecting or closing deals.

Step 6: Ask Yourself, "Will It Hurt Me to Throw This Away?"

Studies show that 80 percent of all filed or stored information is never referred to again. So why hold on to it? To determine whether or not to keep something, ask yourself, "Will it hurt me to throw this away?" Could you get it again if you needed it? If you're a boss, the answer is usually yes. Throw it away. If I don't specifically keep an email, it's automatically thrown away by my system after 45 days. Maybe twice per year there's one that I wish I could get again. And I usually can. One of my staff recently had trouble in that her email was working slowly. The technician looked at her email account and discovered that it had stored some ridiculous amount of old data because she kept every single email. After the technician had her clean out all the files she didn't think she would ever need again, her stored email went from 2.7 gigabytes to 0.5 gigabytes.

Conclusion

As you can see, there are not 4,000 steps to time management and there is no need to track your time for three months before introducing time management into your life and your business. There are six simple steps:

- Touch it once.
- Make daily lists of the six most important tasks to accomplish.

- Plan how long each task will take.
- Assign time slots for accomplishing each task.
- Focus on the difficult projects first.
- Ask yourself, "Will it hurt me to throw this away?"

Master these six steps and you won't believe the difference. Implement them companywide and you will be operating at maximum productivity before you know it.

Of course, even if you stick to these six steps, events and people will interfere and your schedule will be disrupted. Emergencies will come up that will take an hour or even two hours out of your day. As long as you've scheduled some flexible time into your day, some blank spaces in your schedule, you can accommodate those detours. The key is that when something interferes with your schedule, deal with it *and then go back to your schedule!*

Instituting Higher Standards and Regular Training

Preprogram Your Organization to Run Like a Finely Tuned Machine

According to an article in *Harvard Business Review*, only 10 percent of the population has what's called "the learning mind-set." These are people who seek out and enjoy learning. The other 90 percent of the population will not look to improve their skills unless they have to as part of their job requirement. Today, most professions—real estate brokers, accountants, financial planners, stockbrokers, lawyers, healthcare professionals, masseuses, and so on—have mandatory continuing education because they found that, without it, people wouldn't keep current with the information necessary to be accepted as a professional in their field.

What if your doctor wasn't required to keep up to date with medical advances and hadn't looked at a medical text in 20 years? He or she might be prescribing medicine that is now known to be harmful or doing procedures that we've proven ineffective. Yet in most companies there's little or no training and there's rarely mandatory training.

Some managers view training as an interference with "work" to be done. But think of the tale of the woodcutters: Woodcutter A cuts wood all day. Woodcutter B keeps stopping and sitting down. At the end of the day, woodcutter B has three times more wood than woodcutter A. Woodcutter A asks: "How could this happen? You were resting all day!" Woodcutter B says: "I wasn't resting. I was sharpening my saw." Take time to sharpen your skills, your tools, and your resources, and you will be more productive.

The Tribal Method of Training

Joe's Bank just hired Sam, and he's about to go through his new-hire training. At Joe's Bank, they use what I call the "tribal method of training," where information is passed from person to person by word of mouth, like cavemen might have done. Sam is told to watch Betty for two days, and then he will be ready to do things himself. There is no formal methodology, no classroom-style training, no training manuals, no role playing. It's all just one person sitting with another person and watching what that person does. Just watch and learn. If Betty has a bad day, a bad attitude, or bad habits, Sam might think these are acceptable as well. This is the worst kind of training you could possibly have.

On the other hand, banks like Wells Fargo, Banker's Trust, and Citibank—all former clients of mine—have classroom-style training programs with policies and procedures for everything. At one of these companies, Sam goes through extensive classroom training before he ever sits to observe another teller. When he finally sits down to do so, he can actually spot when she's doing something wrong. Sam has learned his job, but the training shouldn't stop there. Improving and advancing the skills and professionalism of every person in your company is an ongoing process, and formal training sessions should be regular and nonnegotiable.

Your industry and competitors might be advancing, but, without mandatory continuing education, your team isn't. In this chapter you'll learn how to set the standards of achievement in your company or department. You'll learn how to implement mandatory training programs and how to make them fun, interesting, and stimulating so your staff loves them. It doesn't matter if you're a one-person army or a Fortune 500 firm; you need to be working on your skills.

I had an original equipment manufacturer (OEM) client who was trying to penetrate the 100 biggest manufacturers in her market using a method you will learn in Chapter Six. A key element to this process was that her sales staff had to toughen up. The grim reality is that without great training, the majority of salespeople will never call a prospect back who rejects them even once. Few salespeople will call back even twice after a prospect has said no. This was definitely the case with this OEM company. Its salespeople would have given up after the first rejection from those manufacturers. But we were implementing a corporate initiative and it was absolutely mandatory that they learn how to persevere.

We knew that it would take a coordinated and highly monitored effort to solve this problem. We had call reports that the salespeople were required to fill out that showed what their activity was, and then every week, I personally selected salespeople for what I call "the hot seat." I drilled them with specific questions about the prospects they had contacted—what their efforts were, what they said, and what the prospect said. Because they knew we were going to be doing this every week, it slowly raised the bar of performance in the whole company.

This was not easy or immediate. Every salesperson started off not really doing the required activities. But when they were put on the hot seat by me, with all 50 of the other salespeople as well as the president of the company, the vice president of sales, and their sales manager all listening, they quickly realized they had better *re*spect what we were going to *in*spect.

For the first three months there was barely any progress and, on their own, this company and its sales team probably would have given up. But after three months of steady marketing to the executives at these manufacturers and more or less forcing the sales staff to keep calling the same prospects who kept saying no, we started to make nice progress. Every week we would go over what the salespeople were saying and what the prospects were saying. In each case, I'd tune up their skills. Within six months the sales crew had gotten in to see 54 percent of those they targeted.

With consistent, relentless, and organized training on just this specific concept, we raised the standard dramatically and then policed it throughout the organization. These salespeople learned that consistency in their approach—no matter how many times they were rejected—results in a tremendous conversion rate of prospects to buying clients. They are now the masters of selling in their industry.

⚙ Exercise

With training, everyone sings in harmony. What kind of music is your organization creating? Write down whether the following statements are true or false in your business:

1. All employees perform each aspect of their job with a high degree of excellence and consistency.
2. Results are somewhat predictable because training and skills are consistent.
3. Each supervisor would give a similar answer for each question or problem.
4. Each employee would give a similar answer for each question or problem.
5. Client treatment is similar, no matter who the client deals with in our company or department.
6. All staff members know what is considered good performance or attitude.

If you answered false to any of these statements, you aren't serious enough about training. Without training, employee activity will be intermittent, inconsistent, moody—maybe even indifferent or rude—because you have not set standards. With proper training, every employee will know the ideal procedure for initial contact with a client, the questions they need to ask every single client no matter what, and the follow-up procedures that you absolutely insist upon. The more proactive training you have, the better the . . . everything in your organization. This book will take you very deep into all these issues, but the purpose of this chapter is to emphasize that the most important thing you can do is to insist upon mandatory and regular skills training.

Training Sets Standards

Deliberate and constant training radically improves employees' understanding of company objectives and helps to raise and set standards of performance. If you don't train, you can't expect people to get to the next level. That's why most companies stay small or have to continually waste time addressing the same issues and problems over and over again.

Training Makes Money

Quality training is guaranteed to make you money. In the case of the company going after manufacturers, it had been in a four-year decline when we started our program. With consistent training it experienced a dramatic and much-needed increase in sales. Your sales team knows what to do and can handle any situation with ease because you've covered it in your weekly sessions together, right? It's the same with customer service (which you will learn more about in Chapter Three) and every other area of your business.

When clients experience consistent top-notch service no matter who they are dealing with in your organization, they will keep coming back. Without training, you'll lose clients that might be saved if you proactively address issues as they arise. Standardized client interaction and follow-up procedures mean that you are constantly building better client relationships that will lead to repeat business and referrals. Again, this book will give you a full formula for all these things in subsequent chapters.

Training also saves you money because it reduces employee turnover. When employees know exactly what to do in any situation, they have the tools to thrive in your organization. Training boosts confidence and reduces stress. Because training also sets a clear path for performance, it will be easier to measure and reward employees for exceeding performance standards. With organized and regular training programs, your company or department will be a better place to work.

Train or Be Derailed

The health of your business is not so different from that of your body. An ounce of prevention is worth a pound of cure. If you were choking, would you rather your friends try to learn the Heimlich maneuver right then and there or would you prefer that they already had training and practice doing it? Training is proactive. It keeps your company healthy and prepared no matter what crisis arises. If you don't train, you force everyone to be reactive, so your chances for survival decrease dramatically.

Training can save lives. I taught self-defense in New York City when I was 25, training many top executives at some of the biggest companies in the world. I remember presenting to a major oil company when the chief of security said that he thought self-defense training was a bad idea. "People will get false confidence and probably get in more trouble." I asked him if he had any kids. He had a 16-year-old and an 18-year-old daughter. Two weeks prior to that meeting there had been a horrible situation in Queens where an 18-year-old girl was dragged onto the roof of her building, sexually abused, and then thrown off the roof to her death. I asked if he remembered the story. He did. The girl had the attacker's skin under her fingernails, showing that she had made a gallant fight. In a life-threatening situation, you're in one of two categories: either you have no training and you're guessing, or you've had training and have very specific ideas of what you can do. I asked the executive which category he'd rather his daughters be in: trained or untrained. He said, "I see your point."

It's the same with any area of your business. When your employees confront any situation, they're in one of two categories. Either you've addressed it and trained them and they have the information they need to deal with it, or you haven't addressed it or trained them and they're going to be guessing. Which category would you rather your staff be in?

Some people fear that they won't remember things when they're in crisis. But your brain has a crisis scan function that kicks in during those situations. When adrenaline is pumped into your system, your brain speeds up, searching for what it has available to get you through the crisis. Over the years of teaching self-defense, I heard many examples of this—where someone in a crisis would not just remember what to do, but would even remember me teaching him the move.

When I was 18 years old, I drove a car off a cliff while racing a friend on a rainy night (not a very smart move). As I was coming around a curve, the car broke from the wet ground and there was another car coming at me. I punched the gas and spun the wheel at exactly the right time to avoid crashing into the oncoming car and regain control. But the road curved again and there was no way I was going to make it. I had sped up to get out of danger and now I was going too fast. The car slid off the road and hit a lawn at 80 or 90 mph. I felt the car double its speed as it careened across a slick lawn. The car hit a tree, spun sideways around the tree, and toppled 265 feet down a cliff. An untrained body would have stiffened up with fear and broken every bone.

The only reason I'm still here is because of my karate training. As my brain signaled "crisis," my body knew from years and years of karate practice not to tense up and resist, but to relax. I was floating around on the inside of that car. I was bouncing off the sides, the steering wheel, the roof, and before each impact, I would block my face from being hit. The car finally came to a crashing halt in the treetops. I survived that night because of training.

The point is that any kind of training can intervene in a crisis or in any situation that you want to change. Here's another example of a situation that was not a crisis but that posed a serious challenge in my company. We have a massive radio campaign that is driving leads to our sales team. People call in response to the ad to get more information sent to them about what we do. We tell them that in order to send them the right information, we need to know a little more about their business. We ask a few questions about what they do and then we ask them what their two biggest challenges are in growing their business. In the process, if it seems appropriate, we mention that, as an alternative to just receiving information in the mail, they can sign up for one of our training programs on the Web.

We had five new salespeople who started in a single week and about five out of 10 prospects responded to that alternative offer by saying, "Well, send me the information and then I'll decide." This went on for a week with hundreds of people throwing up this objection for which the salespeople had no comeback. The minute I heard this, I trained them to use this script: "Well, sir, I'm happy to send you the reports. In fact, they're already on their way. But let me tell you what happens to people who receive our reports. Either they read the reports and are so impressed with the information they end up signing up for the Web seminar I'm talking to you about now. Or they're in such a reactive mode, reacting to their business, that they never take the time to read the reports or to improve their business, and they end up doing nothing. My question to you is: Are you the kind of person who would rather take action and learn how to double your business? Or are you too busy reacting to your current business to take the time to learn the skills to improve it?"

Using this script, the salespeople improved their closing ratio. Of the prospects who would usually use that objection, half would sign up for the Web seminar right there on the phone. So performance improved immediately just by adding another piece of training to the process. This situation was not exactly a crisis, but we were losing half our prospects because no one took the time to think about what would be a logical comeback to that particular objection. This shows that a little training goes a long way.

So let's not have people making up what they're going to do in a crisis or in any other situation in your company or department. Let's have them *know* what to do in every situation because you address it weekly.

Repetition Is Key

When designing your training programs, remember that repetition is the key to preprogramming your company or department to run like a machine. The design of the Ultimate Sales Machine program was conceived with the simple law that no one gets good at anything without repetition. Karate requires tremendous discipline. You're just repeating moves over and over. This is true of tennis, golf, or any other sport. Practice, practice, practice and *then*, when you've begun to master your moves so that you know what to do automatically, it gets exciting. But pigheaded discipline comes first.

Just how serious are you about your company? Are you playing at business or taking care of business? According to Sun Tzu in *The Art of War*, one of the five essentials of victory is this: "He will win whose army is animated with the same spirit throughout all its rank."[3] How are you going to animate your whole team with the same spirit? Three words: training, training, and training.

Most of the better training programs come in and blitz an organization with a lot of information and then they leave. The staff has a nice healthy glow for about a week afterward. The perception is that you received a lot of value, because you gained a lot of information. But in reality, without continuous follow-up, very little sticks from a one-shot training. That said, one-shot training is better than no training, but you're about to learn that there is a better way.

By rotating core material regularly, the same concepts are constantly reinforced and reiterated. Skills are impacted immediately in either training method; yet, over time, skills are impacted permanently with consistent repetition. When you get all of your people speaking the same language and following standardized procedures, internal communication improves dramatically because everyone shares a deep and rich pool of the same knowledge base.

Taking the time management skills you learned in Chapter One as an example, here's what a typical learning curve looks like and why repetition is so essential. In this graph, we see that right after someone does some time management training, there is an immediate increase in skill. What happens after training occurs if there is no follow-through? As you can see here, there is an immediate falloff of the newly learned skill. That's where most companies and programs stop; hence, *some* minor

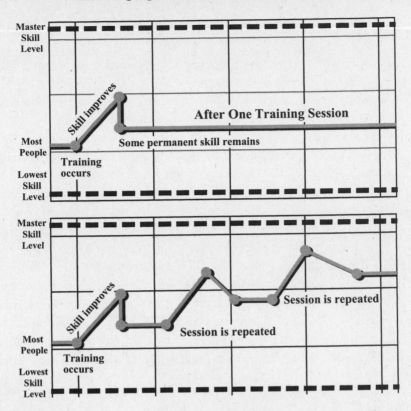

skill remains, but it's not like you're going to magically turn everyone into a time management expert with a single training experience.

What I do, in my own companies and with clients, is constantly teach the same information again and again until the skill is permanent. The skill improves again with another training session, but there is greater improvement because it's the same material being covered. The falloff occurs again, but it's not as dramatic as last time. Then another training session takes place and then another, and the skills improve even more, and the dropoff is even less. You see that, with each training session, mastery is that much closer.

How to Run a Training Session

To begin a training session, people should be told what to expect:

- What will be covered
- How long it will take

- How the information will be covered
- The objective of the particular session
- The obtained skill or knowledge that you hope they will gain

When people have a clear understanding of what they are about to hear and see, they will be mentally prepared and focused for the training.

It is important to create a training environment that is conducive to learning. Make it fun! Create an open environment where people can make comments, jokes, and suggestions without reproach. This isn't military training. People should look forward to it because they know it will be interesting and stimulating. As I mentioned in the beginning of this chapter, learning is not something most people do naturally. Since most of your staff will be reluctant to take time to train, you must make training fun, interesting, stimulating, and even an exciting experience. And above all, training must be mandatory. Put it on a schedule as a nonnegotiable commitment. No doctor's appointments. No dentist appointments. No excuses. Even one-person armies must treat it this way. Set a schedule and commit to following it—no matter what.

As you will learn in Chapter Eight, we retain significantly more information if we both see and hear it rather than just hearing it. But we retain the most information if we are actively involved in our learning such as when we participate in role playing or other learning exercises. At the very least, always use visual aids in your training because they drastically increase retention. Data dumps are okay for initial sessions when you need to relay a lot of information. However, the highest retention will come from practical application and regular and consistent involvement. That's where you get the big gains in productivity. So don't just create a training booklet and hand it out. Set the time, reserve the room, and make the training session mandatory.

Encourage questions, jokes, insights, participation, and humor. Treat all questions with respect, no matter how pointless you think they are! Keep your people focused, but don't make them feel stupid.

There are a variety of training methods and tools you can use to suit your material. It is a good idea to mix a few methods to meet your needs and keep people awake. Let's consider a few.

Lecture Format

This means you talk and they listen. This method is good for a data dump but not for anything that requires substantial input or group processing.

Group Questions

You present broad questions to the group and ask for a show of hands. This method keeps people engaged because it is interactive. Asking group questions is also very helpful when you want to show what is at stake in a given training session. Leading people to their own conclusions is much more powerful than you telling them what that conclusion should be. You might ask the following series of questions: "How many people get frustrated when they don't know the answer to a customer service question?" "How many of you would like to be so much of an expert that no matter what comes up, you are prepared to deal with it?" "Who here thinks that training and role playing would give them additional insights into how to deal with more situations?" Asking these types of questions can guide a group to the conclusion you want them to make.

Group Discussions

As in the group questions format, you are facilitating discussion around a given topic or issue and want specific feedback from your group. This keeps everyone engaged, but here the substance of their answers is crucial to the training session. For example, if I'm teaching a seminar and ask, "Who here has done workshops at their company?" I might get a show of hands. But then I ask, "How's it going?" At this point, I am going to get specific feedback from which I can extract common themes that need addressing in the training session.

Demonstration Training

With this training technique, the supervisor demonstrates how the employee should perform the task. Perhaps you are working on making appointments. The supervisor sets the scenario—she's calling a prospect for the first time and her goal is to get an appointment with the CEO. The imaginary receptionist answers the phone. The supervisor delivers the script of what everyone on the sales team will say to get past the receptionist and through to the CEO. After demonstrating, the supervisor will then solicit questions and probe to determine the level of understanding from the employees. The supervisor will then ask the employees to demonstrate back to the supervisor, which leads to role playing.

Role Playing

Role playing is an extremely effective way to train. Let's take customer service as an example. A company that is looking to be at the top of its game will already have outlined "the seven most common customer service issues." Even though you may have a manual that lays out what to do in various situations, role playing can really drive it home. Role playing helps each person automatically do what he's supposed to do even if he's rushed, challenged, or surrounded by distractions.

The other day I was calling my cell phone company because my phone magically started receiving about six text messages per second—everything from the news to the weather to horoscope predictions. I was calling to get this feature shut off and, I'll admit, I was impatient because the customer service person didn't seem to know what I was talking about, even though I thought I was explaining it clearly. My wife was sitting next to me when the customer service person hung up on me. My wife's thought was that I deserved to be hung up on because I was impatient with the customer service rep. Except now I was furious. If a customer is unhappy, have you trained your staff to hang up on them or to console them?

In reality, this scenario was disastrous but as a role play between a supervisor and a customer service rep it would be a fabulous tool. With the supervisor acting more and more obnoxious, the exercise would serve the dual function of preparing employees for the worst and providing comic relief for the training session. So yes, you can have fun and joke about irate customers (like me), but it sets the tone of how those people are to be treated. Not hung up on, but nurtured. You can tell when you encounter an organization where this training has been done and when you get one where it has not been done.

Hot Seats (Going Deeper)

Hot seats are a highly effective method of improving skills. I use these constantly with my clients. As we work to implement a new program or procedure, I hot seat sales reps. I drill down again and again on minute details until they get everything practically perfect.

For example, we had a client who sold office equipment. If sales reps went to the office manager in a prospect company, they would get nowhere. The typical office manager did not have the authority to approve the budget for replacing the major equipment like copiers and computer systems, even if they were 15-year-old antiques. The attitude was always this: as long as it's working, don't fix it! Office managers might know the long-term advantages of upgrading their office equipment, but often they were ineffective at persuading senior management to spend the money. My client wanted to get to the CFO instead. But reps found that most CFOs bunted them right back to the office manager because that's who's in charge of the office equipment. To get around this, we deliberately went after the CEOs, knowing that they would bunt us down to the CFO. We worked on this "CEO bunt" method and perfected it.

Hot seats were key to implementing the CEO bunt because I constantly found that the sales team had not done some step in the process we had expertly laid out. For example, a key ingredient to an effective CEO bunt is to give that CEO a tool that he or she can pass to the person you really want to reach. Usually that's a follow-up memo, yet I cannot tell you how many times hot seats revealed that the salesperson had not done this step.

I put the salespeople in the hot seat and asked them questions on every single part of this process until I was sure they absolutely had it down and would do it right the next time. I even did this with the owner of this company. Just from this one process, this team went from making four appointments a week to 30 appointments a week. But to be clear, it took five months of pigheaded determination and discipline to turn this company into the Ultimate Sales Machine.

Case Studies as a Training Method

As I just did with the office equipment story and as I do throughout this book, your training should use concrete examples and case studies in which the concept you are teaching made a big difference. People remember stories, especially when they are dramatic or humorous. There are two ways to include case studies in your standard training. One case study should show how someone did everything wrong and how that made the situation worse. Another case study should show how someone did everything right and how well it worked.

⚙ Exercise

Right now, for your area, think of a case study that illustrates a great point about how something should be handled. Write it down in as much detail as you can remember.

Test Before and After

For every concept or skill you teach, develop a test on that area for the staff. And if you really want to see your training stick, give staff the test before they take the training. That shows them how much they're going to learn and, more important, makes the answers stick when they learn it. Then, after the training, they take the tests again and feel accomplished when they get all the answers correct.

The Spot Quiz

In the companies I've run, spot quizzes are an institution. The staff comes into the weekly meeting and I hand out a spot quiz like you used to get in school. The staff groans, laughs, and makes jokes, but little by little, whatever you cover, again and again, eventually sticks. What are the six steps to time management? The 12 steps to get an appointment? The seven steps to selling? The six questions they'll ask every prospect? They know the answers. I have had them so programmed that if you quizzed some salespeople who haven't worked for me in 10 years, they'd probably still be able to fire the answers right off.

Technology Training Can Be a Boon to Productivity

I remember reading that most software programs are used to about 10 percent of their potential. The other day I was watching a consultant who works for us download a file from his email. He opened the email, opened the PowerPoint document, and then went to "save as" in the menu and saved it in a folder. I reached over and, using the mouse, simply dragged the item into the folder. He couldn't believe it was that easy. For years, he had been saving attachments as separate docs, not knowing you could simply drag them into the folder of choice.

Fortunately, this was not a technology consultant, but his company had never had any technology training at all. The skill level was embarrassing. I suggest that every company have some kind of ongoing and continuing technology training so that all employees know how to use the technology they have in the fastest, most efficient way possible. There are excellent tutorial software programs out there that teach you how to use technology effectively.

The best way to conduct technology training is to have mandatory times when this will occur and to make it fully interactive. As the instructor goes through the material, each person should follow along by executing each task for himself. Simply showing employees how to perform some operation does not mean they will be able to do that operation on their own. Those who are good with technology often get impatient with those who aren't—they want to just grab that mouse and show them how it's done. I have a technology person like that on my staff and I constantly swat his hand away and insist that I do the clicking myself so I learn better. And, again, the key here is repetition. Better to teach five shortcuts and repeat them three weeks in a row during your training sessions than to teach five new shortcuts every week and have none of them stick. We are all so busy doing our jobs that we don't take time to learn these shortcuts.

For example, I like to enlarge the type on my screen so that I don't have to use my glasses while working on my computer. And then I have to remember to put the font size back to normal-size type before sending the document on to a client. One day while my tech expert was watching me do this, he showed me that right on the menu bar of Word, there is a little window where you can enlarge the "view" without enlarging the actual type itself. Simple, fast, and I never have to remember to change the size of the type. Over the years I have surely wasted a month of my time enlarging type and setting it back to normal size. There are probably dozens of things you do for which some genius programmer has created shortcuts. Another way to learn technology, if you are a high-level executive, is to go through some of your normal tasks while a more technical person watches over you and shows you shortcuts.

Email is another area where training is key. I was the last person to do email and now I can't live without it. But I learned it by having an expert watch over my shoulder and walk me through it and then come back several times during the course of the week to show me more and more shortcuts and easier ways to do things. Same with PowerPoint. I couldn't live without these tools today. The productivity boost is enormous.

Now let's introduce the most powerful training you can possibly conduct in any company or department.

Workshop Training

Workshops are a powerful way to facilitate training, improve skills, and implement new procedures. This method is so effective for improving any company, department, issue, or skill that we have devoted an entire chapter to it. In the next chapter, you will learn how to use workshops to solve every problem in your organization and improve any skill area.

⚙ Exercise

What's your training plan? Everything works better with a plan, so jot down the answers to the following questions to begin creating your unique training plan. Write down whatever comes to mind even if you don't know where to begin. In the next chapter, you will learn how to get very clear on how to develop your training plan by using these notes to create an organized program.

- What kind of training are you going to provide?
- Who? Which departments or people need what kind of training?
- Why? What's the impact going to be?
- When are you going to conduct the training?
- How? What methods will you use and why are they best for the material you'll cover?

Conclusion

Developing a regular and consistent training program will enable you to effectively and systematically accomplish the following:

Train new employees who can hit the ground running.

Upgrade knowledge and skills of existing employees so that everything they do works better, smarter, faster.

Provide continuous professional development so your staff becomes more and more effective.

Solve any and all problems that come up in your organization.

If you take the time to sharpen skills and improve knowledge in every possible area, your company will start to run better, smarter, and faster—like a finely tuned sales machine. The companies that conduct the best training will own the future, so train constantly, train with enthusiasm, and train as you entertain. Lastly, and this is not to be overlooked, *train or feel the pain*.

With consistent training every week in every area of your company, you can put higher and higher standards into place and raise the bar of performance for your entire staff. If you really want to become the Ultimate Sales Machine, training is an absolute must at every level, no matter how large or how small you might be.

(3)

Executing Effective Meetings

How to Work Together to Improve Every Aspect
of Your Company Using Workshop Training

The best way to build the Ultimate Sales Machine and to keep it running as smoothly as possible is to hold regular, highly productive, workshop-style meetings dedicated to improving every aspect of your business. In each of these meetings you will focus all of the relevant people on fixing just one small part of the business. Together, you will brainstorm plans for how to improve this specific area, draft procedures to test, and ultimately create carved-in-stone company policies that everyone will be trained to follow. This constant attention to what I call the "three Ps"—*planning, procedures*, and *policies*—is essential if you want to easily and quickly grow your business into the Ultimate Sales Machine.

One of my clients became one of the fastest-growing companies in America, hiring 50 new people a week. Here's a question for you: could your company hire 50 people this week and weave them seamlessly into your organization? And, before you answer, could you then hire another 50 people next week?

Whether you're a Fortune 500 company or haven't hired even your first employee, you need to have the systems in place that would make hiring 50 people every week a breeze. This makes the difference between success and failure. A company that thinks like a small company remains small. A company, even a one-person army, that thinks and acts like a big company is going to grow faster, smarter, and better.

Most entrepreneurial companies don't install enough of the three Ps. Larger companies are more likely to have the three Ps in place, but most don't go far enough in perfecting and implementing them. In this chapter you will learn how to take any company or department to the next level through weekly workshop meetings focused on further developing the three Ps in every aspect of your business.

While you are improving the company, you need to be thinking like this: "What if I were hiring 50 people next week and I wanted all of them to enter the business and quickly be able to perform at peak levels? What kind of a training program do I need in place to do that?" So, for example, as you are improving your current sales effort, document everything as you go. You will be creating a training manual for future hires—even if, like this client, you are not hiring a single additional person right now. By thinking this way, you are forced to spell out each and every step. Leave nothing, or very little, for the imagination.

The Large-Company Model

Large companies typically already have training and procedure manuals, but they don't always go deep enough. Far too much is left up to individual interpretation. For example, I've never seen any company, short of those that have had my training, that has well-planned and -executed follow-up procedures after a sales call. That is almost always left to the individual salesperson. When you do that, the quality of follow-up is going to vary widely.

I recently looked to buy a new vehicle to tow my boat. The salesperson took my card, but I never heard from him. Instead, to my surprise, I got a "quality control follow-up call." After a few questions, the person got around to asking why I didn't buy. I told them why (the trade-in offer was thousands below the *Kelley Blue Book* value). I then asked a few questions of my own and found out that the dealer had hired a group to do the follow-up. Here an entire side business has been born: selling telephone follow-up to dealerships that can't seem to figure how to properly manage that practice internally.

This is not to say that you have to dictate what the follow-up is supposed to be. No—that is another mistake most executives make. All you have to do is have meetings where these things are discussed and developed. This is to say that you should have great follow-up procedures, but the folks in the trenches can help develop them. They will buy in much better to procedures that they themselves helped to create. This chapter explains how.

It is essential that you schedule at least one hour a week to work on the three Ps. In the words of my good friend Michael Gerber (author of *E-Myth*), this is working *on* the business, not just *in* the business. CEOs of large businesses, and businesses that want to be large, must do more of this. Here's how.

Many organizations achieve small, if any, real improvement year in and year out and CEOs don't know where to begin to change this. A typical problem I see over and over again is that the CEO or department head believes that he has to think of all the solutions to every problem that arises in his company or department. If you have a good staff, they will fill you with ideas on not just the problems but how to fix them, even ones you didn't know existed. Just ask them. I always tell my clients, "If you have a good staff, the only thing you need to bring to a meeting or workshop is *your judgment.*"

Keep in mind that when you ask your people what the problems are, *they're going to tell you.* You might not like what you hear. But this is the first step to finding and fixing the leaks and glitches holding you back from being the Ultimate Sales Machine.

Workshops

Workshops are an excellent method of focusing your mind and everyone else's on solutions and improvements within your organization. Workshopping means that instead of you talking and your staff listening, all of you get to work together on a problem, developing the ideas and insights to propel the company forward. If you are a medium- or small-sized company, you can invite every employee to participate. You never know from where the big ideas are going to come. Sometimes receptionists offer excellent solutions to problems in other departments because they are the first point of contact with any customer, so they may understand the customers' needs better than the high-level executives. Large companies should have workshop meetings every week for every department.

The Benefits of Workshop Training

Workshops help the company bond together as a team. Often, if you ask six people the same question, you will get six different answers. For example, if you ask six people at many companies what's the most important strength of their company, product, or service, you will get six diverging answers. That is not a good thing, and workshops will help you to unite employees and create a more powerful vision at every level of the company. Even more important, workshops offer an opportunity to create synergy in your organization. You will find that the ideas you generate as a group will be light-years ahead of what any one of you, including the CEO or department head, would have created on your own. At the same time, workshops also give the company or department leader a rare opportunity to influence attitudes, ideas, and the direction of the company.

Step-by-Step to an Outstanding Workshop

The first thing you need to do is schedule your weekly meetings with your staff. If your organization consists of fewer than 30 people, you can have the entire staff in your first workshop. If you have more than 30 people, you may have department-specific workshops. If you are a one-person army, you can do the workshops by yourself and the result will still be profound. Schedule workshops for the next year and put them on the company calendar as nonnegotiable requirements of everyone's job. Start them this week.

Next, you need to decide what you are going to work on in your first meeting. You may have an obvious thorn in your side—like the lack of good time management practices or an ineffective referral program—that you will want to work on right away. However, for most companies and departments, let me suggest an excellent first workshop.

Ask every person in the room to give three examples of how to improve some aspect of the company or department. Do not ask people to give answers immediately. Let them work on it. Give them three minutes to think about their answers and you will get better answers. Tell them that if they come up with three things fast, they can go ahead and write more.

Then go around the room and ask every person what they wrote. Note that the leader of the workshop has the most control over the experience and the outcome. It's important to make this a positive experience. You want people to look forward to these meetings as a time when the group will work together and each person will be listened to with respect. As people state their issues, make sure you are clear on what they are saying. Restate it in such a way that you will all remember what was said. Then write down each issue on a whiteboard or easel pad.

The meeting leader is responsible for keeping the meeting moving. After a few folks have shared duplicate ideas, say the following: "Okay, so we can get input from everyone, if you have something that has already been stated, you don't have to state it again." You will be amazed at how everyone wants to tell you everything they wrote down even after you say that you don't want duplicate input. Don't be impatient. Just gently say: "Good. Those are already up here (on the whiteboard). So, folks, to keep this moving, don't give me duplicates. Next."

If your staff is spread out all over the country, you can still do this workshop by telephone. Keep a list of everyone's name in front of you so that you make sure to get input from everyone. To make this run smoothly via telephone, you need to make sure that everyone numbers each item and writes down the same statement the same way so that you can refer to them later without causing confusion. Here's how your teleconference might go:

YOU: Okay, Kelly, give us your ideas on how we could improve this department.

KELLY: We could use well-crafted follow-up letters after we've interacted with a customer. I can't believe some of the letters I've seen going to customers. Spelling errors, poor grammar, you name it.

YOU: Great. Everybody, write this down for number four: "Create standard follow-up letters."

You can later return to number 4 or 5 or 8 and everyone stays with you. You won't have to read the entire statement every time you want to refer to it.

Taking Action on Workshop Ideas

As a result of your first workshop, you will have a list of things you need to work on to improve your business. In a moment I will show you how to prioritize the idea list into a master list you will use in planning future workshops. Each one of those items needs its own workshop to solve the problems or remove the obstacles. So keep the list and methodically work through each issue until you have solved the problems.

As you do these workshops, many things will surface that are easy to fix, create, or improve. But other things will surface that are worthy of sustained attention, as they are going to take time to fix. Right there on the spot, the boss can assign to-do's for specific people to "own" and get accomplished before the next meeting. Often, larger, more cumbersome items will come up that require several people to work together. These may be things that require technology or involve different systems or levels of staff. In these cases, you need to prioritize and properly delegate.

As the workshops are creating procedures and policies to solve problems, the leader of the workshop puts out a postworkshop memo that says: "This week's workshop solved the problem of customer service inconsistencies. Here are the nine things you can do when a customer is unhappy." That memo goes into a "procedure binder" and that becomes a training manual for new people. Each memo is a page or two and so, at the end of the year, you will have 50 to 100 pages that document an entire year's worth of workshops. As you test and finalize the procedures into policies to address each issue, you take out the old memo and replace it with the new, more thoroughly developed policy. This works best when someone is assigned the responsibility of updating the binder to reflect all of the growth and learning curve of the company.

This simple workshop is the first thing I do as an outside consultant when I go in to improve a company. For many of them, it has opened the door to creating lasting positive change. Here's an example.

Fixing 18 Ten-Year-Old Customer Service Problems in Two Hours Flat

Recently, I sat 20 employees of a publishing company down to do their first workshop. I asked this question: "What are the things standing in the way of this being a much better company?" We put the list up on the whiteboard and then prioritized it. One of the obstacles was that there were "too many inconsistencies in how the customer service people handle complaints." So we took that single statement and focused the next workshop on it, asking folks to list examples of where this occurred. There were 18 distinct inconsistencies noted by the staff where this company had never bothered to create standard procedures or policies by which people could operate. As a result, many of these 18 issues appeared hundreds of times during a given year and most of them ended up being dealt with by the president himself. Yet, like most presidents, he was so busy that he never stopped to create permanent solutions. This was partly because he couldn't immediately and easily think of what those solutions might be. Again, here is a case where the president believed he had to solve all the problems. You don't. Have a meeting with the people dealing directly with the problems and simply ask for solutions.

So I gathered the staff into a room and, in one hour, we collectively solved nine of the eighteen issues. The following week we solved the other nine. Most of these issues simply needed to be addressed one time with the president in the room. In some cases, we created form letters that dealt with the problem. In other cases, we put a section on the Web site that listed standard answers to some of the issues that arose. This particular publishing company had made some choices in its editorial content that often brought about complaints from parents who purchased products for their children. When customers complained, the customer service rep would then say: "Thank you for bringing this up. You are not the first one to do so, and we appreciate your input [honor the customer]. We've addressed this specifically and I'm going to send you a link to our Web site where you can read our perspective on this issue. If after reading that, you are still not satisfied, please get back in touch with me. Issues that go beyond our company policies are addressed quarterly by our president. So if you do not feel satisfied by how we address this issue, please let us know."

On the Web site, the issue was addressed thoroughly with compelling copy that explained why the company operated the way it did. Now, instead of the president dealing with some of these issues daily, he would only need a quarterly meeting to look at cases where someone was not satisfied with the company's policy or position.

The other thing we did was to develop a hierarchy of solutions the customer service reps could offer to keep the customer happy. In other words, each rep was authorized to offer a solution. If the customer was still unhappy, the rep could offer another solution. If the customer was still unhappy, the rep could even offer a third solution. This procedure empowered the customer service people with levels of actions they could take before needing to involve a supervisor.

It is amazing to think that this company had labored under so many basic problems for a decade and we solved them within two hours using focus and communication in a workshop-style meeting.

Imagine if you planned, tested, and established policies for every step of the sales process, from prospecting to cold calling to initiating interaction with customers to rapport building and right on through to every detail of follow-up. When a new salesperson comes in—Wham!— there in one place is the collective input, learning curve, and intelligence of all the salespeople, spelling out "best practices" for every step of the sales process. How much faster can the new salesperson enter the game of selling? And how much better is that salesperson going to be if you had this kind of training in the first few days?

Continuing Workshops

With a training tool like that, pretty soon you'll be able to hire 50 people in one week and turn around and do it again the next week. Workshops help any company at any size get all the current activities working much more like the Ultimate Sales Machine. The key is to do continuing workshops. In fact, here are step-by-step instructions for another workshop with a specific problem you're trying to solve. If you want to get the most out of this, you need to actually do these exercises with your staff. Follow the instructions, in the order presented, doing each step as you go. You'll get more out of the experience.

This is a great workshop for everybody to do: what is something else you can offer the buyer at the point of sale?

Step 1: Appoint the person to lead the group. In small companies, the CEO is often best, unless he or she wants to defer to someone else in the group. If you're a one-person army, do it by yourself. It will be very valuable.

Step 2: On a whiteboard, write down the focus question: "What is something else we can offer our buyer at the point of sale?"

Side Note on This Workshop

In my experience of implementing this particular workshop, after we are done and have tested various offers, we have found that one out of three people will buy something else if offered at the point of sale. The most expensive thing you have to do today as a business is to acquire new customers. Once those customers are in the door, anything else you sell them increases profit margins dramatically. So every company should have add-on sales at the point of purchase. In one case, I worked with a calendar company that got some stores to put "spinners" (racks that hold the calendars) up by the cash register, and the cashier would say: "Have you picked out a pictorial calendar? We have 26 different types and they make great gifts for around $10." About one out of every three people would buy a calendar. Many would buy a few as gifts.

And here's a great spin that you definitely want to consider when you're trying to increase your profits. I know a software company that struck a deal with another software company to add on a complementary product. The first company sold the second company's software and the two companies split the profits. The first company had done the hardest part: acquiring the customer. It was able to increase its "profit per customer" by adding an additional product from another company that it didn't even have to develop.

So as a side note to all companies, this is a very good exercise. Let's continue with how you might get more ideas for this.

Step 3: Now have participants in the group write down on their own pad every single idea that comes to them. Give everyone a few minutes to work on this. Do not let them call out ideas. The leader must participate as well. You'll see that most of the people will run out of ideas after about two minutes, so that is a good period of time. If you're doing this by yourself, the exercise is the same: write down everything you can think of that you could offer your buyers. The benefit, of course, of doing this with a team is that, among everyone in the group, you're going to think of a lot more possibilities.

DO NOT READ AHEAD. STOP HERE AND DO THE EXERCISE.

Step 4: Now the leader of this exercise will ask participants to give their ideas. The leader will write them down on the whiteboard, summarizing them as he or she goes.

Step 5: Prioritize. Now organize a vote to decide which ideas would work best. People's opinions will change as the collective intelligence of the group is shared. Here you want to get a general consensus.

Have participants look at the whiteboard and rank their number 1, 2, and 3 choices. In other words, what do they think is the most important thing to do, the second most important, and the third. Have the group write down their answers, thinking through their choices. You've got 30 seconds, so go.

DO NOT READ AHEAD. STOP HERE AND DO THE EXERCISE.

Step 6: The leader of the group will then ask each person to give his or her choices. Next to each choice on the board, you're going to write three slashes for a ranking of first choice, two slashes for second choice, and one slash for third choice.

Now tally up the totals. The highest number will be the group's collective first choice and so on. The items receiving the highest number of votes are the ones you're going to work to integrate using more workshops to do so. Cut it off at the five top training ideas—maybe six if you must have one more. Your whiteboard will now look like this:

1. Additional service 1 Ⅲ Ⅲ Ⅲ ‖
2. Additional service 2 Ⅲ ‖
3. Additional service 3 Ⅲ Ⅲ ‖
4. Additional service 4 Ⅲ |
5. Additional service 5, etc. Ⅲ

At the end of the exercise, you'll have some clear winners; as you can see, 1 and 3 got the most votes.

Step 7: Implementation: There are 10 steps to implement any new concept for any company. We're going to spell those out shortly.

Once you see what you can accomplish with workshops, you will no doubt be hungry for more. Do them every week, and in a year you'll be an entirely different organization with dramatic improvements in every area of your business. Just stop everything, once per week for an hour, to fix all the things in your business that aren't the way you would like them or to add new improvements to strengthen your business or your profits.

Example

Let's go back to the carpet cleaning company as a great example of each aspect of the workshop as well as the implementation. My carpet cleaner client sent me recordings of some of the salespeople talking to customers. I'm listening to this salesperson talk to a 78-year-old woman who uses a walker to get around. She's calling to have her rug cleaned. They set up the appointment for the rug to be picked up and taken back to the plant (wall-to-wall has to be cleaned in the home), where they have a giant washing machine–like structure to completely submerge, clean, and expertly dry your rug. The conversation with the elderly woman goes like this:

WOMAN: Well, what about the pad under the rug? It's kind of dirty, too.
SALESPERSON: How old is the pad?
WOMAN: It's about 15 years old.
SALESPERSON: Oh, that's too old. If we tried to clean it, we'd obliterate it.
WOMAN: Well, I guess I'll have to go get a new pad.
SALESPERSON: Oh yeah. You're definitely going to have to replace that.

Since I'm the consultant and I know how expensive it is to get new clients, I think: "They should sell pads. Heck, they've got the rug right there in the plant. They can put the rug on the padding, cut it out, roll it up, and send it right back with the rug. It's a great up-sell."

So I get the owner on the phone: "I have a great idea for you. You should sell pads." He says, "We do." I tell him, "No, you don't, actually," and I play him the recording. The owner brings the salesperson in and asks her why she didn't offer to sell this old woman a pad. The salesperson says, "I didn't want to seem too pushy."

This carpet cleaning company actually had six excellent up-sell options. The problem was getting the salespeople to offer them. In addition to carpets, they can clean your couch or your bed. The technology of using hot steam to clean your carpet can be applied to the furniture you sit on (or your dog sits on) all day. Studies show that the average living room has five million dust mites in it. Our bodies are equipped to deal with those mites, but their feces and the bacteria that feed on it can cause bacterial infection. (As you can see here and will learn in depth in the next chapter, market data can be very motivational.) Steaming that bed or couch kills germs.

We gathered all of the salespeople in a workshop and asked them, "What would you say is the best method for offering *every* client *every* service *every* time?" One suggested we put the six services they offer right on the order form. As they're talking to the client, they would be able to check off all six things on the order form to show they offered them. This was a great suggestion, so we decided to test it and implement it as a procedure for the company. We followed 10 simple steps and, after several months of pigheaded discipline and hard work, we had it so that *every* salesperson offered *every* service to *every* customer *every* time.

Now let's go over the 10 steps to implement new concepts, change, and growth into your organization.

10 Steps to Implement Any New Policy

One of the finest executives I've ever known is Scott Hallman of Business Growth Dynamics, who built a company up to be *Inc.* magazine's 59th-fastest-growing company out of 500. He is the executive I mentioned earlier who was so systematized he was hiring 50 new people a week. In fact, at the height of Scott's growth, he was hiring 55 new people every week. Scott has since gone on to become a trainer himself, teaching people how to enhance profit in their organizations and also how to implement. The following uses some of Scott's ideas as a foundation along with some of my experience in the field and as a trainer who has had to master implementation.

1. Get Everyone to Feel the Pain

To create real change in any organization, you have to help everyone, including yourself, to define, outline, and intensify the pain of *not* fixing the problem. When people start to think about their problems, they put themselves in the mood to learn, and that's the mood you want them to be in to get profound results.

The first time I did a Fortune 500 implementation, I went in and conducted an audit. I had good ideas and presented them to the CEO. He was impressed and felt his fee was well spent. He flew his entire sales team—255 people—to Denver, where I presented my ideas to them. They intellectually understood them, but they only half-heartedly agreed with them. The next day, they went out and tried them here and there. The ideas didn't work *right away*, so the salespeople abandoned them almost immediately and the program totally failed.

You probably already know what kind of person I am. Failure doesn't go over very well with me. I don't take on clients and then fail them. I learned right then and there that having a system for implementation was much more important than the ideas I might have for growing a company. The first thing you need to do if you want people to change is to show them why what they're doing now isn't working. Make it as intense as possible.

One of the best ways to put people in pain is to ask them what challenges they are facing. The next time I did a large-scale implementation, I started with this exercise. There were a few hundred salespeople in the room. I began by asking them to list the biggest problems they were meeting in the market. I then had the salespeople form groups to discuss and vote on the group's agreed-upon problems. Misery loves company. I had an entire room complaining about their competition, lack of time, the challenges to get in the door, and so on. I had some rather profound solutions to their problems, but they required a radical upgrade in selling over what they had been doing. In order to get them open for something that needed a new learning curve, I knew I had to put them in a lot of pain with their current model.

After the groups discussed their problems, I had each group tell me the top three challenges that they had voted on. I wrote all their problems on the whiteboard and then asked them if they liked having these challenges. I asked how many people in the room would like to solve these challenges. "What if there were ways to solve these challenges but they required you to gain an entirely new learning curve? What if it took a little extra work in the beginning to gain this learning curve, but, once you had it, it would dramatically reduce many if not all of these challenges? How many here would look forward to the new learning curve?" I used the group questions format, as discussed in the previous chapter, in order to get the buy-in.

I had learned the secret to creating change: you have to put people in pain.

Using the practical example of the carpet cleaner, we first showed those salespeople how they were not serving their clients. Here was this old woman with a walker trying to figure out on her own how to get a rug pad. They could have helped her, but they didn't. Second, we did a matrix that showed them how their commissions would be impacted if only one out of every five people took just one of the up-sells. In the course of the past year of *not* doing the up-sells, they had potentially already lost $20,000 in commissions. Talk about motivation to adapt to a new strategy.

Another exercise to increase the pain of not changing is to simply have everyone work on that. Tell them to each write down, "What are the drawbacks of not changing or improving this behavior?" and then list those drawbacks. Let them intensify their own pain.

2. Hold a Workshop to Generate Solutions

We've already covered this. If you are in a management position or are the CEO, you only have to bring with you to this workshop questions and your judgment. Whatever the problem, your staff deals with it every day. They will have many ideas on how to solve it.

We asked the sales staff what would be the best way to make sure they offered all six services every time they talked to a client. As stated, the solution that ultimately solved the problem was to list the six services on the order form and require salespeople to check them off as they offered them to the client.

3. Develop a "Conceptual Solution or Procedure"

You've isolated what you want to work on (offering the up-sell every time) and you have a plan for what procedures you will follow to do this.

You might even have scripts, outlines, and cheat sheets. In the case of the carpet company, putting the list of services on the order form was the conceptual solution. We say each solution or procedure is "conceptual" until it is "proven" by you and your staff. In this case it is cut-and-dry, but other solutions you attempt may not be so simple. These more complex solutions will need to be worked on in this phase of your implementation.

In order to have the salespeople go through the list of services every time, we had to present them in a way that positioned what we were doing as servicing the customer and not selling to the customer. We developed some dialogue to make this happen, such as, "We feel it's our obligation to alert you to other services that you might want to take advantage of today. So I'm just going to list these for you. If you have an interest, I can go into more detail." The salesperson would then give a sentence or less on each up-sell. Often, this prompted questions.

Recently, I activated a new credit card. Usually, this is all done by electronic recording. This time the recording said, "Please hold for an operator." I thought that something must be wrong, but, to my surprise, the only thing the operator did was try to sell me additional services—protection plans, group buying discounts, and so on. Here's a company that instead of automating the activation process decided to use it as another opportunity to touch down with buyers and thus potentially increase profits. In order to get this implemented, I'm sure they tested scripts and went through the steps I'm outlining in this section.

Back to testing: do this step for any area for which you don't have a procedure. Using up-sells as an example, how many up-sells do you have and how many different ways do you offer them? How does your company or department generate referrals? How do you address customer service complaints? How do you bond and follow up with clients? If you don't have an answer for each one of these questions, or if each member of your staff has a different answer, then you need to create and test procedures in order to implement policies that will be followed by every member of your organization.

4. Leader or Top Talent Personally Performs Procedure or Task

If you're a smaller company, often the CEO or leader of the company can personally test and perfect the procedure. The leader has the biggest picture of how everything fits together in the company or department, but he or she often leaves the details to others. Hands-on involvement at every level enables the leader to create the three Ps with certainty. When Scott Hallman was building his company to be *Inc.* magazine's 59th-fastest-growing company, he personally tested every procedure. No one could snow him on any issue as he did each procedure himself and had a complete and very realistic view of how things should and could be done.

Of course, if you are a Fortune 500 company, the CEO does not usually step in and do a cross-sell or an up-sell. Instead, you pick champions. Figure out who is going to champion this idea. Then that person accepts the responsibility for making that idea effective in the organization.

Don't be tempted to have everyone in your organization test and perfect the procedure at the same time. You will spend a lot of money with lower-level talent trying to figure something out. Instead, have the higher-level talent perfect it and then train the rest. Just keep in mind that you have to constantly figure out how to make it scalable.

For the carpet cleaning company, we worked with the top producers and got the formula perfected enough that we could show the rest of the salespeople that one out of five customers did take at least one up-sell. Some of them took all five up-sells. Then we trained the entire staff on it. I always recommend testing new ideas with your top performers.

5. Set a Deadline for Testing the Conceptual Procedure

Set a deadline so you know that if you aren't seeing results in a certain amount of time, you need to go back to the workshop whiteboard and look at additional options. At the minimum, your weekly meeting will always check in on the progress or lack of it. More on this in step 9.

6. Document Step-by-Step Procedure or Process

You want this to be a repeatable process, so spell it out. Write out your scripts, procedures, activities, and the results you expect to achieve. Make it so 50 new hires could come in today and everything would be clear to them if they followed your three Ps manual. Even if your company or department is small, you need to put these procedures in place as if you were going to hire 50 people because it forces you to detail every step along the way.

7. Have Show-and-Tell and Role Playing

Take your documented steps and work with your staff to test and implement them. Show-and-tell and role playing offer the best methods of gaining experience before you put the process into the field.

Scott Hallman's company processed more than four million medical record files a year. With more than 650 technicians located on-site at client hospitals, managing performance results was critical. Left to their own devices, new technicians might process only four medical charts per hour. However, by constantly working on the process and "proceduriz-ing" it down to the smallest detail, Scott was able to get the technicians to average 9.2 charts per hour! That's more than doubling their performance. What would it do for your company if everyone could produce twice the results they're producing now?

If it's a telephone procedure, demonstrate it or record your high-level talent doing the procedure so your staff can actually hear how it works. Role-play and workshop every possible scenario. Work over your staff, forcing them to approach each scenario exactly as you would have them do it.

I was hired by a company that sold small to midrange technology solutions to IT executives. They bought six companies and put together an integrated and global technological solution to business that changed everything. It was an utterly brilliant design. Instead of selling $100,000 technology enhancement packages, they were now selling $9 million complete technology makeovers. This required the salespeople to sell to CEOs of very large companies up to and including Fortune 500.

The problem was that not one of their 40 salespeople had ever called a CEO at any time for any reason. We role-played with them. We wrote scripts. We told them how to do it. But they were still ineffective. These people were more technology oriented and therefore not the types to call large-company CEOs (a problem covered in Chapter Nine). For the most part, these salespeople were not asserting themselves enough to even get past the receptionists or assistants, so they never even came close to delivering their scripts.

The CEO of this technology solutions company decided to hire me to show them how to do it. I got on the phone and recorded myself. In two hours, I made 50 calls, got two top CEOs on the phone, and talked my way into a meeting with one of them. I played this for the staff. I was winging it all the way because this was my first time pitching this material. The salespeople saw that, although the pitch wasn't perfect, it was still good enough to close an appointment with a $4 billion company. They learned that CEOs of large companies are great visionaries and can be engaged if you have a great promise for their future. Offering this promise wasn't as hard as these salespeople had thought. The next day, every salesperson started calling CEOs, and some of them started getting appointments.

8. Have Another Workshop on How to Improve

You're deep into implementing this procedure. If there are any weak spots or areas to improve, your staff will know about them. With the carpet cleaning company, we did many workshops with the staff, asking *them* how to best implement this strategy. So if you're having trouble implementing something, ask your staff how to do it better. Even on the assembly line, you can gather your people together and ask them how you could increase production. The surprising thing is that you may find that many of them have been frustrated for a while now and have great suggestions that were ignored by their immediate supervisor. So it's worth your time, no matter how large your company may be, to get in the trenches and hear some of the staff's ideas.

People like to be asked their opinion. Then when they give it, they'll have a greater buy-in when you actually take advantage of the ideas they suggest. Make them work at it and perfect it in concept and in practice before you roll it out.

9. Monitor the Procedure Directly

In the case of the carpet cleaning up-sell, the owner of the company recorded the reps so I could hear the actual conversations. We corrected and monitored weekly. Some companies have people test something and then report back a month later. That's crazy. You need to monitor weekly. Or, if it's really important, monitor it every day so you can be sure that your staff is doing it properly and that it is bringing about the desired results. Monitor the procedure closely, observing and correcting behavior.

No matter how well you spell it all out, some people will still miss some things. Monitor. Correct. Monitor. . . .

Think of yourself as a military leader training your troops in the important art of hand-to-hand combat and survival. Do you want to have your people trying to figure out how to fight while they're on the battlefield? Or, do you want to role-play the heck out of them so that when they get into battle, they are skilled and prepared?

Even when you've perfected the concept and are rolling out the policy, you're not done with monitoring. The next phase is to randomly, but consistently, observe and correct the procedure even as it's being implemented company- or departmentwide. Now you have trained your soldiers and they are in combat. The mistakes they make could cost lives. Don't you want to correct and monitor at every turn?

Get in there and make sure the idea is being properly implemented. As previously mentioned, add spot quizzes to the mix. The lowest level of learning is memorization. Start there. Make everyone memorize every procedure by role-playing it again and again. The highest level of learning is synthesis. That's when you've learned something so well that it has become synthesized into the way you think, act, and react. Synthesis only comes from hands-on experience.

Once the policy is in effect and it's second nature to everyone, you're still not done. Continue to monitor and police at regular intervals. If you are a hands-on leader and you've grown your company to the point that you really are hiring 50 new people per week, how can you still monitor your people? Easy. Since you as a leader are disciplined and determined and directly involved in the creation of each procedure, you can easily spot when things aren't being done the right way. You can walk into a site and spot every single flaw in the operation.

10. Measure and Reward the Outcome

You must measure your results intently. People *re*spect what you *in*spect. In step 3, you documented your expected results. Now you have to monitor to make sure everything is being done correctly to achieve those results. Rewarding comes last, after the bugs are out, but it is critical. It is important that you set very specific criteria for rewarding your team. For example, I see companies rewarding employees with more money than they got last year just for doing the same thing they did last year. That's not a very good management idea, is it? Rewards are for increasing performance.

Make a big deal out of the reward process. I learned this in my first job when I was 19 years old. The CEO would come into the company and give $100 to the top producer, $100 if you met your quota, and $100 to the ones who had the most add-on sales (lamps, end tables, etc.). You had the potential to earn three $100 bills. Not only that, but the CEO would shake your hand and make a big deal out of it. You will find that people will work even harder for the recognition than they will for the money. But, no matter how rich you are, a $100 bill is nice.

Conclusion

The three Ps are magical in your operation because they create the conditions for every aspect of your company to operate with subconscious competence. Every person on your staff knows what to do in every situation without having to think about it. As a result, your company or department begins to operate like a finely tuned machine.

We'll continually return to the three Ps throughout the rest of the book, showing you how to build a stronger and stronger organization.

Becoming a Brilliant Strategist

How to Get Up to Nine Times More Impact from Every Move You Make

As we've already established, it's harder than ever to get in front of a potential buyer, so when you finally get your company in front of that buyer, you need to maximize what you can accomplish in that moment. You need to think and plan strategically. This chapter also shows you how being a strategist will make it easier to get to that customer in the first place.

To make sure you understand the difference between a tactic and a strategy, here are some simple, yet essential, definitions. A *tactic* is a method or technique used to achieve an immediate or short-term gain. You run ads or send direct mail pieces to get leads. You go on a sales call to make a sale. You attend trade shows to meet with potential buyers and get more leads. These are examples of tactics.

A *strategy* is a carefully defined and detailed plan to achieve a long-term goal. In business, a strategy is the overall impact, the ultimate position you would like to achieve in the market. To think like a brilliant strategist, you will design and combine your tactics with the long-term strategy in mind. In addition, you will constantly ask yourself and your team, "How many strategic objectives can we accomplish with *each* tactic?" In this chapter I'll show how every tactic can potentially achieve 10 or more strategic objectives.

In my experience, there are three types of executives. A full 90 percent are what I call "tactical executives," while 9 percent are what I'd call "strategic executives." And only 1 percent—the most effective executives—possess the rare combination of both tactical and strategic abilities.

Tactical executives think only in terms of making the sale for today. They don't understand strategy. If you tell them that it's twice as difficult today as it was 10 years ago to get an appointment with a prospect, they will think of ways to make the sales team try twice as hard. Strategic executives will often look at the situation from a global perspective and see if they can develop some high-level strategy that might help to solve the problem. These executives are brilliant. They create concepts, ideas, and strategies that most would never develop. But strategic executives are not good at, or interested in, tactics. Hence, I've seen many big ideas that never come to fruition because strategic executives fail in the implementation of their big ideas.

Now let's talk about the top 1 percent. The executive who thinks both tactically and strategically can develop the big ideas and the big strategies and also use discipline and determination to see those brilliant strategies implemented at the tactical level. And just for the record, the second type of executive, the strategist, can often be paired with a strong tactician and be very successful. However, the strategist may have to keep explaining and selling his or her ideas again and again to the tactical executive.

In my experience a purely tactical executive does not grasp strategy easily. Here's a good example: I have a client who has just started a brand-new magazine. The salespeople find it nearly impossible to reach the advertisers they want in the magazine. This is a market with 80-plus competing advertising vehicles. To meet this challenge, I changed the titles of the salespeople to sound less salesy—for example, "director of corporate communications." This enabled a salesperson to call a prospect and say something like: "Hi. I'm Jennifer Smith, the director of corporate communications here at *XYZ Magazine*. As part of our ongoing effort to continually serve the market, we like to learn more about other companies in our market. I also interface with the editorial staff here, and I'm always on the lookout for potential stories for our magazine. Tell me, how long has your company been in business?"

This approach enables the sales staff to achieve the strategic objective of establishing solid relationships within the market and getting into discussions that build rapport. After they build rapport, the salespeople are able to softly segue into talking about advertising. "One of the other things I do for the magazine is look for products or services that our readers might be interested in." This enables the salespeople to then get into dialogue about advertising and work their way into a technique you're about to learn called "education-based marketing," creating an opportunity to educate prospects. This is a long-term, *strategic* approach to the sales process.

But here's the point: A tactical salesperson would say, "Why do I want to do all that when all I really want to do is sell them advertising?" The strategic executive would understand that this approach would get you into an actual conversation that can build some rapport and interest before trying to immediately sell the prospect an ad. The *strategist* looks at every challenge as an opportunity to out-think competitive approaches. This will be demonstrated 10 more ways during the upcoming pages.

Let's go deeper.

When you or your salespeople get in front of a client, what do you want to accomplish? What are your strategic objectives?

When I ask executives that question, most of them reply tactically: "I want to make a sale." Then I ask them to think strategically: "What else do you want to achieve?" And they say, "What else is there?" The conversation goes like this:

ME: Would you like to be respected?

THEM: Well, of course, I'd like to be respected.

ME: Would you like to be trusted?

THEM: Well, of course, I'd like to be trusted.

ME: Would you like referrals?

THEM: Well, of course, I'd like referrals.

ME: Would you like a preemptive strategy for when your competitors try to undercut your pricing?

THEM: Well, yeah, that's a great objective.

ME: Would you like to be perceived as an expert?

THEM: That could be valuable, yes.

ME: How about influence? Would you like to have influence in that meeting?

THEM (**the tacticians**): What does that mean?

ME: Hang with me here a second. How about brand loyalty? Is that important?

THEM: Heck, yes.

ME: What about some urgency to buy now? Would that be a good thing?

THEM: Yes. That would be good.

If you even *think* about these objectives, doesn't it automatically change how that meeting might go? So much of the sales process and potential strategic objectives are left up to the individual salesperson—every time. What if you, as the leader of your company, could devise a way to accomplish all those strategic objectives, and do them every time anyone in your company is in front of a buyer? How much more powerful would you be over your competition?

Let's go deeper.

Increasing Sales 600 Percent by Adding Just One Additional Strategic Objective

Two furniture stores open up in a town on nearly the same day. One is totally tactical and the other is very strategic. If you go in to look at couches in store 1, the salesperson tries to sell you a couch. Tactical. Over a four-year period, this store grows at about 10 percent per year, mostly driven by the increasing costs of furniture.

In store 2, of course, they try to sell you a couch, but the management constantly trains the salespeople to sell the store. "First time in our store? Well, let me tell you about it." And while the salespeople are on their way to the couches, they pitch the heck out of that store. They tell you about the history, the owner's devotion to service, why they have lower prices than their competitors, how well trained they are on furniture construction, and how that benefits you as the consumer.

The purpose of this buyer education is to create brand loyalty. Over time, this store builds a large and loyal following of customers who automatically come there first when they are interested in any type of furniture. When you shop for furniture, you probably go to various stores with little or no brand loyalty. Or you may see a sale in the newspaper and go because of the sale. But if you had a relationship with a store that stood behind its product like no other and could thoroughly explain the differences in furniture quality (there's quite a bit to know) and even offered expertise in decorating, you might have an affinity, a loyalty, a preference for that particular store. When you needed furniture, you would go there first because of the relationship that it purposefully built with you. Buyer education paid off handsomely for one of our two new furniture stores. Over a four-year period the tactical store remained a one-store location, while the strategic store opened six locations.

People will even pay more if they perceive there is a greater value or a deeper reason for buying from one provider over another. I cannot tell you how many times I've helped companies step up out of the commoditizing world in which they live by being more strategic. In a moment I'll have you do an exercise that will pound this idea home. Let's do a little more setup so you get as much as possible out of the exercise.

Here's a question I want you to answer: when your buyers look to purchase your type of product or service, how much of an expert are they? When I ask this question in front of a large audience, everyone pretty much admits that in any given purchasing situation, the average buyer is not much of an expert. For example, you are probably not much of an expert at all about carpet cleaning, are you? If most of your buyers are not experts at what to look for in your product or service, this opens a gaping strategic opportunity for the brilliant strategist to capitalize on.

I call this the science of *setting the market's buying criteria*. Basically it means that every buyer can be taught how to be a better buyer of your type of product or service. Using the carpet cleaning example, the buyer calls in with loose or few buying criteria at all. The salesperson then *resets* the buying criteria by educating that consumer about the EPA studies on the importance of clean carpets to the quality of the air and life in your home. You can do this for your company with profound results. To further explain, let me introduce you to a powerful concept that really tunes up the strategist in all of us:

The Stadium Pitch

Imagine that I could put you on stage in a giant stadium where the entire audience is composed of your most perfect prospects, giving you the opportunity to present to them all at once.

First question: Are you ready right now? Could you walk out on that stage and present to every one of them and do it perfectly?

I give speeches all over the world where I ask this question. Usually about three to six people raise their hands (out of 1,000 in the audience). When I drill down with the few who raise their hands, I find that they are usually not ready, but sometimes I find someone who is ready. They've got a killer stadium pitch and it's expertly tuned. I compliment them, saying, "Wow, you are really prepared." The response comes back: "Thank you for the compliment, but I have to thank you because I got one of your training products years ago."

The audience will laugh, thinking the person has to be working for me, but, boy, does it make a point about the strategist. As you will soon see, a well-prepared stadium pitch will enable you to attract a lot more prospects and close a higher percentage of tire kickers into actual buyers.

The first thing you need to think about and plan is who the ideal person would be in your audience. For example, my client who sells products for manufacturing production lines would work for months to build their case with the production manager—the one on the front line of production—only to have a higher-level executive say no to the increased costs. So I shifted their entire strategy to selling to the owner or CEO of the company. So in their stadium, they would want CEOs. Who is in your stadium, ideally? The challenge is how well you can keep that person in the audience.

Right now, take a few minutes and write your stadium pitch title.

LADIES AND GENTLEMEN, THE TITLE OF TODAY'S TALK IS:

Twenty years of research has shown me that there's always a very small percentage of folks "buying now." Three percent. I gave a lecture recently in front of 1,200 CEOs and said: "Let me prove this to you. How many people in the audience are in the market for a car right now?" About 30 people raised their hands. "How about tires?" A different 30 raised their hands. "How about furniture?" Thirty hands up. "How about home improvements?" Yet another 30 hands. "Office equipment?" You see my point. About 3 percent of potential buyers at any given time are buying now. Right now. That percentage drives all commerce.

My research further concludes that 7 percent of the population is open to the idea of buying. This is the percentage who may be dissatisfied with their current item or provider and are not opposed to change, but who may not yet be "buying now." The remaining 90 percent fall into one of three equal categories. The top third are what I call "not thinking about it." They are not against it, not for it, but just "not thinking about it." So if you sell office equipment and you ran an ad, this 30 percent would not respond because they're just not thinking about office equipment right now.

The next third are what I call "think they're not interested." So at first pass, they are not neutral like the first third. They would reply, "I don't think I'm interested in office equipment." And then the final third are what I call "definitely not interested." These folks are happy with what they have or just simply know they don't need it. They may have a 10-year-old copier, but if it's not broken, why fix it?

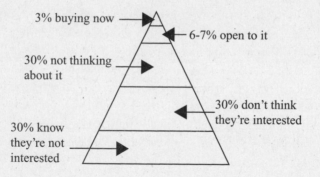

With this in mind, let's put you back in that stadium. Right before you walk out there, the audience is told: "You had to come, but you don't have to stay. If this person [you] talks about something that is of no interest to you, you can simply get up and leave."

If you walk out there and say, "I'm here to tell you why we have the greatest office equipment in the world," you're going to have 90 percent of the audience get up and leave. And anyone who's ever spoken in public knows that you do not want that to happen.

So now let's rethink that stadium title. What could you say that would keep virtually everyone in their seats? This is important because whatever that title is that would get all those potential buyers to stay and hear more is the same approach to use in your advertising, direct mail, or Web site. What can you write as your stadium pitch title or ad, for that matter, that would appeal to the entire pyramid of potential buyers?

Let's imagine that you sell office equipment. It's your turn to give your speech and the audience is full of CFOs. If you're a little strategic, you might go with something like "The Five Ways Our Office Equipment Can Benefit You." Again, an approach like this appeals only to those who are "buying now," and possibly those who are "open to it," but pretty much 90 percent of your audience is leaving.

So what title would have a broader appeal? How about "The Five Ways You're Wasting Money in Your Operations and Administration"? I'm not saying this is going to rivet the executives to their chairs, but they're not leaving either. They'll stay to hear a little more. This is also true for an ad with that headline. It's definitely going to appeal to the top two tiers, but it also appeals to *everyone in that stadium*. Everyone is interested in saving money in their operations and administration costs. Certainly every CFO is interested in that, so they'll stay in the stadium. And if everything that follows has some substance to it, you've now taken your marketing and selling activity to an entirely new level.

The hardest thing we need to do today is grab the attention of potential buyers and keep their attention long enough to help them buy your product. This approach of offering some education of value to them gives you a significant opportunity to attract more buyers and build more credibility. I call this "education-based marketing," and here's a line you should write down: you will attract way more buyers if you are offering to teach them something of value *to them* than you will ever attract by simply trying to sell them your product or service.

As another example, I had a merchant services company as a client. They primarily target retail stores. So in the stadium pitch scenario, their audience are retail store owners. If they walk out there and start off with, "I'm going to show you why our merchant services are better than anyone else's," the 90 percent are leaving since they are not in the market for merchant services right now. So what could you say to keep every retailer in the stadium to hear a little more? Here's a great title: "The Five Reasons All Retailers Fail." The tactical executive reading this is already saying, "But if all I really want to do is sell merchant services, then why would I bother with all this?"

Here's the answer:

1. Offering an education that helps the buyer is going to get more buyer interest.
2. If the information is actually good and useful, it automatically re-positions you in the mind of the buyer as much more of an expert than all your competitors. (You're teaching them things about their own business that they might not know.)
3. If you think and plan strategically, you will find a way to weave that information in such a way that ultimately sells your services far better than you could ever sell them by simply flat-out pitch-ing your product. Examples will follow.

More on Education-Based Marketing

One of my clients was a multinational newspaper company that had four bad years in a row, dropping from $1.4 billion to $1 billion in annual sales (approximately $100 million per year) and going from $400 million in profit down to no profit.

Enter the strategist. The new CEO was one of that 1 percent club—the ultimate executive—who is both strategic and tactical. The man is brilliant at spotting the big-picture strategy. He is also a total master at seeing a strategy implemented at the tactical level.

I was brought in as a sales expert. I audited four of the company's more troubled newspapers and presented my strategy for turning around advertising sales.

Before I instituted anything the company model was purely tactical. It owned more than 100 community daily newspapers in midsize cities. An ad salesperson would call up a prospective advertiser and say, "Hi. I'm with *XYZ Gazette* and we'd love to come and talk to you about your advertising." If the prospect was not "buying now," this was a very short conversation: "No thanks. I'm not interested."

It's the same in the circulation department of every newspaper in America: they are all tactical. "Hi. I'm with the *City Chronicle*. We have a special right now for subscribers." If you're not someone who reads newspapers, you're hanging up on these poor tactical telemarketers. A strategist might devise an approach that would make you want to read a newspaper. But that's another project, so let's stick with the ad sales example for a moment.

Picture yourself as the owner of a small-town ad agency, a body shop, a haircutting salon, or a restaurant—all mainstay advertisers every community newspaper should have. With my program the call from the sales rep now went something like this:

REP: Hi. I'm with *XYZ Gazette*. We have a new program to teach business owners like you how to be more successful. Have you heard about this program?

PROSPECT: No, I haven't.

REP: Well, since we rely on the success of local commerce, as do you and everyone else in this community, we feel it's our obligation to make sure local businesses are as successful as possible. So we've actually underwritten the cost of an educational program that shows you the five most common reasons that businesses fail. It also shows the seven ways to become the most popular [name the type of business here: hair salon, restaurant, etc.] in the community. In the next few weeks, we're going to be showing this to every other [name the type of competitor here] in the community and thought you might want to make sure you're learning the same things they're learning. Would you be interested in being more successful in your business and guarding yourself against the types of things that put [your type of business] out of business?

PROSPECT: Well, duh. Of course, I would.

REP: Great. Here's what we do. I'm one of the speakers who put on this program. [Do not call your salespeople *sales*people.] I'm going to be going around to all the [type of business] over the next few weeks and presenting this information. The content takes about 38 minutes to cover and then usually you'll have some questions, so most of these sessions last about an hour. Since this is a community program, we even come to you. You don't have to travel. But we only do these at a time when we won't be disturbed, so we can get in and out quickly. What's a time when you can sit and have a good educational experience without being interrupted?

PROSPECT: Well, we start at nine and then all hell breaks loose around here—so either at eight or after five.

REP: We have another program where we buy you lunch. We call it a "lunch-and-learn." You have to eat anyway, so you might as well learn something while you're eating. In this case you come to a restaurant. We rent out a room. You get to sit with several other business owners, have a nice lunch, and get a terrific education on how to ensure the success of your business. Which would you rather do? Have us come to you during off-hours or attend our lunch-and-learn?

PROSPECT: The free lunch sounds good.

REP: Great. We're doing three of those this week. We have one today at noon at [restaurant name]. Then there is one on Wednesday and one on Friday. Which day works best for you?

PROSPECT: Can't do it today, but Wednesday looks good.

REP: Great. I'll put you down for Wednesday. Now this is a very expensive program for us, but there's no cost to you. Like I said, we thrive if our local community thrives. So we have only one condition for you attending. You've agreed to attend on Wednesday. When we fill up that day, we will start to turn people away who want to attend. So once you commit, all we ask is the professional courtesy that you attend or at least give us 24 hours notice to fill your seat if you can't come. Does that seem fair?

PROSPECT: Sure.

REP: Great. Write my phone number on your calendar so if you need to reschedule, you'll have it handy.

END SCRIPT.

Now the business owners gather to see the information. Here is the basic content. The session begins with overall data on businesses: how many businesses there are in the United States, how many start each year, the failure rate of business, and so on—just good general information of interest to any business owner. This data is eye-opening because it shows that 96 percent of all businesses fail within 10 years, with 80 percent failing within the first two years.

From there the session goes on to show five common reasons why businesses fail. This data is very easy to gather and you can tailor it to your needs. For example, according to *Entrepreneur* magazine, the top reasons for failure include bad customer relations, bad budgeting, lack of staff training, failure to anticipate market trends, and poor and inconsistent marketing.[4]

When we get to the last—poor and inconsistent marketing—we go into some core ways to market. Again, not hard to assemble. The last section of this educational program teaches that "advertising" is one of the best ways to get customers. And guess what. There are studies that show this. There is no need to make up anything. The section on advertising compares the various ways to advertise (the yellow pages, radio, TV, direct mail, etc.), brilliantly showing why each has its drawbacks to an advertiser—except, of course, newspapers.

To be very clear, everything until this point is educational. This is not a veiled sales pitch. All the data is legitimate and so good that people take notes. But then, of course, the last part goes into "the power of newspapers." We found that newspaper readers tend to be more educated than the average consumer. Newspapers are a major driver of commerce in their communities. The presentation is very compelling.

In my experience with my newspaper company client, by the end of the session, everyone who saw the orientation wanted to advertise in the newspaper. No one felt sold. They felt educated. Why? Because when you *sell*, you break rapport, but when you *educate*, you build it.

In the words of my good friend and fellow sales trainer Andy Miller, sales is all about building rapport, not breaking it. When people feel they're being "sold," they automatically resist you. When people are being educated, they have no resistance—especially if the information is good. Sales is an art form, and that's why we dedicated Chapter Ten to just that skill. But this chapter is about being a brilliant strategist before you deploy a single tactic. And it's also about creating vehicles that more or less force your salespeople to build deeper and stronger rapport, by making sure they are highly educated with information that serves the buyer.

Let's look at all the strategic objectives accomplished by education-based marketing:

1. It made it a lot easier to get appointments.
2. It enabled you to get in to see just about anyone—including the 90 percent who were not buying now.
3. Since the information was so good, it established the salesperson as an expert rather than merely a salesperson.
4. Since the information was so good, it gave credibility to the salesperson.
5. When you begin any meeting with real data and hard facts, the sales material at the end of the meeting has a lot more credibility.

6. Because we have control over the material covered, it artfully unseats every type of competitor we have. For newspapers, this would be the yellow pages, TV, radio, and so on.

7. It created brand loyalty.

8. If someone gives you something of value, you want to give back. People who saw this orientation wanted to advertise, if only to honor the devotion of the newspaper that provided such useful information.

9. Part of the education taught the importance of consistency in your advertising. This addressed another strategic problem the newspapers were having. Folks would try advertising once and, if it didn't yield results immediately, they would pull out. This program taught that it takes time to build a presence in the eye of the community.

10. It made people feel that advertising in the community newspaper was almost a moral obligation to support your community. "The more support we have, the more programs like this we can bring to the community."

11. The expert and strategically designed presentation made selling idiot-proof for the salespeople. The sales reps went around to business owners with a three-ring presentation binder that stood up on the desk. They flipped through the panels and showed the information to all the prospects. I recommend using PowerPoint whenever possible, but the point is that every rep had the same material to present.

12. The presentation says everything the top management would want every prospect to hear and know. Most sales organizations leave 90 percent of the sales process up to the rep.

13. It made the reps smarter. Even if some reps weren't using the exact material provided, it gave them insights on business success that they never had before. This automatically made them more consultative in their selling.

So even if it's not practical for you to go out and start doing educational seminars for your prospects, you should build a stadium pitch that has every possible piece of data you can put in there. Then you can have a contest with your salespeople to give them the incentive to memorize the information. Arming your salespeople with powerful insights will dramatically elevate their status in the eye of any buyer. Implementing a comprehensive program like this, however, can elevate you to a level where virtually no one can compete with you.

How This Could Fail: The Tactical Executive

Even after building this elaborate program and explaining it to everyone with a national rollout, we still had salespeople who responded: "You've got to be kidding me. Why would I go through all that when all I really want to do is sell advertising?"

And you will have those reps working for you, so let's go at it another way. What is your strategic position? Madison Avenue ad agencies and many others call it your USP (unique selling proposition). The problem with this thinking is that it's focused on you. It asks the question, "What is special about us or what do we have or do better than our competitors?" In addition to this internally focused approach (which is the minimum every company should know), you should also know that your best possible ultimate strategic position is to devote yourself to helping your clients succeed. So this newspaper company might go from a Madison Avenue–style unique selling proposition of "reaching more people in the community daily than any other media source" to an ultimate strategic position of "helping businesses and consumers in our market live better lives." This is an example of going from being focused on yourself to being focused on your buyer. In the more strategic USP I give, we focus not only on the advertisers but also on the readers. This is a broader, more outwardly focused USP.

Going Deeper

Now it's time to further implement the education-based marketing approach. This requires absolute pigheaded discipline and determination. I watched this newspaper company's CEO work his magic. I started the process by gathering groups of the newspapers' staffs to come to centrally located meetings and participate in two days of training on every aspect of selling smarter and presenting better. The CEO then put two people on the road whose full-time job was to integrate this strategy deeper and deeper into the fiber of the company.

I recall one meeting where I was presenting to this CEO and his team of regional presidents—the presidents who ran newspaper "groups" so that the CEO could get greater control. So here I am presenting some of the concepts and the CEO turns to one of the presidents and says, "What did you think of the training?"

PRESIDENT: I didn't attend any of the training. I didn't want to intimidate the staff by being there.

CEO: Well, how are you going to reinforce something that you didn't learn yourself?

The executive was speechless. No comeback. He just squirmed. And so did the other presidents in the room who had also not attended the training.

So learn the lesson yourself. Change—real change, dramatic improvement—in any company starts at the top and works its way down.

Souping Up the Strategy

Today, the Internet makes it possible to do programs in almost every type of situation and circumstance you can imagine. I have a client, American Art Resources, that's the number 1 provider of artwork to hospitals. One would think that art is subjective. Pick the kind of art you like, right? Wrong. Art has an emotional impact. It's been clinically proven that some art actually helps patients recover faster. Plus, art has an impact on your staff, who see it every day. So this company sponsors Web seminars on "The Five Most Dangerous Trends Facing Hospitals." This program has been presented to more than 400 hospital executives. All of this has happened over the Web. No one has had to travel.

The information the company provides is stunning, well constructed, and highly educational. Hospitals have serious challenges, and this lays them out. It then goes on to offer suggestions on how to solve these problems, showing that there is great research available to make hospitals more effective. The key point the program is making is that everything matters, especially the design of the hospital, and even the artwork. It uses artwork as an example of how every detail counts. As a result, my client has educated the market about why it's the most knowledgeable provider of artwork to hospitals.

You can go on its Web site and select from thousands of pieces of art (www.americanartresources.com). Its consultants are highly educated. Where it previously could not get in front of hospital CEOs and top executives, it now has "top-of-mind awareness" among the biggest hospitals in the world.

I worked with a very large chain of shoe stores where I got the owner to do a study on feet, fashion, and footwear. There are 214,000 nerve endings in your feet, for example, that connect to every organ in the body. Your feet sweat about a cup of moisture per day. The quality of the shoe makes a huge difference in whether your shoes will allow this moisture to properly escape or build up bacteria—which is tracked into your home. This chain of shoe stores trains every single salesperson with a massive amount of information on feet, fashion, and footwear. In addition, in every store it puts a handy binder with all this information so salespeople can take any customer through any section. This helps them accomplish the following strategic objectives:

1. Sell more shoes.
2. Sell better shoes.
3. Build brand loyalty.
4. Establish expertise.
5. Build a relationship where the buyer only wants to come to their store.

And so on.

Why I Also Call a Stadium Pitch a Core Story

I refer to the stadium pitch as your *core story* because, if it's done properly, this core story will provide data that will make all your marketing work harder. The data becomes the *core* of all your marketing. The data sets the buying criteria in your favor.

For example, I'm working with a company now that sells incentives to other businesses. These are used by its clients to increase brand loyalty, motivate more purchasing, as well as increase employee retention and performance. The salespeople of every other company in this field will present you with all the incentives you would ever care to see. My client offers a stunning education on "Four Ways to Increase Profits, Performance, and Sales."

During this magnificent education, the prospect learns a ton of information about all these areas. The end result is that the prospect becomes much more educated about the power and use of incentives in the running of his or her business. Prior to seeing this data, the prospect's buying criteria may be extremely loose and uninformed. After seeing this data, the client is highly educated and motivated not only on why and how to use incentives but also on my client's company in particular. This company is perceived as more educated and sophisticated than any of its competitors. So the market's buying criteria shift in favor of the expert every single time.

You should have this goal for your product or service. What information will help set the buying criteria in your favor? No matter what you sell, data makes your information work harder. Also, it needs to be said that the more complex your product or service, the better the opportunity to appear as an expert.

Important Point

If you come from the place of truly wanting to serve your buyer, then being a market expert—not just a product expert—means being more knowledgeable than any of your competitors. This is easy to do as most of your competitors will be more concerned about selling product than about positioning themselves as experts. In every case where I have personally run companies using these strategies or helped clients do the same, we have literally slaughtered our competitors. Even after they see what we are doing, they cannot grasp it. Truly, building a core story or stadium pitch is working smarter, not harder. The one who gives the market the most and best information will always slaughter the one who just wants to sell products or services.

Here's the key to choosing which data to include: market data is way more motivational than product data. Most people think that a shoe is a shoe (*product data*), but when you learn that your feet connect to every organ in your body, that's *market data*. It makes your choice of shoe much more important. So think about what market data is there that makes your products or services much more important.

Two More Examples of Education-Based Marketing

I worked with a company that sold research aids to tax experts (accountants and lawyers). It was focused on product data: "Here's our research aid and here's what it does." I got them to focus on market data: "The IRS now requires you to take these 22 steps in your research. These are steps you can't possibly bill to the client, as no client will pay for all this. So what you can do instead is use our products. These products speed up this process." Market data made the product data much more important.

Example 2: I had a client who sold pictorial calendars that ranged from puppies to Pamela Anderson. We did some studies and found that, per square inch, bookstores were outselling massive retailers by 40 percent more volume. Why? Bookstores were putting the calendars right by the cash registers. When do you buy calendars? At the end of the year. So there you are, standing in line waiting to pay for all your Christmas gifts, and you see a calendar on Mustangs. Your boss loves classic Mustangs. You buy him a calendar.

The mass merchants were putting the calendars in the stationery department. They weren't moving nearly as many calendars per rack or spinner. By showing this data to more and more stores, my client increased sales 20 percent in a single year whereas the company had not had an increase in sales for four years prior to using this market data to motivate better positioning of the calendars.

And it goes on and on. No matter who you are or what you sell, you need to take the time to collect market data and build your core story or your stadium pitch.

Today the Internet makes market data readily available. Sites like www.census.gov and www.CNN.com have great information on just about any subject you can imagine. You will have no trouble gathering massive amounts of data for your core story. The problem is finding the time to put it all together. Luckily, there is a company called Empire Research Group (www.empireresearchgroup.com) that can actually do all this work for you.

The Smoking Gun

In the legal market, the term *smoking gun* refers to that piece of evidence that makes it so your opponent cannot win. You've found the smoking gun that makes the other party guilty. It's the same with research. There's always that smoking gun that positions you above everyone else. The fact that art actually facilitates healing and that calendars sell like crazy when you put them at the register are both smoking guns. I can list hundreds of examples and I can tell you this for sure: there's always a smoking gun. Always.

I had a client who sold lawn care services, and every year some of his workers would break off on their own and steal away his clients by offering to do the same work they were already doing for less: "Just pay me personally instead of my company." The research team turned up a case in which the state of New York actually sued a homeowner, forcing that homeowner to pay worker's compensation on the lawn care person who hurt himself while working on the homeowner's lawn. Take that piece of data to a customer who's switching for $5 less per month and ask them: "Are you sure that your new lawn care person has worker's compensation insurance? Because if he doesn't and he gets hurt on your property, you could actually be responsible for his worker's compensation payments for as long as he's injured." This is definitely a smoking gun—a single fact that makes it unlikely that any client would want to switch to a single worker who didn't have all the proper licensing and insurance.

To get the most powerful market data and to uncover the smoking gun, the trick is to look at things over time. That's where you'll find the big breakthroughs. I had a client who deliberately avoided selling his products through the big mass merchants like Wal-Mart. The company was doing all its sales through gift shops. A little research revealed that there were 36,000 gift shops. That looked like a big number until you looked at how many gift shops there had been in 1985. There were 96,000! That means 60,000 gift shops had gone out of business, while Wal-Mart was adding more locations every day. That made the client change strategy in a hurry. Go look at data over time. It's amazing.

I had a client who was selling alternative therapies to doctors. A study showed that consumers were spending $460 billion on alternative therapies. Good stat, no doubt. But if you went back 10 years, it was only

$46 billion. It had grown tenfold in 10 years. In fact, today, there are 350 million visits to an MD every year. But there are 420 million visits to alternative practitioners. Yes, 70 million more visits to folks who don't prescribe drugs. These are trends, and, for some reason, almost no one ever looks at them. Yet buried in those trends are strategic advantages that slaughter your competition, get you in the door more easily, and give you something of great interest to your buyer.

⚙ Exercises

1. List your strategic objectives. Look at those listed for the newspaper company as a guideline. Then do a workshop with your team on each one of them. It will be profound. Ask your staff, "What would make us more respected?" Do a workshop on it. Then ask them, "What would position us as an expert in the eye of our buyer?" and so on. Go through all 13 strategic objectives listed for the newspaper example, and workshop each of them with your team. Those will be very fruitful workshops.

2. Do some market research on your industry over time. Keep track of everything you find out that could be of value to your customers. Dedicate some time to this every week until you're sure you've found your smoking gun.

Conclusion

One of the most strategic things you can do is to find market data that makes your product or service more important. I don't care if you sell shaving cream or overnight delivery services—there is market data that will make your product more vital.

Now go back to those strategic and tactical executives. The strategic executive understands that a core story or an education-based marketing approach opens doors faster and more easily and allows you to build more rapport and close more sales. The tactical part of that brilliant executive will then make sure that he or she is implementing this approach with piercing effectiveness at the tactical level. If you want to build the Ultimate Sales Machine, you need to think and plan like a strategist and implement like a great tactician.

5

Hiring Superstars

How to Accelerate Your Growth by Using High-Octane Talent at Every Level

If you want to build the Ultimate Sales Machine, one of the key pieces of the puzzle is to understand the personality profile of top producers. Breaking it down, you need to learn how to recruit them and keep them and then apply all that you've learned so far from this book. And as you'll see, every subsequent chapter goes even deeper.

This chapter will reveal 20 years of secrets in finding, interviewing, testing, motivating, compensating, and managing superstar employees. You will learn essential insights into hiring only the best people for any department. If you are an employee, you will learn how to perform and behave in order to be a superstar.

The average bad hire costs a company $60,000, yet most hiring decisions are made from an hour-long interview—if you're lucky. I've talked to CEOs of companies who estimate that a single bad hire costs them millions. In this chapter, you will learn some unique and effective methods for finding people's faults before you hire them. Most companies do not find out any of the problems until after people have worked for them for several months. By then it's a painful extraction process, or worse, you leave them in the job because they know how to do it and you don't have the time or energy to replace them.

When I was top producer everywhere I worked, I thought the only reason I was top producer was because companies didn't usually hire people like me who were difficult to manage. You know the type: eager to please, always looking for more to do, always wanting more responsibility, always wanting to know more than you think they need to know. I was like that—a pain—but they're worth every penny if you properly channel their energy. So I swore that when I got into a position of authority, I would hire this type of person.

Then I went to work for Charlie Munger and had the freedom to hire anyone I wanted. When I tried to hire nothing but superstars, I discovered that they're an incredibly rare breed. Consequently, I spent the next 20 years studying the phenomena that make top producers and superstar employees.

One-person armies may think they are not in the position to hire anyone, especially superstars. But you'll learn otherwise. Think of what just one top-producing salesperson could do for your business. What could you focus on and accomplish if you had someone else who was expertly handling your sales? How much faster could your business grow? I've shown many entrepreneurs who didn't think they could afford salespeople how to hire a whole team of salespeople on straight commission. This is a profound breakthrough for most businesses and can reshape your entire company almost overnight. So if you think you can't possibly hire or don't need a superstar right now, think again. This chapter spells out how to grow any company or area faster if you're wise enough to share the wealth.

⚙ Exercise

For one-person armies and smaller companies: Take a moment to list three initiatives that you would love to hire someone to execute in which the reward could be great if the person did an excellent job for you. Next to each initiative write down what it could mean to your business and your bottom line—estimate its monetary value. Now list what you could afford to pay such people if they really performed. If the reward is big enough, you can always get people who will share in the reward.

For large or medium-sized companies: List up to three jobs for which you should be hiring right now even if that requires replacing someone who is not performing at the superstar level. Next to each job, write down what it would mean to your business to have a superstar in that position. Give your best estimate of the monetary value of hiring that superstar. Now list what you could afford to pay him if he performed. We'll return to this throughout the chapter.

Example

I had a client who sold Internet Web listings to plastic surgeons. For example, if you are considering breast augmentation, you can go to www.breastimplants411.com (breast implant info) and look at hundreds of before-and-after photos and then choose a plastic surgeon in your area to talk to about it. This Web listing company was started by a top producer. When we met, he was doing all the selling himself. Since he was a superb salesperson, he resisted hiring other salespeople for a number of reasons:

1. He didn't want to give up the commission he could be making himself.
2. He had no experience hiring others and wasn't sure how to proceed or structure it.
3. He thought hiring salespeople would cost him more money than they would be worth to him.

We did the math. If he paid just 20 percent commission to the salesperson, he would get to keep 80 percent of the revenue. Plus, if the salesperson sold as many accounts as he did each month, the salesperson could earn a six-figure income.

Based on that, we put an ad in the paper using the highest possible figure as bait. It's amazing how so many companies put the average income a salesperson can make in their ads. That's how you get average salespeople. Put the highest possible number that a top person can make in your ads. More on this later.

Within a few months, this entrepreneur had five salespeople working for him and it increased the company's revenue nearly fivefold. What's more, the owner himself went from working *in* the business to working *on* the business. He has since built a number of highly successful companies and has forever altered his thinking about hiring superstars.

What Makes a Superstar?

The type of people I'm talking about are those you can put in a bad situation with poor tools, no training, and bad resources and still, within a few months, they begin to outperform your best people or build your company in ways you never dreamed possible. Hiring someone like this is not about luck. It's about understanding the personality characteristics that fit the job for which you are hiring and having the tools to identify the candidates that possess those characteristics.

Personality profiling is the key to finding superstars. Many companies offer tests to determine psychological profiles. Only now they don't call it psychological profiling. The correct term is *behavioral assessment* or *personality profiling*. For the purpose of having one term, I will refer to this method of understanding a person's psyche as a personality profile.

Just as an example, let's focus on one of the most developed, validated, and popular methods, DISC personality profile. DISC is based on the studies done by Harvard psychologist William Moulton Marston in 1928 and has been developed and perfected by dozens of companies over the years. DISC stands for four aspects of the personality: dominance, influence, steadiness, and compliance. DISC tests use word association to measure the intensity of each characteristic in the tested candidate.

Dominance is a personality trait that has to do with the strength of your ego. It is a measure of your personal power, your desire to control situations, and how well you assert yourself in every interaction. Candidates who exhibit *high dominance* have strong egos. Although the word *ego* tends to have negative connotations, it is actually a good thing in certain situations. Donald Trump has a strong ego. Do you think that's helped him go from the $25 million his father was worth to the billions he's worth today? Then there are others whose ego is less obvious, but it's clearly working hard for them. Do you think that Steven Spielberg is a wallflower? No, he has a strong sense of self (ego) that has guided him to becoming one of the most powerful producer/directors on the planet.

Strong ego is crucial in sales because it means you will have the drive and personal ambition to close as many sales as possible and the armor to not take repeated and even harsh rejections personally. Such drive and ambition mean that high-dominance people are decisive in taking action and making decisions. They like control, can't stand inaction, and thrive on challenges. Most successful CEOs are high-dominance. That's how they get the job done! Someone who exhibits *low dominance* is much more cautious, consultative, and nondemanding.

Influence has to do with how you interact in social situations and how well and how much you communicate. *High-influence* people love people. They are naturally empathetic, easily putting themselves in other people's positions and understanding their points of view. They work well on teams and are fast and energetic. They are also persuasive, communicative, and verbal. *Low-influence* people are serious, logical, factual, and probing.

Steadiness is all about how patient, persistent, and thoughtful you are. *High-steadiness* people are deliberate in their actions and decisions. They work steadily and cohesively with others, but are most happy behind the scenes. They are good listeners and have the ability to gain support from others. *Low-steadiness* people are incessant multitaskers. They move fast and initiate action.

Compliance has to do with how you relate to structure and organization. *High-compliance* people always plan ahead. They are cautious in their actions and decisions and they work well alone. They like organization and structure, and they work accurately and precisely. *Low-compliance* people think of the big picture and are not as cautious in their actions. They will wing it more than a high-compliance person. They see gray areas and are more general and independent in their thinking.

The recipe for a superstar is not just a high level of one trait. It is a combination of different intensities of each trait. To understand how these traits work together, let's think about sales. Top producers exhibit high influence. They are empathetic and have a psychological need to bond with others, to find something likable about every person. This is a wonderful trait to find in a salesperson. They just keep going at the client every which way, trying to find more and more ways to serve and please that client. They also see everyone's best side, which helps them make friends out of their clients.

But make no mistake; influence by itself is not enough. People who are very high influence and strongly empathetic are too understanding and they don't close sales. However, if your candidate's personality combines high influence with high dominance, you've found your sales superstar. They will bond like crazy with the buyer, but the high dominance makes them expect a sale and they will keep selling, if only for that buyer's own good. In other words, high-dominance or ego-driven people may passionately believe that you should have their product and feel compelled to sell it to you, no matter how much you resist. This sounds pushy, but if blended with empathy, this person will close with perfection.

Further, high dominance may not be the ideal characteristic for a superstar receptionist or administrative assistant or anyone who needs to be more team-oriented. But for sales it's a perfect fit. Only a person with an extra dose of strong ego and a psychological need to take control of every situation barrels into a client eight times after the client has said no. People with weak self-esteem and low dominance go away after only a single rejection and are likely to never actually close a sale.

About half of the salespeople I've worked with over the years gave up after a single rejection. They would call a client, the client would say no, and the salesperson would never call that person back. Very few, perhaps only 4 percent to 5 percent, keep trying after four rejections. Yet, as you learned in the previous chapter, I've found that it takes about 8.4 rejections to get a meeting. And what makes the difference between people who will face that rejection one time and quit or 40 times and never quit is determined purely by the strength of their ego.

However, since it's difficult to find people who will face eight rejections and keep trying, I now build in *procedures* that require salespeople to try again and again and again. In fact, I build in 12 attempts that a salesperson will make, and I educate the salesperson in advance that the client will say no at least eight times. This sets up the expectation in the salespeople to receive rejection and not take it personally. They're trained on the first day of the job that they are going to go after the client 12 times, even after the client has said no every time.

Yes, you can teach some people to go back again and again, which we'll cover in Chapter Nine. But it's great when you hire someone who, without you ever asking or training, is built that way. These people will be way more persistent to close that sale. They also have the personal ambition that drives them to continually improve everything they do. Wouldn't you love to hire people who innovate and expand upon and improve every single task you assign to them?

If you don't understand the personality profile that makes top-producing salespeople, you might just turn them away after interviewing them. A high-dominance and high-influence candidate can seem overly eager in a job interview—maybe even come on too strong. Don't let a little bravado put you off; it is the essential ingredient in every superstar. During an interview, the person is the product, so they must present themselves with confidence and assure you that they are the one for the position. This aggressive behavior will scare some employers, but it is exactly what you need in a salesperson.

Using personality profiling will enable you to single out the superstars in your applicant pool. DISC profiles and other "behavioral assessment" tests are good tools to evaluate a candidate. Coming up in a few pages, I will give you a method for profiling that you won't find in any of these tests, and in five minutes, it will tell you if you have a person with high dominance and high influence. As I've said, I'm obsessed with becoming more and more accurate about hiring, especially about hiring salespeople. After taking a half-dozen "behavioral assessment" profiles and examining a half-dozen more, my staff and I have found one that is remarkably accurate—so much so that we negotiated to have this testing mechanism added to several of my Web sites. At www.chetholmes.com you'll find a blue button that says, TEST STAFF AND NEW-HIRES W/AMAZING RESULTS.

⚙ Exercise

Look again at your list of initiatives or jobs for which hiring a superstar could change everything. Write down the personality profile you think would make someone succeed in each job. If you get stuck, think of someone you know or a famous person or character who would do well in the job and list the traits that you associate with that person.

Now we are ready to give you the full guidelines for how to advertise, interview, and screen the weak from the stars.

Guidelines to Hiring Superstars
Design Your Ad to Attract Top Producers

My ads begin like this:

SUPERSTARS ONLY $50K to $300K

Don't even call unless you are an overachiever and can prove it. Come build an empire within our fine, progressive company. We are in the XYZ industry, but we don't hire backgrounds. We hire top producers. If you're average, you can earn $50K with us. If you are a *star, you can earn $300K plus. Young or old, if you have the stuff, we'll know. Contact us at . . .*

Notice this ad does not request a résumé. It does not ask for a minimum number of years of experience. There's no mention of computer skills or degrees or certificates required for the job. The ad is challenging people to apply only if they are the best. What kind of person does an ad like that draw? A person with a strong sense of self.

When I got a paper route as a 14-year-old, it had 26 people on it and covered one neighborhood. When I took another job and turned the route back over to the newspaper, it covered four neighborhoods and had 126 people on it. It took three kids to take over my route. The point is that I had the qualities of a top producer even at 14 years old. Hence the line "Young or old, if you have the stuff, we'll know." That tells young people who think they're hot stuff, but haven't proven it yet, that you'll recognize their greatness. I've often helped companies who can't afford to pay for top talent to look for young people with the characteristics of top producers but who may not realize yet how great they are. But I've also hired 70-something-year-old fellows who still had the stuff, but whom most companies would pass over because of their age.

Age and Background Are Not Relevant

It's all about personality profile. I've hired 24-year-olds who have outsold 20-year veterans. One of my greatest finds came from a stereo store. Here was an awesome salesperson whom I never would have even noticed if I didn't know about personality profiling. I saw immediately that he had the stuff of superstars, so I recruited him out of the stereo store and set him on a path that ultimately made him a millionaire. The point is to be on the lookout for those superstars everywhere you go. If you're looking for them, you will find them in the oddest places and they themselves might not know they have the stuff of greatness. Another great find was a salesperson who tried to sell me a sweater in a clothing store. I snatched her right out of there and she ended up managing three divisions of a company I ran. I recently found a 73-year-old man who has the best skills I have ever seen for getting top executives on the telephone. He had been a line producer for feature films. So disregard age or background. All you really need to be concerned about are those superstar qualities, and personality profiling can help you identify them.

The Prescreen—the Method You Won't Find in Any Human Resources Manual

Here's how to spot flaws in salespeople before you even interview them. The first thing you do to anyone who applies for a job in your company is to reject them, telling them why you don't think they can do the job. It's not that you don't want to hire the person. It's that you're looking for the unique personality profile that becomes more effective in the face of adversity. This is the most important lesson I can offer for hiring people. If you reject candidates and they quickly crumble and go away, you see right then and there, *before* you hire them, what they are made out of. A superstar will start to question your reasoning—and may even tell you that you are wrong. It's a very powerful exercise in determining people's strength.

When I'm interviewing for salespeople, we call or email each person who responds to our ad. Here's the script: "Thank you for responding to our ad. We are doing a prescreening call of all candidates who contacted us. The prescreening takes place at a set time [such as Tuesday, 5:00–6:00 PM] and in that hour we're going to talk to people to determine whom we will bring in to interview. Would you like to be at the beginning of that hour, in the middle, or at the end? We'll call you within 10 minutes of the time you select." Some of these prescreening calls take two minutes, some last a little longer, and some take seconds.

When you call them, the prescreening conversation goes like this:

YOU: Okay. You read our ad and it said, "Don't even apply unless you think you're the best." So tell me why you think we should interview you.

THEM: Well . . . uh . . . Can you tell me a little bit about the job?

YOU: That's a much longer conversation. I'm happy to have that conversation if we determine that you're someone we want to interview. So tell me, why should we interview you?

(Notice that we are testing their ego in the first 60 seconds of the conversation.)

THEM: Well . . . um . . . Let's see. I've been in sales for two years. I really like it and I like interacting with people. I feel that if it's a good product or service, I can sell it.

YOU: I'm not really hearing it.

THEM: What do you mean?

YOU: I'm not hearing superstar. I'm not really hearing top producer.

THEM: You're not?

YOU: No.

(This rejection is intentional. It makes most HR executives cringe, but it works really well for determining, right then and there, what kind of person you have.)

THEM: Oh well . . . okay. Um, um . . . I guess you would know.

YOU: Yes, I would know.

THEM: Well . . . okay. Thanks very much. Bye.

Most people, particularly well-trained HR executives, will interview everyone in a loving and nurturing environment. In that kind of environment it is easy for people to present themselves well. When you put people like the person I just prescreened in the field where prospects are regularly rejecting them, they quickly give up. By using this technique in the first two minutes, you can very quickly determine who will rise to the occasion and perform in the face of adversity and who will crumble.

Here's how the conversation should go:

YOU: Okay. You read our ad and it said, "Don't even apply unless you think you're the best." So tell me why you think we should interview you.

THEM: Well . . . uh . . . Can you tell me a little bit about the job?

YOU: That's a much longer conversation. I'm happy to have that conversation if we determine that you're someone we want to interview. So tell me, why should we interview you?

THEM: Well let's see . . . In my last job, I was the new guy and I had never sold widgets before, and, within three months, I was bringing in bigger accounts than they had ever had. In six months I was outselling people who had been there for five years.

(See how they start selling right away.)

> **YOU:** That sounds good, but I'm not sure I'm hearing top producer.
> **THEM:** Well, maybe you're deaf.

It sounds funny, but I actually had a person say that to me and I hired him. The egos of the top producers will not let you tell them they can't do the job. The ideal candidates will try to qualify you just as they would a prospective client. They will be tactful and start asking questions: "What kind of person are you looking for? What kind of a job is this?" Or they might say, "Well, what makes you say that?" Or they might start to sell you on them. They keep trying. That's the bottom line. Their egos step in.

If you're selling a product or service that is a one-shot sale and that's all your people do and there's no follow-up or bonding needed, people who have a strong ego but don't naturally bond with or relate well to others might be ideal. They will care more about closing the sale than anything else. These people do not make good team players, but you can't have it all. They will produce. So you have to decide what's more important—a lot of nice team players or a lot of sales. Again, such a candidate is not ideal for sales where you need to build a bond with clients and keep them buying.

Three Steps to Interviewing Superstars

Now that you've narrowed down the applicant pool, you're ready to interview the top candidates. Here's a three-part interview structure designed to draw out the superstars: relax, probe, attack.

Relax

Once candidates talk their way in for an interview, begin by giving them every opportunity to show their best side. Help them relax. You should be friendly and be a great listener. This will throw them after you treated them so harshly in the prescreen. They come in loaded for bear, and here you are supernice right from the start. Another technique I use is to ask them to "write down five questions you want to be asked in the interview that will show your best side."

Probe

The purpose of this portion of the interview is to get to know the person. Before you begin, you must tell prospects that they don't have to answer any questions they don't want to answer. Explain to them that your company hires based upon personality profile rather than background and ask them directly, "Do you agree that this is more pertinent?" When they answer yes, you say that you'd like to find out what shaped them, so you're going to start with their childhood.

Additionally, this portion of the interview tests the level of their empathy. If they become stiff during this section, you don't have a natural bonder. Tell them that you are going to ask questions about their mother and father as well as questions about how they grew up. If they become uncomfortable, you don't have a superstar. Superstars like to bond with others. But this is only part of what you are probing for in this interview.

Legal notice: You have to get their permission to ask questions about their childhood and you need to explain how these questions are related to the job. The candidate must understand and agree that personality profile is more important than background. Otherwise, the interview can get you into trouble. Legally you cannot ask any question that isn't relevant to the job (such as "Are you married?" or "Do you have children?") because it could be the basis for discrimination. It is your responsibility to think through whether or not your questions might (even unintentionally) screen out any particular group by race, gender, or disability. For example, if you ask whether or not they have or plan to have children, an applicant may understand that this has bearing on your decision to hire them and that the question may mean discrimination. But if you establish that personality profile is what you're after and get their permission to probe "what formed you," then you're probably okay asking about their childhood.

The questions I propose here are not designed to discriminate against anyone. They are designed to draw out the superstars from the applicant pool. However, the questions you ask are your responsibility, so please check with your lawyer, HR department, or the Equal Employment Opportunity Commission (http://www.eeoc.gov) on this point. This book is not intended to provide legal advice.

Probing the candidate's childhood is crucial because self-confidence is often shaped very early in life, so you want to find out if the candidate's background contributed to building up self-esteem. An encouraging parent who really believes in the child will help to develop strong self-esteem in that child at an early age. My mother was so blindly encouraging that if I'd told her, "I want to be a bank robber," she would've said, "Oh son, you'd make a GREAT bank robber." Parents who are overbearing or what I call "quick to caution the child" will raise a child who will not be effective in challenging situations.

The term *quick to caution* means that when children want to try something new—climb a tree, jump off the diving board, be adventurous—the parent holds them back, rather than encouraging them and being there in case they fall. My parents would have let me march into hell for a heavenly cause. That's how I raised my children, and they are both strong and fearless about what they want and how to get it. If you find a person who has not had what I call blindly encouraging parents, then you are likely to find a person who does not have the self-esteem to withstand the rejection that comes in a sales position. Naturally some people develop self-esteem in spite of not having encouraging parents, but in my experience that is the exception, not the rule.

To determine your candidate's background, ask the following questions:

- What events or influences from your childhood shaped who you are today?
- What are some of the biggest challenges in your life? They need not be work-related.
- What was the toughest sale you ever made? (Make sure you ask for all the details and step-by-step specifics of this experience.)

Now you want to look for areas of accomplishment to gauge just how much of an overachiever your candidate really is. Use these prompts and questions:

- Tell me about a time in your life when the odds were stacked against you but you overcame them and succeeded.
- Tell me three or four things of which you are most proud.
- Have you ever practiced and reached a high level in any area beyond just getting by in life?

Areas of achievement might include music, sports, writing, or art. Many top producers have other areas of overachievement. Sports are a big one.

Once I had a salesperson who was an absolute master at astrology. It takes discipline to develop any area of competency. This particular fellow had software programs that helped him do a chart, and he was scary accurate at telling you about yourself—a great tool for bonding. This guy had it all. He was a serious closer, too.

To test empathy and the candidate's ability to bond with others, ask these questions:

- How would your best friend describe you?
- Of everyone you know, who has the most faith in you? Why?
- What are your best memories?

People with weak empathy skills will give one-sentence answers to such questions. They are just not great at "sharing," and it will be obvious. Bonders will talk your ear off. They need approval as part of their profile, and they will win you over with tales of their past.

People with a strong ego will have no problem telling you how good they are. Contrary to conventional rules of etiquette, this is actually a positive thing in a top producer and you want to give them the opportunity. Ask candidates to rate themselves on a scale of 1 to 10 in these areas:

- Ambition
- Confidence
- Ability to face rejection
- Establishing rapport
- Qualifying skills
- Ability to create desire in your prospects
- Closing skills
- Time management
- Presentation skills
- Strategic thinking
- Market knowledge
- Self-improvement
- Getting around gatekeepers

Top producers will rate themselves very high in all areas. But so will dreamers, so be careful. Some people have what I call false bravado. This is a cover for a deep insecurity that will eventually make them cave in the face of adversity. So getting examples from them of why they've rated themselves so high is a way to go deeper and see what you really have. I hired a sales rep who came on so strong, I thought, "This guy is either truly great or completely full of it."

On his first day in the job, all that bravado worked well for him. He got three sales. He was on cloud nine. The second day, he hit nothing but no's. On the third day, I noticed he was writing a lot of letters. That was it. I pushed him with everything I could, and he just avoided the telephone after that day. My philosophy with salespeople is to keep the pressure on constantly. One of two things will happen: they will cave under the pressure or rise to the occasion.

I had a client who did all hiring through group interviews. The "team" members all had to agree before they would hire any new salesperson. The results? They hired a lot of nice people who could not sell. One superstar in that environment stirred up the entire place. He started outselling even the veterans within just a few months. That superstar got that job because I rammed him down the throat of that particular CEO. I convinced him that he needed to put some heat in the kitchen. He listened, and after that star salesperson started selling like crazy, several of the weaker people quit.

My philosophy is that the sales environment should be structured where the strong survive and thrive and the weak go do something else. This is a race and you need champions. Put the people who aren't sales superstars in customer service.

Next you want to find out how candidates measure themselves against the best of the best. Ask them who is the best salesperson they have ever met. If a candidate names himself as the best, offer him the job. Most likely your instincts will tell you to do the opposite. If they name someone else, ask them what differentiates them from the person they named. This is another way to force candidates to self-evaluate and for you to make judgments about them as they do so.

The best of the best are always seeking to be better, so another area to explore with them is how dedicated they are to self-improvement. Ask them what was the last self-help book they read or CD they listened to or

DVD they watched. When I was a sales rep, I studied everyone. Name a few top sales trainers; I had their CDs and was listening to them in my car or reading their books. I also constantly sought out self-help gurus. Some of their books and tapes—*Think and Grow Rich* by Napoleon Hill, in particular—changed my life. I read that book six times cover to cover.

This method of probing candidates' personal lives and experiences from childhood opens them up in many ways. You will get a true sense of how people think and feel.

Now that they are more honest and unguarded, go through their résumé with them. Ask them the following questions:

- Why did you leave your last three positions?
- Were you unhappy? Why?
- Tell me about a disappointment or disagreement you've had with a boss and what happened.
- Name two weak points of previous bosses.
- Name two instances when a supervisor criticized you.

The point here is to determine how they think and if they have good judgment. Recently, I was sitting in on an interview when a candidate gave this reply: "One time I had to get a boss fired because he was ruining the business." After the interview, the sales manager told me that he wouldn't hire that candidate because he feared the candidate might do the same to him. What would you do?

I asked him for all the details and I have to admit I thought the candidate did the right thing. His boss was a jerk and needed to be fired. We've all had bad bosses. But instead of just complaining, this guy stood up for the good of the company. Still, this is a difficult admission to handle as an interviewer because it may also indicate that the candidate is a troublemaker. Keep in mind that if you react negatively to anything candidates say, they'll clam up or adapt what they are saying to what they think you want to hear. On the other hand, if you react positively, candidates are likely to expand on their comments. So be like an open book in this phase of the interview.

It's easy to make mistakes in hiring; you will find that the "probe" approach reduces the number of bad hires. I start with their childhood and then go over their business background last. You'll get more truthful answers that way. After you've bonded over their childhood, you're more likely to get the straight story on everything else.

Attack

Now we are at the end of the interview. You're probed deeply. You may sense that you've found a high achiever, but you'll often be surprised at what happens when you "attack." Try saying something such as, "You seem like a nice person, but I only have one opening. I need a real superstar. While I'm sure you would do well in many endeavors, this is a very competitive industry and I doubt your particular skills and personality will hold up in this position. To be truthful, I don't get the impression you're really a superstar."

Be tactful, but don't be soft. You've be amazed at how many people crumble. Here you thought you had the perfect candidate. But when you tell them you don't think they have the stuff, suddenly they agree and thank you for your time. Let that person go. Superstars never crumble. They have tremendous faith in themselves, and nothing can convince them they can't do *any* job. When you tell them you don't think they have the stuff, be prepared that they may think otherwise and may even be thinking, "Screw you, you jerk." So sometimes you have to prompt them to come back. Simply say, "How do you feel about what I just said?"

Be careful to use a strong rejection instead of a weak attack like, "You haven't convinced me yet." This is an easy invite for candidates to keep selling. When you use the attack, there must be a moment where they really believe you think they don't have the stuff.

Rewarding Your Superstar

The last aspect of hiring top talent is to create a performance-based relationship with little or no base pay. There are countless ways to do this. Let me give you an example. I had a client who paid $9 per hour plus commission. He was even putting this in his ads for new salespeople. This base pay is not much—certainly not enough of a reward to attract superstars—but his commission structure was so good that his top producer was earning $92,000 per year. He could definitely find a superstar in his industry who would work for that amount of money. But to get top producers, he had to be clear on how he would reward them. I put it to him this way: "Do you want to attract the kind of person who will be like your top producer or do you want to attract $9-per-hour-type talent?" We put, "Can earn as high as $100K if you are a star," right in his ad. This dramatically changed the type of person he started to attract.

You must reward top producers handsomely. Years ago I walked into my boss's office to quit and he—the CEO of the company—jumped up on his desk and pointed down at me and said, "This is God talking and you are not leaving my company." I laughed out loud. He then called the bookkeeper and wrote me a $5,000 check to stay. That was probably a $1 million check he wrote to himself. I brought in another million. He made me feel great and I stayed.

I have all my clients put together what I call a "recruiting document," where they flesh out the most money a person can make, maybe even over several years. I have a client who sells apartment buildings. I had him put together a compensation plan that showed that after four years a salesperson could be earning $330,000. Using this recruiting document, we then went after recent college grads. He only pays a base of $2,000 per month, so we had to give new hires the incentive to work for that little money while they got up to speed. Picture your kid coming home with a sheet of paper in her hand showing how she would be earning $330K in four years. (See sample on next page.) Do you think you might help your kid get that job—maybe even subsidize her income or let her live at home longer if the payoff looked like that?

Another client of mine was in the insurance business. It takes an insurance salesperson a lot of time to build up income, but the rewards are fantastic if you get a big book of business. And the ongoing clients provide residual income. But the salespeople were always given incentives to get new business. We reduced the percentage that the rep could make from residual business each year. So for the first year, salespeople earn 30 percent commission on all business. For the second year, they continue to earn 30 percent on *new* business but earn only 20 percent on the ongoing business from the client's firm the previous year. The third year and thereafter, new business is still 30 percent but ongoing business drops down to 10 percent. The new business is where the bucks are, so reps have a powerful incentive to get new business all the time.

Sample Recruiting Document

	Calls	Leads	Appointments	Listings	Closings	Avg. Commission	Total Commissions	You Earn
Year 1								
Average mail leads		124	93	55	23	$34,044	$783,012	$156,602 (20%)
NOTE: Base year 1 of $2,000/month to be deducted from commissions earned.								
Year 2								
Average mail leads		124	93	55	23	$34,044	$783,012	$195,753 (25%)
Year 3								
Average mail leads		124	93	55	23	$34,044	$783,012	$234,903 (30%)
Take on intern earn 10% of gross							$100,000	$10,000 (10%)
Total								$244,903
Year 4								
Average mail leads		124	93	55	23	$34,044	$783,012	$313,205 (40%)
Intern 1 earns 10% of gross							$200,000	$20,000 (10%)
Intern 2 earns 10% of gross							$100,000	$10,000 (10%)
Total								$343,205
Year 5								
Average mail leads		124	93	55	23	$34,044	$783,012	$313,205 (40%)
Intern 1 earns 10% of gross							$300,000	$30,000 (10%)
Intern 2 earns 10% of gross							$200,000	$20,000 (10%)
Total								$363,205

Plus 10% of gross commissions invested in company investment account for the purpose of buying investment properties.

How Even One-Person Armies Can Hire Top Talent

In the audience at a seminar I gave, there was a graphic designer who had never had salespeople. He was the salesperson, so his life was feast-to-famine on a regular basis. When he had no business, he'd chase to get some. Then he'd get business and would have to deliver the service, so no one would be working on getting more business. When the project was over, he'd have to chase to get more. Here's our dialogue:

ME: What's a dream project for you?

HIM: An identity package for an emerging and well-funded start-up or growing company.

ME: How much would a gig like that get you?

HIM: The right project, $25,000.

ME: And how much of that are you willing to give away every day to get a project like that?

HIM: I could give 20 percent and still be happy.

ME: That's $5,000.

HIM: Right.

ME: And how many of those could you handle per month?

HIM: Probably four per month.

ME: So $5,000 times four projects per month is $20,000. Put that in the newspaper and see what kind of talent you pull.

Here's how the graphic designer could get someone to work full time at getting him more business and keep the projects going. Later, we'll show you how to get a constant stream of new and big clients no matter what business you're in. But let's play with this for a moment.

Say you're a chiropractor and you're seeing 100 patients per week now. Hire a person who gets 20 percent of everything above that number and put her out there to form relationships all over your community—in gyms, community groups, companies, and so on. No matter what kind of company you have, there are ways to get more business flowing than you can handle if you follow all the advice in this book. So far, we've only covered the high-level, more strategic aspects. Subsequent chapters get down into the nitty-gritty of getting you more buyers than you can handle.

As long as you're willing to pay, even just on performance, you might be shocked to learn that there's someone perfect who will build your company for you as long as you share the wealth as she does so.

How to Manage a Superstar

Once you've hired a superstar, you need to be very strategic in order to keep that person in your organization. Top producers share a number of traits that easily translate into restlessness in most companies. They are original, intelligent, and sure of themselves. They are generally frustrated in most organizations and usually end up starting their own companies.

The key to keeping superstars is to never say no to them. Instead, redirect their energy or give them a few hurdles to jump in order to get what they want. Here's an example of how to respond to a superstar.

SUPERSTAR: Hey, boss! If we had better communication between departments, I believe our sales would increase. Could I put together a program for that?

YOU: Great idea! Tell you what. You get me three more sales per month for the next three months and I'll let you run with that idea.

While many people are turned off or get offended by a little ego, you need to be grateful for your superstar's ego and let go of your own for a minute. Here's how to handle a superstar who is criticizing something you created.

SUPERSTAR: This promo piece is terrible. We should have a better one.

YOU: I designed the one you're criticizing, but great! Let's see what you can come up with.

There is no need to react or get defensive. Just direct their energy, challenge them, and see what they create. Great managers know just how to capitalize on a big ego.

SUPERSTAR: I could definitely increase sales.

YOU: I'll believe it when I see it. Talk is cheap.

The more you challenge superstars, the more you encourage them to overachieve. But don't forget to compliment them when they meet and exceed your challenge.

A Note on All Hires

This chapter focuses primarily on sales talent, as they are the drivers in most organizations and a critical component of your success. But much of what is outlined here can be customized to fit other departments. For any position you are looking to fill, break it down into all the different skill areas needed to do that job and have the candidates rate themselves in those skill areas. The relax-probe-attack method is a great interview tool, but go soft on the attack when not looking for salespeople. Say things like, "I wish I had more than one position because I really like you. But I've only got the one position and I'm wondering if you're really the right fit." Make all candidates sell themselves at least a little for every position. This is really just a test of how people meet adversity, whether it's a receptionist who must handle 100 calls per hour or a finance executive. A little attack is very telling of what type of person you are interviewing.

In fact, everything said here about hiring superstars also applies to nonsales positions, including how you reward them. For example, one of my clients owned a massive framing business (framing paintings and prints). I suggested that the company structure its compensation plan for the framers based upon how many frames per day they could build with no mistakes. We based the performance around the best framer and made it so everyone could earn more money if they performed like him. Can you structure income around performance, no matter what the position? Today, it's all about performance.

⚙ **Exercise**

> Now look again at your list of initiatives or jobs that need superstars. These are things you'd like to do to help your company or department grow or improve that someone else could do for you and a superstar could do better than you. Read over what you wrote about what these would mean for your organization and what their value would be in terms of your bottom line. Write a great job description of what those people would be expected to do.

Then think about how much they would earn. If it's a sales job, as previously mentioned, how much of what they bring in can you give to them? For other positions, can you change the incentive to be about performance rather than hours?

Now, take out an ad in a newspaper or online that says, "Can earn as high as [insert number here] if you are a star." Follow the steps above to attract a superstar.

To make it easier for you, here's a complete ad we ran to get top talent for a client.

SALES SUPERSTAR WANTED $50K TO $300K

Don't even call unless you are the best and can prove it. Earn $50K if you're average, $150K if you're good, and $300K plus if you're great. This is in the [type of industry here], but we hire star performers, not backgrounds. Young or old—if you have the stuff, we'll know. Will train someone who has everything we want. Small base, but huge performance rewards to get you to $300K and beyond each year. Must be awesome at opening doors and getting appointments from a cold start. Must be highly self-motivated, a terrific presenter and communicator, and a barracuda closer. Come and build your own empire within our fine, progressive company. We have a superb reputation and need real stars to bring in the best accounts. Email résumé to:

Think about that ad. That ad is the dream for any top-producing salesperson.

Conclusion

If you want to have the Ultimate Sales Machine, you need to have the ultimate salespeople. Use the blueprint in this chapter to set your company's or department's procedures for hiring. But don't forget to add your own pigheaded discipline and determination to the mix. It takes time and persistence to create a superstar team. Resist feeling put off if your first hire or even your first few hires don't work out. At my old company, we went through eight new salespeople for every one who worked out. We knew this was going to happen, so we even had a procedure for speeding that process up and getting rid of the ones who weren't going to get the job done. If they weren't great, they'd burn out fast.

Workshops can help you create procedures that are tailored to your individual company or department. Keep at it. I've doubled the sales of many companies with this simple strategy to identify, hire, and keep superstars. Put some top-producing talent in the company and watch it grow.

6

The High Art of Getting the Best Buyers

The Fastest, Least Expensive Way to Dramatically Increase Sales

The following strategy has probably helped more companies double their sales faster than any other single concept. In a sentence: there's always a smaller number of "best buyers" than there are all buyers. That means that marketing to them is cheaper than marketing to all buyers. A direct mail effort to 100 "best buyers" is obviously less expensive to market than a direct-mail effort to an entire audience of 10,000 "all buyers." But it's how you market and sell to them that determines whether or not you will ever get them. When Charlie Munger put me in charge of ad sales for one of his magazines, it had a database of 2,200 potential advertisers. I did a market analysis and found that 167 of them bought 95 percent of the advertising in the top four magazines. This was especially important because these four magazines were getting all of the valuable advertising in this market. None of these advertisers were in our magazine and we were all the way down at number 15 in terms of market share in our field.

By focusing intently on those dream 167 buyers, I was able to get 30 of them into the magazine in the first year. Suddenly executives who had never heard from us before were now hearing from us so intensively from every direction that within six months we had 28 of them in the magazine. That alone doubled the advertising sales of the magazine. These were the big advertisers. When they came in, it was for premium positions—full-color spreads, the inside front cover, back cover, and so on. Up until that point, we had been scraping by on revenue from quarter-page, third-page, and a few half-page ads. We doubled the sales the next year by keeping those best buyers in the magazine and bringing in another 30. We doubled it again, a third year in a row, by bringing in the rest of the 167 best buyers.

When I doubled sales three years in a row, Charlie Munger said, "Are you sure we're not lying, cheating, and stealing? In all my years, I've never seen anybody double sales three years in a row."

Naturally, we weren't doing any such thing. We were just marketing and selling better than any of our competitors. That, and we truly had built the Ultimate Sales Machine with procedures and policies for selling that all the salespeople had to follow. This book will cover every aspect of this in the ensuing chapters.

Best buyers buy more, buy faster, and buy more often than other buyers. These are your ideal clients. No matter what else you are doing, you should have additional effort to capture them. I call this strategy the *Dream 100 effort*. It is your program for targeting your 100 (or whatever number is appropriate) dream clients constantly and relentlessly until they buy your product or service. The goal of the Dream 100 is to take your ideal buyers from "I've never heard of this company" to "What is this company I keep hearing about?" to "I think I've heard of that company" to "Yes, I've heard of that company" to "Yes, I do business with that company."

In this chapter you will learn the strategy for getting your dream clients. You will also find a plethora of creative ideas to capture the interest of those best buyers. You'll see how to focus your efforts on the best buyers or the best neighborhoods (if you sell to consumers) and how to maintain that focus over the long term with pigheaded determination and discipline. Master this and you will see breathtaking growth in your revenue. The fastest way to grow any company is to focus a special and dedicated effort on your dream clients.

Business-to-Business Sales

One of my clients sells research aids for law firms. In large law firms, a managing partner acts like a CEO of the firms. They have an executive committee that helps to manage the firm and make decisions. Next in line are the senior partners of each specialty—intellectual property, litigation, bankruptcy, and so on. Then you have the lawyers, then the paralegals, librarians, information systems people, and so on.

Since my client was selling research products, he was dealing with the librarians because that's who manages research tools. If you've got a revolutionary product, you can probably get an appointment with a librarian and you will probably impress that librarian. Librarians in some firms have great influence with partners, but many do not. You can spend an hour selling to that librarian and the librarian might get 5 or 10 minutes to try to explain your product or service to the lawyers you want to reach.

So the challenge with this client was to build a program that would skip the librarian and go straight to the management committee. If you called a law firm partner and said, "I have a great research aid that will help you be more effective," he or she would usually bunt you to the librarian. We designed a core story educational seminar: "The Five Most Dangerous Trends Facing Law Firms." We called the managing directors of the top 50 law firms to offer the free education. Here's the script: "I'm sure you're aware of our company. We've been helping law firms be more successful for more than 50 years now. We recently commissioned a study on what's going on in the legal market and we've learned there are some pretty serious challenges facing lawyers in the new millennium. Since our survival depends on your success, we wanted to make sure that you saw this information and had every opportunity to be ahead of the problems. We put this information into a very succinct executive committee orientation and we're now showing this to all the top law firms. In fact, we're in touch with [name several other top law firms] and are in the process of arranging to show this in one of their management meetings. We'd love to arrange to make sure you also see this important information."

There are several factors that made this approach very successful. First, note how we used fear as a motivator. It's far easier to get in to see top executives if there are "dangerous trends" facing them than if you offer some currently unrealized benefit. Also, the term *social proof* was heavily at play here. That means, "When others are doing it, it's okay for me to do it, too." Let me give you a great example of how social proof shapes society. For those of you too young to remember, there was a time when it was a shame in society to live with someone without being married to the person. And surely, you would never have a child out of wedlock. Today, other than very religious families, everyone I know lived with their significant other before they married them. Hollywood stars were the first to break this taboo, paving the way for the rest of society to follow suit.

Or to put that in a business context, "When best buyers buy, other best buyers buy faster." In the script above, note the language: "We're now showing this to all the top law firms. In fact, we're in touch with [name several other top law firms] and are in the process of arranging to show this in their management meetings. We'd love to arrange to make sure you also see this important information." Note that we didn't say, "We have shown this to so-and-so." We said, "we're in touch with" and "arranging to show this to . . ." This was the truth.

I have a rule about selling: never lie. Make sure you're telling the truth. By wording our telephone approach carefully, we were telling the truth, but the impression we gave was that it was already happening. By mentioning names of other top firms, we got interest from their competitors pretty darn fast. We also made certain that it was the truth. We were in touch with all the large firms. In fact, we called all of them on the same day. If someone checked, another firm might say, "Well, yes, we've heard from them, but we haven't set anything yet"—or whatever—but the point is that we were, in fact, "in touch" with all the large firms all at once.

Prior to all this, my client once could not get in to see even a single partner. Now the company was presenting to the entire management committee of law firms with astonishing results. For example, I accompanied the salesperson to present for the executive committee of the largest law firm in a major city. At the end of the presentation, that firm bought almost everything that rep had to sell.

From a structural standpoint, when you use a selling approach like this, you have to make sure that your first objective is to truly serve the buyer. That "stadium pitch" or "core story" was rock solid and full of terrific and useful data about law firms and their challenges. If you want to have a disaster, go ahead and promise an outstanding educational experience and then don't deliver on it. You'll find every person in the room squirming with anger about their time being wasted.

In this case, however, the data was superb. We even built in some humor. It showed that the lawyer growth per capita, according to the American Bar Association, has gone from 1 out of every 700 people being an attorney 30 years ago to 1 out of every 300 people being an attorney today.[5] Then we showed how in San Francisco, one out of every 66 people is an attorney and in Washington, D.C., one out of every 23 people is an attorney. And then the next panel said, at this rate, by the year 2052, every other person in America will be an attorney. That got a good laugh, but the data revealed that while the number of lawyers was growing, the billings had leveled off for several years. What did this mean? More attorneys, less money per attorney. The orientation went on to show that lawyers weren't the only ones suing. Corporate clients were now suing law firms at an alarming rate. Forty percent of all large law firms will face a major litigation from one of their massive clients.

All this information was available in hundreds of sources, but what we did was put it all together into one source—our orientation—and the results were an amazing educational experience and snapshot of the legal profession from a very high level. The last part of the education centered on the burgeoning research challenges for lawyers. There are over three million cases now in the databases from which lawyers can draw. That's not good news. We organized the presentation so that the section on law firms being sued was followed immediately by the section on how easy it is today to miss an important precedent or case. This really amped up the importance of having great research aids. The results at the end of the "education" were that every lawyer in the room wanted to have these aids—if not for themselves, then surely for their staff. This illustrates how the learning curve in Chapter Four ("Becoming a Brilliant Strategist"), when combined with the learning curve in this chapter, makes for a formidable force for gaining access to dream clients.

I had another client come to me because his company wasn't getting enough leads and appointments. It sold office equipment to businesses. Its current tactic was to send a letter to every single prospect in our area. It did a search and found that there were 20,000 businesses in its area. So it sent out 20,000 direct mail pieces and it didn't get a single response. Not one. Today, because of the onslaught of direct mail businesses receive, direct mail effectiveness has fallen off dramatically. In our newspaper orientation (in Chapter Four) we showed that the quantity of direct mail has doubled over the past 10 years—meaning, the average household receives twice as much direct mail today as it did 10 years ago.

In Canada, I recall (as the client had newspapers in Canada) they even put trash receptacles by all the mailboxes in apartment buildings so that folks could throw the direct mail away before going back into their homes. So this client had spent what was a lot of money for them on a massive direct mail campaign, expecting to flood its salespeople with leads. (In Chapter Seven, "The Seven Musts of Marketing," you'll get some ideas on direct mail that might make it more effective.) But let's get back to this client's Dream 100 discovery.

I reviewed the sales from the previous year. The company had a number of sales ranging from $10,000 up to $28,000 for computer systems it had installed. But then I got to a sale of $160,000. "What's this?" I was told that that was a big company. The way business-to-business computer system sales works is that if you have 100 employees at desks, you need 100 computers. Each computer can cost about $1,600 per workstation (fully installed with hardware, software, the system, and so on). The client had been focusing on small companies but occasionally got a big company. My natural reaction was "Why don't we just go after big companies?"

I'll state it again: while you're doing everything else, have a special effort dedicated to just the dream clients. We started a side effort to target massive sales. This company is not going to get a Fortune 500 client, but it could easily target companies with 100 to 300 employees and compete quite effectively at that level.

So we did a search of all the large companies in the area. You can do this easily online. Go to www.zapdata.com and in minutes you'll find all the companies of a given size in any industry in your area. For this company, there were 2,000 companies in the area that were within its dream client range.

I asked this client what the criteria were for companies to buy new computer systems. "Well, if their system is old, they may be spending more on the maintenance than they would on a lease for a brand-new system that has 10 times more features than what they have now." I marshaled the four salespeople to call every one of the 2,000 companies we had identified. They simply called each one and spoke right to the receptionist. They said: "Hi. We're doing our annual survey and we've got just two questions: can you tell us what type of computer system you have and how old it is?" A full 99.9 percent of the receptionists just answered the question.

In two days flat, we found out there were 508 dream companies in the area with computer systems that were at least five years old. Many of them had computer systems whose original provider was now out of business. This meant that prospects were now buying used computer equipment in order to replace broken desktop units or to expand its current number of desktop units. They might not even realize they could replace the system that would cost less in the long run and, moreover, might serve them several times better. Naturally, folks in this position don't even think they need a new system. So you are surely not going to get an appointment with them by just calling and asking, "Do you need a new computer system?"

As you learned in Chapter Four, there's probably about 3 percent of that group who are buying right now anyway. But, just because people are buying now does not mean they are beating a path to your door. Even if you send out a direct mail piece, they still might not notice it. Remember, this company had sent out 20,000 direct mail pieces with not one response. We know some of those companies were looking to buy right then, but they didn't respond to the direct mail piece. So one direct mail piece doesn't do it. You need to really get their attention.

The first thing we did was send out a Rubik's Cube to those 508 companies. In the accompanying note we said: "Puzzled about how to double or triple employee productivity? We guarantee to find you 12 ways to reduce costs or increase productivity or we'll give you a $5,000 gift for your trouble." This time they got only one response. It just so happened that that one response was from a company with 355 employees. This would be the biggest sale in the client's history.

We then called behind the offer and got another 15 appointments. Within six weeks this company had more business in play than it had the previous year—all big deals. Also, before using this approach, the sales reps would struggle to get a single appointment each per week. In fact, in some weeks they did not get a single appointment. With four sales reps, they were getting maybe three appointments per week. Using this approach (with details to follow in Chapter Nine), we got them up to one week where these four salespeople set 30 appointments. That's a tenfold increase in appointments per week.

We sent the dream companies a little gift with a clever tie-in every other week for the entire five months I worked with this client. When I left them, they had nine times more business in play than they had done in the previous year. If this client was wise, it would have continued to hammer those 508 large companies in its area. Over time, whenever any of them need a computer system, who do you think they are going to call first?

If you continue to market to someone with great vigor, they will absolutely get to know who you are. If they tell you no again and again and you keep marketing and selling to them, here is what will happen: they will go from not knowing who you are to knowing exactly who you are to maybe even being annoyed that you won't go away to starting to respect you because no one has ever marketed to them with such force to even feeling *obligated* to give you some business. Yes, obligated. If someone keeps coming after you again and again and again, even if you are not interested in that person, you start to feel like you want to give something back.

I've used this approach in hundreds of cases, especially for myself. I've gotten 60 of the Fortune 500 as clients through the pigheaded determination I'm recommending for you. And to tell you the truth, most of them were not that difficult to get. The point is that massive and diligent follow-up can penetrate just about any company if you are determined. One of the hardest of all was Jay Abraham, author of *Getting Everything You Can Out of All You've Got*. I have training programs for business owners and he has a large database of business owners that buy his training programs. I decided that I wanted to partner with him to mutually co-market to his and my list. I hit this guy with a phone call or letter every other week for two solid years. Finally, after two years, Jay's then business manager called me up and invited me to have lunch with Jay. I flew to Los Angeles and had lunch with Jay, and the game was afoot. I've estimated that the first lunch with Jay has easily been worth over $15 million to me over the years. Jay became an extraordinary partner who not only made me a ton of money, but also taught me a great deal about thinking out of the box.

Most all of my other large clients were much easier to get—most within three to six months, some with one phone call. Here's how I got the chairman of a $100 billion company on the phone with a single try.

I decided that I wanted Wells Fargo Bank as a client and called the chairman and CEO of the company. To my utter shock, he called me right back 10 minutes later. Here I was expecting my usual three to six months of hard labor, and the man just called me right back. He tried to turn me down for a meeting about four or five times on that phone call, but I persisted until he finally said, "How's tomorrow at 3:00?"

I sputtered and took the meeting. On my way to the meeting, I stopped at three of their branches, looking to open a business checking account, and was able to report to him about my experience and how I thought I could improve it. I got the account. This is to say that you will be pleasantly surprised at how easy it is to get 99 percent of your dream clients. There will be that 1 percent that take forever but even those can be had if you're committed.

Penetrating Hollywood

I wrote a screenplay entitled *Emily's Song*, a touching, sweeping drama about a singer who goes from rags to riches. After getting many very positive reactions, I decided that I was going to sell this screenplay in Hollywood. I knew nothing about the entertainment field, the players, how everything worked, and so on.

I bought the issue of *Premiere* magazine that lists "the 100 most powerful people in Hollywood." Gee, there it was, my Dream 100 list, and someone had already done the work for me. Then I subscribed to *Hollywood Creative Directory*, which gives you all the contact information for anyone of substance in Hollywood. Next I had one of my assistants make up index cards for me with all their contact data, and I began my process.

I called the CEOs of all the major studios, including Paramount, Disney, Warner Bros., Universal, and Sony Pictures. Using the techniques we'll go over in Chapter Nine, I was able to get seven out of 11 of the biggest CEOs in Hollywood on the telephone. I then went after every major agency and, finally, after the agents who represented the artists that I thought would make great leads for my movie. Basically, I was turned down 38 times with various methods of rejection, the most common being the words, "We pass, but thank you for your submission."

Then one day I got a call from perhaps the most powerful music agent in all of Hollywood. At the time, I approached him because he handled Shania Twain, Céline Dion, and Faith Hill, among others—any one of whom would've made a great lead to play the main character, Emily Evers. He said: "I read your screenplay and I think it's pretty good. I mean, it made me cry." These were the most wonderful words I think I've ever heard. He continued, "I have the perfect person to play Emily: LeAnn Rimes."

This is several years ago, when LeAnn was dominating the charts. She was at the pinnacle (so far) of her career and red smoking hot.

I gasped and just repeated, in shock, "LeAnn Rimes, hmm."

I think he thought that I was cold on the idea—but I was just in shock—so he proceeded to pitch me on why I would want LeAnn to play Emily. And it was a great pitch indeed, showing me why this fellow is so successful. He ended by saying: "And Warner Bros. wants to make a movie with her, so I think you might get a deal over there. Do I have your permission to let LeAnn read the script?"

My permission to let LeAnn read the script . . . ? Hmm, let me think. "YES, YES, YES!!!!" The story goes on. It took her a month to read it, while appearing on every award show known to man—and me watching all of them, thinking: "That girl is reading MY script right now. How cool!"

Ultimately, LeAnn liked the project and we walked into Warner Bros., where they bought the screenplay from me. This certainly would never have happened if I had not first been completely systematic in getting the script into the hands of the most powerful people in Hollywood. They were my Dream 100. While it would have been easy to get discouraged and give up after a few initial rejections, my experience showed me that with determination and discipline to keep targeting the most powerful potential buyers, I would get a deal for my movie. The Dream 100 effort strikes again! One of the lessons for you is to build that list, organize your approach, and never say die.

No matter what you sell, there are dream prospects out there. If you're committed and stay in their face, you'll be surprised how easy it is. Really. My clients have included the largest companies in the world. These are companies that do $200 billion per year, and the toughest among them took about six months to penetrate. Chapter Nine will give you step-by-step instructions on how to build your full-on Dream 100 effort. For now, however . . .

Business-to-Consumer Sales

If you are selling business-to-consumer, you need to learn the *best-neighborhood strategy*. If you're a dentist, an accountant, a jewelry store, or a chiropractor, for example, you could take out ads in the paper and reach everyone. (In Chapter Seven, I'll offer some great ideas on how to make those ads as effective as possible.) But while you're doing that, and for a lot less money, you could send a special direct mail effort to just the best neighborhoods where the best buyers live. The secret is to do it continuously so that you build top-of-mind awareness among those best buyers.

A real estate broker followed this advice and focused on the area where I lived for 16 years as her dream neighborhood. It had 2,200 upscale homes. Every single month she sent a simple mailer that listed the houses that sold in the neighborhood and their selling prices. When do you look at a flier like that? Only when you're interested in selling your house.

When we were ready to sell, she's the person we called. This woman had top-of-mind awareness. She made the commitment that these 2,200 homes in this neighborhood were going to know who she was. What does that cost her? She sends a very simple three-fold flier that probably costs her $0.60 so she's spending about $1,320 a month on this effort. These are $1 million to $5 million homes, so if she gets one client a year, she more than pays for her effort. The commission on a $1 million home, at 5 percent to 6 percent, is $50,000 to $60,000, easily paying the $15K or so she's spending. But she doesn't get just one client a year. When she came over to our house, she showed us a three-ring binder listing all the homes in the area that she'd sold. She'd sold nearly every house in our neighborhood—and next to many addresses she'd noted, "sold twice" or "sold three times."

If you sell to consumers, target the best neighborhoods with great consistency. And remember that you should be willing to do more to attract them than you'd do for everyday buyers. Give something away; make a lot of attractive offers to get them in the door. Once they are there, what can you do to keep them? There is more coming up on this in other chapters to help you fully flesh out this strategy.

Dream Affiliates

Dream affiliates are another excellent growth strategy. Is there a company that could partner with you to send you more business than you could handle? Jay Abraham taught me the strategy of *affiliate marketing*. Who sells to the exact buyer you want to reach but doesn't sell your type of product or service? Here's an "affiliate strategy" that I used to get hundreds of clients all at once. Harv Eker (author of *Secrets of the*

Millionaire Mind) has training programs that are complementary to ours but not competitive. We cut a deal where we'd offer one of his programs as a bonus when people buy ours. Since most of our products are sold to business owners, Harv was only too happy to have us promote him to all our buyers. At the end of our seminars and Web seminars, right when we are going into our close, we put up three panels talking about Harv and how brilliant and valuable his programs are. We then build value around his programs, showing how much it would cost to buy them. Then, when we give our price, we tell them that if they buy our program, we'll sell them Harv's programs as a bonus.

This serves everyone. He gets excellent exposure to an entirely new list of buyers and we get one of his programs as a bonus to induce more sales. Harv has promoted us to his database for a cut of the profits as well. So has Tom Hopkins, author of *How to Master the Art of Selling*, as have Brian Tracy, author of *The Psychology of Achievement*, and Jay Levinson, author of about 56 books, including all the *Guerrilla Marketing* books. These affiliates have helped us gain thousands of new buyers and millions of positive impressions on future prospects and all in record-breaking time. And we have done the same for them.

Affiliate marketing means you ride in on someone else's well-established relationship. This is far less expensive than trying to acquire a customer on your own. Dream affiliates can increase your sales dramatically overnight; therefore, you can afford to share generously with them. We run radio ads every week to drive just 60 business owners to one of our ventures. When Jay Levinson wrote a strong endorsement letter to his list, we got 450 new leads in a single day.

When Jay Abraham first promoted me to his list, we sold $2.3 million worth of product within 30 days flat. The cost of selling that much product was one tenth the normal rate. Jay took a generous portion of the revenue and we both walked away very happy.

So can you go to a company that has ideal buyers for you and work out an arrangement where they will help you sell your products faster? All the major companies have relationships like this. Fly on United and get points for Hilton Hotels. I know a fledgling software company that convinced a well-established software company to give away a sample of its product as a bonus to all its buyers. The established software company was thrilled to be able to offer a $1,000 bonus and the fledgling software company got 1,000 new clients almost overnight.

There's a company called www.Pro2ProNetwork.com that will set up appointments for chiropractors, dentists, optometrists, and financial advisers to go out in their community and meet with other professionals who might send them referrals. Chiropractors will meet with medical doctors and teach them about their work. They will also meet with attorneys who are dealing with accident victims and help those lawyers' clients get the care that they might need. Financial advisers meet with accountants who might have wealthy clients, etc. The point is that affiliate marketing is a much faster way to grow than traditional advertising, direct mail, or other forms of driving cold leads. That said, what does it take to get these ideal affiliates? Jay Abraham took two years, but he was worth every phone call, letter, and approach.

It may take you some time, but there is no market in the world that you can't penetrate if you're committed and willing to do something on a regular and consistent basis. Throughout my entire career in the trenches, I simply picked the clients I wanted and went after them with constant marketing. I "decided" that they would be clients and then just went after them until I got them.

⚙ Exercise

First, take five minutes to create a bullet-style profile of your ideal buyer or neighborhood of buyers. Think about specifics such as income range or company size (if you sell b-to-b), location, size of sale, and frequency of sale.

Next, list your ideal affiliates, partners, or lead sources. In Chapter Nine, we will lay out your Dream 100 effort for you and you can customize it to fit your particular needs.

Lifetime Value of Client

Once you have one or more dream clients, what are you going to do to keep them? What is the follow-up going to be like? What level of service are you going to provide that is special because these clients are special?

I worked with a company that owned a chain of upscale restaurants. On my advice it hired a bunch of high school kids to go around to all the upscale homes in the neighborhood with the following script: "Hi.

I'm with XYZ Restaurant. We have a special effort going right now to get people like you to become our clients. In fact, we'd like to buy you a dinner at our restaurant as a way of putting our best foot forward." The kids would then give them a certificate for one free dinner. Others have done this with a "buy one, get one free" approach to ensure that people will bring someone else with them. When someone showed up with one of these certificates, the restaurant staff knew to treat this person like gold. The manager of the restaurant would go over and personally introduce himself to make the person feel special. Who wants to go to a restaurant where you get treated like everyone else when you can go to a restaurant where you get treated like a king?

Using myself as an example, let's see what the lifetime value of a client can be. I eat out four or even five nights per week. I frequent three restaurants whose staff I have trained to treat me like the "frequent diner" that I am. I make sure they know who I am and that I am a good customer. Since I always want to get a table and the finest service, I tip heavily. I even tip a few hundred dollars every Christmas to the manager of my favorite restaurant. If I eat at a restaurant just once per week, spending $100 each time, and I go there for five years, I'm worth more than $25,000 to that restaurant. If you own a restaurant, do your waiters treat your customers like they are worth $25,000 in business or like they are just worth the $25 meal they're buying that night?

⚙ Exercise

How are you going to treat your best buyers when they buy from you? What can you do that is special that you wouldn't do for all buyers? A jewelry store where I have spent more than $100,000 over the years gives me 25 percent off and throws parties every year for customers just like me who spend a lot there. Write down three things you can do for your best clients to keep them feeling special.

The Power of Referrals

What if you only sell items that are one-time sales or sold very infrequently, like boats, cars, and houses? Car companies have become pretty slick about trying to maintain brand loyalty. One dealership we've purchased from many times has a prepaid maintenance program. It gives you such a remarkable deal on price when you pay in advance for maintenance that you're definitely going to take your vehicle there for oil changes and even tires. The woman who sold us our house was so excellent that I have since referred her to three other people, whom she has helped as well. This book is not going to focus on referrals per se—they are so important, I should devote an entire chapter to them—but I do want to emphasize that you should have a specific strategic objective to gain referrals. And you can even soup that up by offering incentives to your current buyers when they refer others to you.

Conclusion

The Dream 100 strategy has doubled the sales of many clients and it can work for you. You just have to have the pigheaded discipline and determination to build a great Dream 100 program and stick to it like white on rice.

7

The Seven Musts of Marketing

Turbocharge Every Aspect of Your Primary Marketing Efforts

Before you can obtain the Ultimate Sales Machine, every aspect of your business must run with razor-sharp precision, and that includes your marketing. Consider this a $50 million learning curve on the absolute necessities of marketing, along with how to use them as part of that machine. If you build that stadium pitch or core story as outlined in Chapter Four, all of your marketing weapons will work more effectively and more as a united front. Here are what I call the *Seven Musts of Marketing*. Every company that wants to be number one in its industry or profession must deploy them:

1. Advertising
2. Direct mail
3. Corporate literature: brochures and promotional pieces
4. Public relations
5. Personal contact: salespeople and customer service
6. Market education: trade shows, speaking engagements, and education-based marketing (as described in Chapter Four)
7. Internet: Web sites, email efforts, and affiliate marketing

Most large companies are doing all of these already, but often how they are doing them can be dramatically improved. In small companies, you may not be able to afford to do them all, so you have to pick and choose which weapons will get you the most impact for the least money. This chapter is going to show you how to maximize each of these weapons separately and then how to coordinate all of these weapons as a united front. In the companies that already use all seven marketing weapons, I usually find that each is treated as a separate little island. This is especially true in the biggest companies, where there is often no synergy between the ads, the brochure, the look and feel of their trade show presence, the direct mail effort, the PR activity, the sales team's work, and the Web efforts. You may *think* you've got synergy or, at the very least, a uniform "look" to all your marketing, but this chapter will show you how to soup it up even more.

Often the PR staff has collected and put into a lovely photo album all of their press releases and the articles they've gotten placed in various newspapers and magazines. When PR people proudly shows me examples of their accomplishments, I frequently reply: "Gee. That's a great article. It points out a lot of the benefits of doing business with your company. Have the salespeople ever had that as a sales tool?" By the look on the face of almost every PR person I've said this to, I can tell that the salespeople haven't seen it and that they will get that article within minutes of my leaving the meeting.

Additionally, those same pieces may be powerful when used with direct mail or at trade shows, yet no one may be coordinating that effort. Another example of this lack of coordination comes when the marketing department assembles a brochure without asking the salespeople what sales points would make the brochure a more effective communication piece. In essence, these marketing weapons are not working together as a highly strategic and organized attack. But when they do, they all work more effectively as part of the same machine. I call this *stacked marketing*. It involves coordinating all of your marketing weapons rather than having varying and even conflicting messages from each separate weapon. With stacked marketing, you develop a consistent message, look, theme, and slogan that carries throughout all of your marketing efforts.

Also, your core story or stadium pitch will provide you with data that will make all of your marketing weapons work harder. In the case of the carpet cleaning company, the owner put all the EPA data in his brochure, radio ads, TV spots, and every conversation. Market data (being more motivational than product data) now dominates all his marketing weapons. As we soup up each of the Seven Musts of Marketing, keep thinking of how you can use market data and concepts from your core story or stadium pitch.

Marketing Weapon 1: Advertising

If you have the budget for it, advertising has the broadest reach and creates the most top-of-mind awareness. When I worked for Charlie Munger, I headed up a four-year study of what kinds of ads got the best response. Every so often we'd find that one ad was pulling 10 times more response than other ads for similar products in the same magazine. Invariably, the best-pulling ads all followed a specific formula. Using this insight, I started designing ads that helped our clients pull a much higher response. Over the years, I've designed more than 500 advertising campaigns and, because of the learning curve from our study, have maintained a very consistent ranking among the best-pulling ads in the magazine.

There are four rules for creating high-response-generating advertising:

Rule 1. It Must Be Distinctive

The first important thing about your ad is whether or not it attracts attention. The best response-generating ads catch the eye and hold it. There must be something in the ad that is distinctive and really stands out. I recall an ad in an airline magazine where there was a fellow looking into the camera and behind him were two velociraptors about to pounce. It stopped you cold. Another ad that stands out in my mind was for a graphic design firm. It was a shot of a herd of zebras and one of them had all different-colored stripes, like a roll of Life Savers—this, against a sea of black-and-white zebras. The headline that went with that ad was great, too: "In the corporate jungle, identity is everything." Clever, distinctive. But we'll get to headlines in a moment. So the first question is, what can you do to really stand out?

Let's talk TV for a moment. We all know that the majority of people at least mute their commercials if they're not already fast-forwarding through them using TiVo or DVR. This challenges TV advertisers to be creative, to develop ads that stop you dead in your tracks. They need ads that are so intriguing that you'll unmute to hear what goes along with the bizarre images on the screen. Or ads that, as you are fast-forwarding, make you stop and rewind to see what the ads are saying.

As of this writing, there is a Gap campaign that features Audrey Hepburn wearing skinny black pants and dancing to AC/DC in and out of scenes from her movie *Funny Face*. This ad stands out. Victoria's Secret ads also stand out, with amazon-sized women in provocative stances, emphasizing the romance or sexy appeal of the image Victoria's Secret wants to create. Yet, there aren't many TV ads that make you stop to watch or even make you curious about the content that might go with the images you're fast-forwarding through. Every company using TV must stop and ask the hard questions: How can we be distinctive? What can we do to stand out and stop people in their tracks?

Rule 2. Capture Attention with a Screaming Headline

Back to print. The most effective ads have a headline that follows this important rule: "Tell me what you want to tell me in 3.2 seconds." The headline should give a benefit and focus on the prospect by using "you" or "your" instead of focusing on yourself by using the word "we." It should communicate its message immediately and make you want to read on for more information. It amazes me that companies will spend $100,000 to be in a national magazine and a prospect has to work to figure out what the ad is selling.

I had clients who ran more than one million dollars' worth of ads in *Forbes*, *Fortune*, and other prominent business magazines. The ad pictured an executive thinking about something and the headline was vague, along the lines of "Thoughts are things." What is this ad about? You have no idea. Worse, the body copy didn't really explain much more. This company offered advance technology systems, but you were hard-pressed to understand that from the ads. Now what if that headline said, "Your future is in danger unless you read this important notice"? Even that is a little vague, but it's moving in the right direction. Even more on point, the headline should be specific: "The Internet is reshaping our world and you're in trouble if you are behind the curve instead of in front of it." Now let's throw in a "benefit" and watch how it makes the ad even more appealing: "The Web is creating the leaders of tomorrow with better ways to capture and interact with clients than you've ever imagined." The benefit is "better ways to capture and interact with clients."

Or here's one that's even stronger: "How would you like to capture three times more clients and lock them in so securely that no one could take them away from you?" That would've pulled them more leads than they could've handled. Instead, they blew a million on what they called "image ads." I was brought in to help their salespeople penetrate more clients because they were wasting $1 million on ads that didn't say anything or drive a single lead. I tactfully tried to discuss the ads with the ad director of the company, hoping to drive thousands of leads to the struggling sales force. When I asked the ad director if he got much response from those ads, he told me they weren't designed for response. So I asked him what was his philosophy behind running the ads, and he said the campaign was designed to build awareness. But when I wanted to know if it was working, he wasn't sure.

This kind of waste makes me crazy. Well-designed ads can pull leads like crazy. They just have to be compelling. Advertising is a way to add power to everything else you're doing. I often refer to ads as "long-range bombing" because they soften the market before you send in the troops.

That said, some companies are using advertising just to maintain, protect, and further their brand. A Coke or Pepsi commercial, for example, might not be designed specifically for direct response. There the company is propagating its brand and must pay attention to the first rule of great advertising: be distinctive. Obviously the above example is for those interested in driving leads from their ads.

Rule 3. After Your Headline Hooks Them, Your Body Copy Has to Keep Them Reading

First, the body copy must focus on your prospect, not on you. The biggest mistake most advertisers make is focusing on themselves. I'm working with a company that does a lot of advertising. Every ad its people send me to tune up is focused on them instead of the prospect. Every single time. And every single time, I point that out and show them how to focus on the prospect. And every time, the executive I'm working with says: "Wow, you're right. That's stronger." Then, a month later when it's time for a new ad, here it comes again, focused on them instead of the prospect.

Next, each sentence should unfold the "story" you want to tell and make the prospect want to read on. Like the headline, the body copy should be benefit-oriented. Don't tell me *what* it is. Tell me *why* it is valuable.

Rule 4. Include a Call to Action

A reason to act now is always great: "Call us now for a free report (only 100 left)." "The first 100 who respond receive a $XXX bonus." Another discovery from our print-ad test that amazed me is that a coupon in the bottom right-hand corner of the ad actually increased response. It might be a little box that says, "Yes, send me more information," and then a few lines where prospects fill in their contact information. To my utter amazement, executives would tear the page out of the magazine and hand it to an assistant, saying, "Fill this out and send it in." So coupons increased response in print ads. My theory is that a coupon provides a noncommittal way of responding. To actually make a phone call means you will have to engage with a salesperson—something you might not want to do at the time. But filling in a coupon is noncommittal and always increases response over ads that don't have them.

As the economy tightens and the competition heightens, you will need to be more and more creative to draw new customers as well as motivate existing ones to buy more. With the effectiveness of TV, newspaper, radio, and magazine advertising dropping every year, people on a budget may want to consider much less expensive methods of reaching your customers. Many of these methods are spelled out in this book, such as the Dream 100 effort and education-based marketing.

Other Advertising Insights

If you're on a budget, you can take an ad one time and use it in all your other activities, which adds credibility. We once took a one-time, full-page ad in *Forbes* with the condition that they give us 100 copies of the magazine for free. Next we included those 100 copies with a letter to 100 dream prospects with a Post-it flagging the page with our full-page ad. The salespeople also got copies of the magazine so that they could flip open the magazine and show prospects the full-page ad in *Forbes*. We then used the same ad at a trade show with a banner across the right corner that said, "as seen in *Forbes*."

We're running a radio campaign right now and the spots are pulling a steady stream of leads. But to our dismay, we have to chase the heck out of the leads to get them back on the phone to take the next step in our process. Looking at it on a week-by-week basis, the ads were not paying off and I was thinking of pulling the campaign. Then we noted that continuing the ads (on the same radio station—reaching the same audience again and again) was helping even old prospects respond to our follow-up.

So let's talk about radio. I have two stories. Traditional wisdom, as taught by radio guru Dan O'Day, says that on the radio, since you only have 60 seconds, you should try to give one main message. And most of the time, I've found this to be very true. In fact, if you talk at a conversational pace, a radio spot should have between 187 and 200 words.

Here's a radio spot that we ran recently that got good response:

Hi, I'm Chet Holmes. If you own a business, I'd like to help you double your sales in 12 months flat. We've doubled the sales of more companies than anyone else. We teach 12 concepts that will double sales in 12 months. Here's just one of them: If you sell to consumers, there's a way to market to only the best neighborhoods, reduce your marketing costs, and increase the quality of your buyers dramatically. Or, if you sell to businesses, it's even easier to double sales. I doubled the sales of a company three years in a row for a well-known billionaire by focusing on only 167 dream clients. While you're doing everything else, you need a concentrated effort to get your dream clients. No matter how big they are or how small you are, you can get dream clients if you hit them every two weeks without fail. Call us and we'll send you to a free Web site where you can learn three of the 12 concepts for free. 212–555–1234. To double the sales of your company, call 212–555–1234. Again, that's 212–555–1234.

This script is 185 words and it works well. But we ran another ad that was 387 words and just heaped benefits on people at a blinding pace with no time to breathe. The announcer was falling over himself in order to squeeze it all into a one-minute spot. Here's a fact: while the average person speaks at only 125 words per minute, the brain can take in information at an average rate of 400 to 500 words per minute as we listen.[6] This 387-word ad proved it. It went on for a blistering minute and included several endorsements as well as a list of 20 benefits from this particular service. It worked great, but I have to tell you that I've never been able to duplicate that success since. Most of the ads we run now are under 200 words.

For some, it is crucial to stay with these tried-and-true formats for exposure. Movie companies are a good example. TV is definitely the best advertising medium for the entertainment industry because you can tell a rich story in a short period of time by combining visual and audio communication. People like movie commercials because they're like a free minimovie slotted into the other programming you're watching. That said, I'm always amazed that a studio will spend a bloody fortune to advertise a movie and then not tell you what the movie is about. Nine times out of 10, when I see a 30- or 60-second spot for a feature film, I turn to my wife and ask, "Do you know what that movie is about?" Movie TV spots should be like a minimovie, telling a story. And the better the hook in the story, the more interested consumers are going to be.

The power of storytelling in advertising is not limited to movie companies. I recently saw a very clever ad for clothing that looked like a movie trailer. Tell a story that intrigues the imagination and you stand a better chance of people actually watching your commercial.

Here's a 60-second TV spot for my upcoming feature film, *Emily's Song*. See if this TV spot makes you want to watch the movie. Try to visualize it as you read. This is an example of where TV is so much more powerful than print. Try to imagine these characters, great music, and gripping drama. (The actors mentioned are not attached to this film at this time and are only given as examples to enhance the script.)

SCENE OPENS and we're seeing a father (Tom Hanks) and daughter (Dakota Fanning) sitting at a piano. They sparkle—a loving and perfect father-daughter relationship. The father teaches his beautiful daughter the title song ("Emily's Song"). They laugh and sing. (That's 12 seconds of a 60-second spot.)

ANNOUNCER: Emily Evers had the perfect childhood, surrounded in love and her father's love of music. But then tragedy strucks.

SCENE: The father is being mugged. We see the knife flash to his throat and then him lying in a pool of blood on the ground. (6 seconds)

ANNOUNCER: Leaving Emily alone.

SCENE: Her house is now empty. A social worker takes her away as she cries. (3 seconds)

ANNOUNCER: Emily lives a lonely life—the only keepsake of her childhood, her music.

SCENE: Enter the adult Emily now, depicted by Kirsten Dunst, singing and playing piano for quarters on Venice Beach. (6 seconds)

SCENE: Three quick flashes of her being rejected by music executives showing that she struggles. But then . . . (9 seconds)

ANNOUNCER: Emily Evers touches the world with her music.

SCENE: Emily Evers on stage blowing the audience away, fans screaming her name, cameras flashing from every direction. We get that she has become a huge star. (6 seconds)

SCENE: She is with a friend. She is crying, a tortured soul. Her friend is trying to comfort her, but doesn't know how. (4 seconds)

ANNOUNCER: The tragedy of her youth still haunts her. But in her darkest moment . . .

SCENE: Emily is hiding from paparazzi in a piano bar and suddenly hears the melody line from "Emily's Song" playing in a darkened corner. She turns and goes to the piano to find her father, who is just as stunned to see her. Now grown up, in shock, Emily mutters, "Daddy?" as she is stunned to see him—alive. (10 seconds)

SCENES: The screen grows dark and comes up on four more lightning-quick flashes of rock star moments and other drama, including Emily about to jump to her death. The last image is Emily (rock star) and her screaming fans. (4 seconds)

END SPOT

That's a total of 60 seconds. A minimovie. Wrap some great music around that, do some slick editing, and you've got a movie with what I call commercial appeal. A minimovie like that isn't going to appeal to everyone, but it does show a lot in 60 seconds and it has a good hook that makes you want to learn more. We've also shown a rags-to-riches story along with a powerful father-daughter story. And if it's done right, you're going to get chills when she finds her father still alive.

Mind you, this isn't the whole story. Not even close. And we can't possibly tell the whole story in 60 seconds. But what this is, in just 60 seconds, is a minimovie that elicits emotions and intrigues the imagination. It's a miracle what you can do with pictures in 60 seconds.

Let's talk about TV advertising that's affordable for almost anyone.

Cable Television

Cable television is also a great way to advertise to consumers. It has become so inexpensive that almost anyone can do it. In some areas, you can buy for just a specific neighborhood. In my area, the local cable company can break out your TV ad to only appear in the city where you might have a bike shop or bakery.

The power of TV advertising is amazing. I know an entrepreneur who offered the simple service of installing all your entertainment components for you. For a busy person, this might be a godsend. Instead of trying to figure out how to make your DVD, DVR, CD players, and newfangled plasma screen TV all work together, it might be worth $85 per hour to have this person come in and do it all for you. He also shows you how to use them. The company was called Mr. Tim's Home TV, Music and DVD Service.

He went on local cable stations with a fast-paced ad announcing his services. He was running about 40 spots a week for only $200. It was dirt cheap because the ads were only reaching 20,000 homes. But they were the 20,000 homes in a very wealthy area, so it was perfect for him. He was on TV during reruns of *Friends*, right there with the spot ads purchased by national brands like Coke and Paramount.

As stated, the key to creating a great cable television ad is to make it as visual as possible. Remember to put the phone number on-screen as well as in your announcer's script. You can even insert important copy points on-screen as well. Mr. Tim's ad showed a man drowning in wires around his TV, VCR, and DVD player. The guy looks into the camera cross-eyed while the screen flashed the words "Let us figure out all this wiring *for you*." So this visually told the story at the same time that the announcer was telling you what Mr. Tim could do for you.

Here's another spot that worked well. Imagine this: you're watching commercials, but you have the TV muted. A woman pulls up to a car and gets out of her own car with a baseball bat in hand. She then proceeds to totally trash the car she's pulled up beside. Right there, you're wondering what the heck is going on. Then a man in an identical car pulls up near her and says something to her. She looks over at the man in the identical car—realizing she has trashed the wrong car. Just then the owner of the trashed car comes out and sees what she's done.

The logo comes up and it's for a local body shop. Clever, visual, no sound required. But after seeing that spot several times, I had to turn on the sound to hear what the man says to her when he pulls up. So the ad worked on every level. Just for the record, the man in the identical car is obviously the boyfriend or husband, and she's obviously enraged over something he did. He pulls up and sarcastically says, "Hon, what're you doing?"

I didn't need to hear that to know what the ad was about, but I just had to hear what the guy says to her.

Today, you can get your ads made for very little money. Mr. Tim paid $400 for his ad and the local cable company did everything for him. I know several local companies that have had spots created that look pretty darn good for under $1,000.

Billboard Advertising

This is the final area of advertising. Obviously, everything I've already covered applies here. Billboards must be remarkably distinctive or they are a waste of money. They are not practical for direct response. In an area I drive through frequently, there is a billboard ad for a local mortgage broker. When I called him to ask if he got response from it, he said that he did, but he wouldn't say how much. This made me think the response wasn't overwhelming, but he did say that it helped him close a lot of deals and to build his "brand" among real estate brokers he was trying to penetrate. So the billboard helped with folks who were already hearing from him. It was like they were dealing with a celebrity because he had this billboard along the highway right in their town.

A little further down the road, another mortgage broker copied him, but made his billboard way too busy. He was trying to squeeze a TV commercial into a billboard. The billboard must have one single message and it should be communicated visually. Obviously, all over New York and Los Angeles billboards are used primarily for fashion, branding a specific designer. So there will be a sexy image and one word on the billboard.

A recent client of mine has a stage show in South Carolina called *The Carolina Opry*. It has been in that area for more than 20 years and is a virtual institution for folks who go to Myrtle Beach. The assumption of folks who had not been there before was that it was some hillbilly country hoedown experience, but quite the contrary. Those who have seen it know that it has a little bit of everything and a lot of heart. Remember, you only have a few seconds to communicate an idea on a billboard. So I designed one that looked like this:

$$\begin{array}{l} 20 \text{ percent country} \\ 80 \text{ percent "other"} \\ \hline 100 \text{ percent pure excitement} \end{array}$$

This conveyed that the show was not all country and that it was exciting. I then picked some images that showed a massive 40-person production in full swing. Additionally some 60 percent of the people who go to Myrtle Beach have been there before. So I created some billboards that encouraged people to see the show again with taglines like "I see *The Carolina Opry* every time I come to Myrtle Beach"—a straight, simple idea communicated in just a few seconds.

So there's a good tune-up on various types of advertising.

Marketing Weapon 2: Direct Mail

Now, if you've done a good job with education-based marketing (Chapter Four), you can use it to make your direct mail much more powerful. Going back to the carpet cleaning company, it has created direct mail that shows a superimposed image of a dust mite with the words, "Five million of these can live in your living room carpets if you don't get professional cleaning." The dust mite is an ugly creature. It looks likes a creature from the movie *Aliens,* starring Sigourney Weaver. What market data did *you* gather for your stadium pitch that would make a good "wow" for your direct mail piece?

A successful direct mail campaign absolutely depends on how regular and consistent your mailings are. In Chapter Nine ("The Nitty-Gritty of Getting the Best Buyers") you will learn, step-by-step, how to run a direct mail campaign for dream prospects. For now let's go with some fundamental rules from my own experience about how to make your direct mail pieces stand out.

First, use color as much as possible—either on the envelope itself or in the lettering on the outside of the envelope.

Second, put messages on the envelope. You've got to get the prospect to open the envelope. So a message on the outside—which should follow the above rules for writing a great ad headline—is a good way to go. Make it benefit oriented and focused on the prospect.

Third, think about the way you sort your own mail. Which item are you going to open first: something that looks like a greeting card or the bill from the phone company? I've seen many companies use greeting-card-, invitation-, or even wedding-announcement-style mailers to great effect.

Countless books on direct mail are better sources of information, so I will limit my comments to using direct mail as a weapon for attacking your dream prospects. But don't forget that this weapon, when combined with other weapons, can be made much more effective. I had a client who added direct mail to the same audience he was advertising to and his response went up 35 percent. Every magazine will let you send direct mail to their subscribers. So if you're in a trade magazine, try mirroring your advertising campaign with a matching direct mail effort to that magazine's subscription base.

Marketing Weapon 3: Corporate Literature

Again, the key to using these marketing weapons to their maximum potential is to coordinate them so that the look, feel, and content of each weapon is consistent with the others. Like your direct mail pieces, your brochure should draw from your education-based marketing efforts and should be a miniature version of your stadium pitch or core story. That means it will have riveting data that sets the buying criteria on your behalf. It will use the same exact graphics that you use in your presentations, advertisements, and direct mail pieces to enhance the cohesion of your marketing efforts.

Here's a practical scenario: You go out and present your core story. This is the educational orientation you have built with market data that you give to potential clients. It goes well and the prospect now wants to present the information to his boss or at a committee meeting. He asks for a copy of your orientation. If your core story is a masterpiece, you might not want to give it to your prospects, many of whom may have a relationship with one of your competitors. But you can give them a brochure that includes the highlights of your core story. This is important because in giving them a brochure, you're giving them a sales tool that turns them into a core story presenter for you.

I'm working with a company called United Multi Family (www.umf. com), which sells apartment buildings. Their core story is a masterpiece of information that not only encourages owners to sell their buildings now but gives many reasons why you want to list your apartment building with this particular company over all others. This core story has an 80 percent closing ratio. The company brochure is a miniature version of the core story, highlighting the main data in the core story. So now, when a rep meets with an apartment building owner and that owner wants to talk to the spouse or partners, the rep can leave the brochure, which acts as a minicore story. Or if the rep can't present the entire core story for some reason, that rep can pull out the brochure and do a minicore story right on the spot.

Let's flesh this out a little further. Most brochures are a waste of money. They are totally focused on you instead of the buyer. I call them ego pieces. Let's imagine that you are an apartment building owner. You're at a trade show for apartment building owners and on one of the tables there are dozens of brochures. Most say something like "Kimberly and Wayne: Why we're great." The only people who will pick these up will be people who already know about these companies and are interested in contacting them. But there's one that says, "The five most dangerous trends facing apartment building owners and how to maximize your apartment building asset." Who wants to know about that? *Every* apartment building owner at this trade show would want to pick up that brochure. Which brochure are you going to want to read?

When done properly, brochures are awesome sales tools. Also falling under this category of corporate literature are promotional pieces. We have more than a dozen superb reports that we use as marketing tools. When people subscribe to our email list, they begin to receive these reports every few days. The reports offer excellent information, and at the end of the report there is a subtle plug for the service we want to sell. It will say, "To learn even more about building your sales, go to www.howtodoublesales.com." Subtle, but very effective. As of this writing, 30 percent of those who get the reports end up clicking on that link at the end of the article. It's an outstanding method of driving traffic.

When I sold advertising, we had a series of excellent one-page promotional pieces, each explaining another sales point. These were used for our regular campaigns, but the sales staff also deploy them on a case-by-case basis for specific objections they would get from prospects. For example, if someone only wanted to take one ad, we had a promo piece that made a case for why you should advertise with frequency. If someone wanted to run only a black-and-white ad, we had a promo piece that gave excellent data on why color was a much better way to go.

⚙ Exercise

Write down 5 to 10 major sales points for why a prospect would want to buy your product over another, or why you would want prospects to go deeper and/or do more than they might initially do. Then create a series of one-page promotional pieces that take on each case. Again, make sure each piece focuses on them, not you, and tells them why, not how. Use color. Use graphics if you can for each promotional piece. But if that's not practical, you can make a great promo piece with a large headline. See below for a sample of one we use when another company wants to promote a mass teleconference with me as the trainer.

FOUR WAYS TO DOUBLE YOUR BUSINESS IN JUST 12 MONTHS

Join me on a mass teleconference with celebrity business growth expert Chet Holmes to learn how to double your sales in 12 months flat. Yes, this man actually teaches four different concepts that will double your sales—EACH can double your sales in 12 months flat. This will be a rocket ship ride of an experience, and all in about 70 minutes flat, no travel required—attend right over the telephone.

The Speaker: Chet Holmes is the only trainer in the world to have personally sold his services to more than 60 of the Fortune 500. His client list includes Estée Lauder, Warner Bros., American Express, and Citibank. He has 65 training products selling in 23 countries. *Success* magazine reports, "Chet Holmes breaks sales records wherever he goes." To see a two-minute intro on Chet, go to www.chetholmes.com.

Here is a sneak preview of our teleseminar THIS coming Tuesday:

1. Chet teaches how to focus like a laser beam on what he calls "best buyers," reduce marketing cost, and dramatically increasing the size of your sale.
2. How would you like to get all your best possible buyers into one room, all at once, and get to present to them all at once? Learn the magic of a concept Chet teaches called "the stadium pitch."
3. Superstar growth strategy: Chet teaches how anyone, no matter how small, can hire an army of commissioned salespeople to radically grow a business.

4. Zero to $100 million: Chet teaches the traits and skills YOU need to grow your company to $100 million. Even if it's not your goal to go to $100 million, you'll learn things that will change everything. Most businesses get stuck at a certain level. Chet's material gets you unstuck and growing like a weed.

So join me and celebrity business growth expert Chet Holmes on Tuesday, October 10, promptly at 11 AM (Eastern Standard Time) and get the ride of your life in just over an hour. Only 1,000 can attend. The last time he did one of these, there were more than 1,000 people who could not get on the teleconference, so you'd better register now to hold your spot: [Web site link here].

This has a good headline and "curiosity-driven" copy, lots of teasers, and enough information to make you want more. And this does focus on me, because, in this case, I'm the "celebrity" trainer, but the copy has a heavy focus on the prospect as well, giving a lot of promises.

You should have a dozen or so pieces like this with a good headline, good focus on the benefits to your prospects, and a call to action.

Marketing Weapon 4: Public Relations

What is public relations? You are doing PR work when you throw splashy events such as trade show parties and benefits for your clients. PR also includes press releases, building relationships with the press, getting articles written by or about you, and affiliating with strong forces that can help you, such as trade associations and community groups. Most companies don't have a cohesive, highly effective public relations effort; yet, it can work miracles for building your fame even if you are a very small company. This is especially true today with the prominence of the Internet.

As I mentioned, we have more than a dozen reports that we use as promotional pieces for our email list. Well, we also use those reports as articles and have our PR firm place those articles everywhere. In any given month, an article written by me will appear in more than 100 Web site ezines. That's every month. If you Google my name, you will find articles in thousands of places on the Web. As of this writing, 56,000 Web sites contain articles by or about me. What are the places in which an article by you can appear?

⚙ Exercise

Write down several ideas for articles that could be published in magazines, trade publications, or ezines on the Web. These same articles can become free reports that you use to market to prospects. This is how you beat the competition with your brain, not your wallet.

A great core story will make this easier. Right now I'm working with two women farmers who've created a way to put images on fruit. Yes, that's right, the apple you give your kids could have Sponge Bob on it. Their core story is about the health of Americans and how eating more fruit increases your life expectancy. Here is one of their press releases. Note that it is full of interesting information—one of the keys for getting your press release picked up.

PRESS RELEASE: OBESITY IN AMERICAN CHILDREN QUADRUPLES; FAST-FOOD COMPANIES TO BLAME?

A study conducted between 1963 and 1970 showed that obesity among children ages 6 to 11 years old was at about 4 percent of the child population. A similar study conducted between 1999 and 2002 shows that obesity is now at a staggering 16 percent.

Many trends have contributed to these factors. Among them is that large corporations have become much more aggressive in their marketing to children. And with good reason. In 1960, children influenced about $5 billion in spending. Today, that number is $500 billion—quite an increase.

The number of products corporate America markets directly to children has gone from 52 products in 1994 to more than 500 products today. A study of grade-school children showed that 96 percent of them could recognize Ronald McDonald. The only other figure with recognition that high was Santa Claus. The golden arches as a symbol are more recognized than the Christian cross.

One company's solution: Two women in Burlington, Washington, who run a small farm called AMF Farms have lobbied and received a grant from the U.S. Department of Agriculture to see if images on fruit can spur on children eating more fruit.

AMF Farms began by offering minipumpkins with cartoon characters painted on them. These products gained national distribution with such chains as Wal-Mart, Kroger, Safeway, and Albertson's. Once they perfected the art of mass-producing painted pumpkins, they made the next step, which was embossing edible images on fruit.

AMF Farms can paint just about any image on fruit, particularly apples and pears. States Michelle Younquist of AMF Farms, "Imagine how much more likely your child would be to eat an apple if it had Dora the Explorer or Sponge Bob on it."

AMF Farms is currently working with large growers of fruit to spread the usage of cartoon characters on fruit. They can also emboss logos of famous sports teams and corporate logos of companies that want to promote the eating of more fruit.

According to the *Journal of Agriculture and Chemistry*, people who eat the USDA daily recommendation of five or more servings of fruits and vegetables are half as likely to get cancer and 20 percent less likely to get heart disease (America's two biggest killers).

"This is just something we can do to help, but we're a small company," says AMF Farms cofounder Liz Mitchell. "We're trying to do our part to get children healthier. If this one thing can get a child eating an apple per day, it's worth everything we're going through."

To learn more, go to www.fruitdeco.com.

This is an effective PR piece because it starts with a newsworthy pain point. Every day there are articles in the news about the problem of obesity in general, especially child obesity. The PR piece is also effective because it uses mainstream and well-respected sources for its data. It reads like a news article without needing much editing. The article presents a company doing something right by offering one small solution to getting kids to eat healthier. Because the article is not focused on AMF per se but on important issues that will be of greater interest to editors, it's much more likely to get picked up by the press.

Make the News

The press consists of people who are just like anyone else whose attention you'd like to capture. Just as the Dream 100 strategy works to penetrate impossible accounts, it can be used with great effect to penetrate even the largest media sources. If Oprah's producers hear from you each and every month with yet another idea, they will get to know exactly who you are. The same is true of any publication or news source.

If you are national in scope, you can target national publications with such consistency that they will get to know exactly who you are.

⚙ Exercise

Make a list of dream media outlets that you'd like to write about your company or publish your articles. If your market is local, hit your local newspapers constantly with ideas or items of interest. A great core story that is packed full of data will give you a lot of fodder for press releases that will attract the attention of editors or news sources.

Ever notice how the entertainment media all cover the same shows all the time? There are tons of entertainment choices, but only the same 10 shows or movies get covered. That's because the people who determine the content of entertainment shows and magazines have relationships with the PR folks responsible for getting those shows covered. You, too, can form relationships with the important media people covering your industry.

In fact, according to *Guerrilla Marketing*, 70 percent of what is published as news is actually "placed news," or news that comes directly from press releases and PR initiatives. Most media sources are besieged by press releases. A sharp editor can see a story in those press releases and assign a reporter to flesh it out.

Every press release you send should be followed by a phone call. That's how you build relationships. Here's what you say: "Did you receive our press release about the amazing amount of pollutants in the home? We were wondering if there was anything we could do to help with that story." Often at that point, you'll be asked to resend your press release. Or you'll be brushed off, but the following month, when you call about the five million dust mites in everyone's living room, the editor will start to remember: you're the guy who knows about indoor air pollution. If a story comes up along those lines, guess who they are going to call first? Also, editors are just like anyone else. They respect someone who continues to call them with story ideas on a regular basis.

Earlier I mentioned American Art Resources (AAR), the people who sell art to hospitals. If they targeted the press for hospitals with pieces like "Why AAR is great" or "AAR gets another major hospital client," how effective do you think they'd be? Those are ego pieces and are of little interest to anyone except AAR. Instead, they use data from their core story for their press releases, so they have received remarkable coverage in national magazines and in many of the trade journals that cover their industry.

Their core story goes into data about hospitals and their struggles—everything from lawsuits to injuries caused in hospitals to lack of staff and waning profits. They cite data like this: 2,000 of the 5,000 or so hospitals are operating in the red (*AHA News*); hospitals accidentally kill more than 200,000 people per year (*Journal of American Medicine*). Their core story contains a massive amount of very disconcerting data that makes for very interesting information to editors of magazines and newspapers. Their PR effort has been astonishing.

But make no mistake: PR isn't just press releases. What about speaking at an industry event? You're not likely to get a speaking gig just to talk about your product or service. But, surely, if you've got a powerful core story, you'll certainly get a gig. AAR's core story was so packed with great data that they ended up being keynote speakers at several major conferences with their Dream 100 all in the room, all at once. Masterful PR for sure. In one speaking engagement, they got more than 300 of their dream target audience seeking more information from them.

Tying some of this together, they also created a brochure that mirrored the data in their core story. It also featured beautiful art of interest to hospitals. This company executed at the top of the game, showing remarkable pigheaded discipline and determination to see the vision come to fruition.

⚙ Exercise

Look at your core story and make a list of the data that would be of great interest to the readers of your target publications.

It's even easier if you are in a specific vertical market. Let's say you market to dentists or chiropractors, or even manufacturers. Every market has trade publications that focus specifically on that market. For most markets there are only a handful of these outlets and you can get to know the editors well if you talk to them every single month.

One article, properly placed, can work for you for years. I got an article in *Success* magazine that said, "Karate master Chet Holmes breaks sales records wherever he goes." A photo showed me doing a karate kick while standing on a table in my office overlooking the Bay Bridge in San Francisco. Yes, I wish this article had given more substantive information, but I've used it 1,000 times in other media activities. If you go to my Web site, you'll see that article represented there prominently. I've also used it as a mailer to my dream clients. It has been a nice bonus to my career—but only because I used it properly in all my marketing efforts.

⚙ Exercise

List all the ways you could use an article that has been or will be written about you or by you. Here are some ideas:

1. Use it as a promotional piece.
2. Have salespeople show it to prospects.
3. Use it as a direct mail piece.
4. Include it in your brochure or core story.
5. Hand it out at trade shows.
6. Use or quote it in your advertising.

PR newswire (www.prnewswire.com) is an amazing tool if you're writing press releases. It goes to every single media source on the planet for hundreds, not thousands, of dollars. I used it twice and ended up in *The Wall Street Journal* both times. The staff helps you write the press release because they know what will be picked up. Another secret to writing an effective press release is to mention a Fortune 500 company in your copy. You have to be very careful about liability here—and that is your responsibility—but if you have a legitimate reason to mention them, it helps in getting your article noticed by the media.

Marketing Weapon 5: Personal Contact

You can advertise to me, direct mail to me, or send me an article, but now I'm on the phone with your company. This is the most potent form of marketing. None of your marketing efforts will have as much impact on your client as personal contact with your salespeople or customer service reps. Since personal contact is such a powerful marketing weapon, we've devoted several chapters to it specifically and included more tips to help you improve this area in your business throughout the entire book. So for now, let's move to . . .

Marketing Weapon 6:
Trade Shows and Market Education

Done properly, a trade show can take you from obscurity to the top of the market in a single event. Trade shows offer an awesome opportunity to really stand out and get noticed. Done improperly, trade shows can be a waste of money. You can't imagine how many people tell me that a trade show they went to wasn't worth it. Then they learn what you're about to learn and it changes everything.

There are only three rules to having a great trade show, but there are 100 ways to capitalize on those rules. In order of importance, here are the rules:

1. Get noticed.
2. Drive traffic.
3. Capture leads.

Now let's go deep.

Rule 1: Get Noticed!

What can you do to really stand out in the crowd? Nothing, including great products and superb selling, will matter if you can't get noticed. Most trade shows are boring—booth after booth of folks hawking their wares. What you have to do is be the fun booth—the place that looks more interesting and exciting than any other booth.

With my help, one of my clients chose a Hawaiian theme. The crew all dressed in identical Hawaiian shirts so that they would stand out. Plus, think about the prospects who are at the trade show. If you go to the trade show with a show of force—another thing I recommend—and you've got 5 to 10 folks at the show in Hawaiian shirts, everyone starts to notice you. People even say to other people, "What's with the people in the Hawaiian shirts?"

Rule 2: Drive Traffic

Let's soup up the strategy even more. So one, we've got Hawaiian shirts. Two, we've got a backdrop of a Hawaiian beach scene at the booth with giant letters saying, "Win a free trip to Hawaii." Three, we are serving tropical drinks all day long. So now we're getting noticed, but let's go further. We want to "drive traffic." The free trip to Hawaii and the tropical drinks are designed to drive traffic.

Rule 3: Capture Leads

Now people get to the booth and, in order to enter the drawing, they need to give you a business card and fill out a quick little form that asks just a few qualifying questions. And here's a tip about getting data from folks. If you ask, "What is the size of your company?" they will either lie or leave it blank. But if you put the same question in multiple-choice form, you can get a lot of information. For example, your simple form could say:

Size of company (check one):
_____ Under $1 million
_____ $1 million to $5 million
_____ $5 million to $10 million
_____ $10 million plus

If you are selling to a lot of small companies, you could start your choices with

_____ Under $100K

Or you might ask,

How many widgets do you buy every year?
_____ Fewer than 5
_____ 6 to 10
_____ 11 to 15

You get the idea.

Ask them two or three questions, all with categories of choices so that they can just check the box that applies to them. So now, not only are you capturing leads, but you know just enough about them to prioritize your follow-up. And naturally, while you are serving them drinks and encouraging them to register, you strike up a conversation and look for the pearls—the great opportunities for your particular business.

To get even more attention at the trade show, another client hired a very attractive model to walk around with the drinks on a tray and send folks back to the booth to register for the free trip to Hawaii. Every major city has modeling agencies enabling you to go online and choose a model to work your trade show booth. You can get an attractive model or two (a man and a woman is a good idea) for about $300 per day per model—a small price to pay to drive traffic.

Also, to soup this up even further, you can throw a luau party at a popular club. Then your model can say to folks: "Hey, we're having a luau later tonight that's going to be a ball. It's by invitation only, so make sure you get your invite at booth number 2372—right over there."

One of the best things you can do at a trade show is throw a party. But for Pete's sake, if you do that, you'd better make sure you do it right! In one industry in which I worked, we became famous for our parties. Every booth in the entire place would buzz about our parties, and our clients would seek out my sales staff to get those coveted invitations.

The secret to throwing a great party is to do it at a popular club. Here's how you do that for very little money. A week or two before the trade show, you call the most popular clubs in the town where the trade show is being held. Call your hotel and ask the concierge to name the hottest clubs. Call during the day and ask for the manager of the club. Here's what you say: "I'm throwing a party in your town in two weeks and I'm going to have 200 people with me. I'm going to pick up the tab for them to drink all night. I'm trying to decide which club I want to use. Can you tell me about yours?"

You can see where a wise club manager would want you to come to his club rather than someone else's. And most trade shows are during the week, which means on a Tuesday evening when a club is usually slow, and you're going to fill it with 200 partying trade show attendees. Things to negotiate: no door charge for your patrons. I've never had a club yet that wouldn't happily waive the door charge. So that saves you a lot right there since door charge is $20 a head in some clubs. Another thing you need to make sure the manager agrees to: Your guests don't wait on line. They go right in. That makes them feel like the stars who don't have to wait in long lines to get into someplace swank.

Next, you want to print drink coupons that your sales staff (and models) hand out. This makes your sales staff very popular. Everyone gets two coupons with the invite, but when they want more, they have to come to you. This also enables you to control the bill and make sure that strangers aren't telling the bartender: "I'm with the XYZ party. Put it on their tab." Then, at the end of the night, the club owner can count the coupons and you just pick up the bar tab. I usually negotiate a flat fee— say, $6 per drink. Some folks will drink scotch but many will drink water or club soda. So if you get a low prenegotiated price, knowing that most people will not drink the really expensive drinks, the manager will usually agree to a set price for all drinks. Do the math. If you have 200 people who drink an average of three drinks, that's 600 drinks at $6, so you're talking about a bar tab of under $4,000. Not a lot to pay for the "best party at the trade show."

Here are a few more things to think about. Usually a trade show will have one night when the organizers are throwing a party or event. It's not wise to go up against that. Also, if you're a small company and some major player is renting out Disneyland, you can get lost. So try to find out what else is going on before you choose the night of your party.

And make sure you make it hot—*the* party to attend. You do that by being slightly stingy with the invites and telling everyone, "This is going to be the hottest party at this trade show."

The first place I threw one of these parties was Toronto. I cut the exact deal mentioned with the club that was at the top of the CN Tower— talk about the ideal place to throw the party. I had five charming superstar salespeople who went around and promoted that party like it was going to be amazing. I hired an incredibly attractive model to help promote it, and we went from obscurity in that market to top of the buzz in one single trade show.

The most important rule about throwing a trade show party is that it has to be fun! That's one of the benefits of throwing a party at a club that is already open for business. You have some built-in potential dance partners. Make sure everyone is dancing and having a great time. Models are a great idea here, too, and only cost about $100 extra to attend the party. Heck, they might go just because it sounds like fun. They will draw attention and get people dancing.

Your role at the party is important to the overall success of the party as well. Be very friendly. Boldly walk up to people and shake their hands. Then introduce them to others. Make sure no one is standing around looking uncomfortable. The bottom line is that you want trade show buzz the next day with everyone talking about your party.

Some more themes that I've used to great success in the past include setting up a casino in the booth, hosting a magician, hiring a fortune-teller, and creating a Roaring Twenties theme. The possibilities are endless, but the most effective themes tie into what you sell. That's more entertaining and ensures that your message won't be lost amid all of those tropical drinks or fortune revelations.

I had a client who chose a *Star Trek* theme. We all dressed up in high-quality *Star Trek* uniforms, complete with the beeper on the chest that made that little sound when you said, "Beam me up, Scotty." It was a huge success. The CEO had the admiral's uniform, so he was especially distinguished. This company was trying to establish that it was the future in that particular industry.

Another client, who sold investment property in England, did a trade show where investors of every type came to look at various investments. They chose James Bond as their theme. They called it "License to Make a Killing." All the men dressed up in tuxedos and the women were in evening gowns. They handed out squirt guns at the trade show and got models to hand out invitations to a Bond party on a yacht they had rented for the night. Because they were restrictive on the tickets, they generated a ton of excitement for the party. The average booth at that trade show came away with 15 leads or so. They had a blast at the trade show and left with 550 leads.

Another client sold products that help farmland yield more crops per square foot or yard, reduce erosion, and produce stronger, more nourished crops. I suggested that the company do a doctor theme and call it "The Dirt Doctors" as, obviously, its product improves your dirt. The staff did not want to do it! Not one of them, not even the CEO, wanted to dress up like a doctor at a trade show full of farmers. But they finally did it and had stunning results. When I was encouraging yet another client to follow this advice and he, too, was timid, I had the dirt doctor client write to the other client about the results. Here's the dirt doctor story from the lips of the CEO:

When Chet came up with this idea for us he said: "Trust me. Just do it." We did it. This particular show is one we had done every year for seven years. With this approach we got more leads than we had gotten in all the previous seven years combined! We did not look like idiots as I thought we would. We were the life of the party. We decided to completely go for it, and it was a big hit.

As Chet mentioned, we sell soil additives. My VP and I dressed in white lab coats and wore stethoscopes around our necks. My name tag said, "Dr. Dirt," and his read, "Dr. Soil." We had a massage therapist in our booth giving complimentary neck and back massages and we had our lovely blond "nurse" walking around the show handing out "prescriptions for relaxation." People were told to bring the prescription to our booth for a free relaxing massage and a chance to win a relaxing trip to Maui. All they had to do was get the prescription signed by one of the "doctors."

They came in droves and lined up for their massages. Because they had to get their "prescription" signed by one of us to be entered into the Maui giveaway, we guaranteed ourselves an opportunity to talk to everyone. While they waited for their massage, we had time for substantive conversation. What happened was everyone was in a great mood when they came to our booth. We were the life of the party.

They were already on our side because they were having so much fun. We focused on the fun, and the prospects genuinely wanted to know what our company and product were all about. We also discovered that, after a massage, people were really friendly (and appreciative) and they would linger to ask questions about the product. Also, our massage therapist was familiar with the product, so she could talk it up while she was working on them. I could go on forever and I would be happy to answer any specific questions you might have, but I learned that when Chet says, "Trust me," that's exactly what you should do.

Tim Alderson
President
AgriGator, Inc.
www.agrigator.com

Of course, you can go to a trade show in your normal clothes and calmly talk about your product or service to whoever happens to come by your booth. But if you really want to turn your trade show booth into a lead-generating machine, you need to completely go for it. Tim followed the rules for a successful trade show as laid out in the paragraphs above. Take the extra steps to get noticed, drive traffic, and capture data about your prospect. Hire extra people like a massage therapist or a palm reader or models to join your staff and make your booth a magnet for everyone at the trade show. Tim's company got more leads than it had in seven previous years combined. It takes careful planning and some creativity, but it's worth every extra effort.

⚙ Exercise

You can do this as a workshop with you staff. Let everyone think about themes or ideas around your product or service that might make a great event at a trade show. You can put up a lot of the ideas already offered in this book. But be open to new and different ideas.

Charity Events

Charity events are amazing PR vehicles. You may want to structure your trade show party as a charity event or do such an event separately. There are two primary reasons why they are an awesome opportunity for your company:

1. Charity events can get tons of publicity for the charity. It's much easier to get publicity when it's for a good cause than when you are trying to get publicity for your own company. The publicity will also mention your company in a very positive light.

2. In most cases, the event pays for itself. Only the profits from an event go to the charity. Ask restaurants, travel companies, and other trade show attendees to donate prizes, gifts, or entertainment so the value of the event for those attending goes beyond giving to charity. A charity event lets you bond like crazy and be a celebrity among your Dream 100. And you do a good deed in the process.

Here are some charity event ideas: You could set up a film premiere with a local theater without involving the distributor. When I worked with 680 chiropractors for a year and a half teaching them how to grow their businesses, we created an event to benefit them and a local charity of their choice. I got the president of Sony Pictures Distribution on the phone and told him: "I have 680 doctors across the country who are willing to promote your movie. Interested?" He was, and we set up film premieres in more than 200 of these chiropractors' cities.

A chiropractor who lived in Dallas went to the Dallas Cowboys and told them he was doing a charity event—a Hollywood film premiere right there in Dallas. They said: "Great. We'll send the cheerleaders by." The film was *Dance with Me* and the chiropractor got the Dallas Cowboy cheerleaders to dance in the parking lot for free. Do you think you could get your Dream 100 clients to an event like that? This chiropractor did, and dream clients even paid to attend the event!

Here's another concept related to the Dream 100 concept: I call it the *market influencer sell*. Market influencers are leaders in your particular market: community leaders, presidents of the biggest companies, anyone who by showing interest in your product or service increases the interest of others. Another good example might be celebrities. I remember a friend of mine owned an antique shop where he sold handmade lamps. After Barbra Streisand started collecting these lamps, their price tripled. In the case of the chiropractors, MDs are important targets because they are a great source of referrals. Many of our participants marketed the event to every MD in their town. Another chiropractor got a presidential candidate to come to the function. Having that market influencer enabled that chiropractor to get still other important people to his event.

Holding a charity event that was attended by such notables raised the public stature of the chiropractor sponsoring the occasion. In addition, these were truly great charity events because they were fun for everyone and they raised a lot of money for a good cause. Some were the talk of the town for several weeks. These chiropractors decided they wanted to be famous in their communities. If you want to be famous in yours, put on a charity event and then get your Dream 100 and market influencers involved.

⚙ Exercise

Who makes it onto your market influencer list? Put together a list of the most influential people to promote your product or service and add them to your regular marketing.

The most obvious and easiest thing to do is to put on a classic cocktail party, dance, or dinner dance. It's simple: book the place, hire the DJ, get companies to donate gifts and prizes, and invite highly influential people. Charge $50 per head or more, and you can throw one heck of a party.

Another great idea is putting on an awards ceremony. With one of the companies I ran, we put on a ceremony called the "Lammies" for the Legal Advertising and Marketing Awards. We had as many categories as we could think of so we could honor as many of the guests as possible. Judges and winners and the entire audience were filled with our Dream 100 list. We charged to enter for an award, and we charged a per-plate fee to attend the lavish black-tie affair, so the event didn't cost us anything. We had dinner, dancing, awards, and then more dancing. A big group of us even ended the evening in the hot tubs at the hotel, partying to the late hours. This was a killer event.

Award categories included best ad, most creative ad, best trade show booth, best new product, overachiever of the year, and CEO of the year. We put together a panel of notable judges from popular ad agencies and, of course, a few members of our staff. We wrote clever scripts for my staff to introduce all the nominees and give great little sendups for the winners when they accepted their awards. This still stands out in my mind, 15 years later, as a marketing accomplishment beyond anything I've ever seen. You have to have enough clout to put on an awards ceremony for your industry or area, but, boy, is it great fun and rewarding if you do it right.

⚙ Exercise

Write down an awards ceremony idea that you could pull off at your annual trade show, in your community, or for your profession. Who are the most influential people in your area and what kind of awards could you give them? The more categories, the better.

Your Own Trade Association

Trade shows are great, but there are other ways to gain top-of-mind awareness through market education. You can create a trade association of your very own that would benefit your industry. You can even involve your competitors. They'll love to come to your events because their dream clients will be there as well, but you'll be in the catbird seat because it's your trade association. Ask your Dream 100 to be on committees, serve as chairmen of subcommittees, and sit on the board of advisers. A trade association with worthy objectives is effective. Is there some problem in your industry that you can rally around? If you organize industry players around an important issue, you will rule your industry.

Other Educational Ideas

I once put on an industry seminar for all my clients. I charged them to attend (and they gladly paid). We had 54 speakers, many of whom were from my Dream 100. We had 27 seminars with breakout sessions and two heavy-hitter keynotes, one of whom was Jay Levinson, author of the *Guerrilla Marketing* series.

You can also create a mass teleconference for your clients. I do these for nearly every company that hires me. One of my clients has one of the largest duck farms in the country. He sells primarily to Chinese restaurants, but wanted to expand into all restaurants. We put on a mass teleconference for him where restaurant owners could learn many tricks for building their traffic. And at the end of the conference, we talked about the growing popularity of duck as an entrée.

The client who sells carpet cleaning services wanted to expand his reach to interior designers because they are market influencers in upscale homes. In his case, we put on a mass teleconference showing interior decorators how to get more clients and get more revenue from current clients. One way was to recommend this carpet and rug cleaning company, which in return would pay a commission for every client sent to them. The carpet cleaning client also has a product that protects furniture and carpets against stains and spills. So the last part of the conference was about how these interior designers could make additional revenue by offering this protective coating as an add-on and how they could set their clients up for the Gold Service to schedule semiannual cleanings.

⚙ Exercise

What kind of mass teleconference can you offer your clients that they would happily attend? And what kind of a speaker would attract a good number of these clients? You will only need the speaker for one hour on a teleconference. If you can attract a big crowd to the teleconference, there's almost no speaker who would refuse to take part for very little money.

Marketing Weapon 7: Internet

In 1995, only five million people used this marketing weapon. That number jumped to 105 million just four years later. Today, virtually everyone uses it. Amazon.com may have struggled in its early years, but it still took $1 billion in market share from other booksellers. Because Amazon grew with the Internet, the company reached $1 billion in sales in four years flat. Predating the Internet, other booksellers (bookstore chains) took 50 years to reach $1 billion in annual sales. The Internet can create an awesome opportunity or it can become your worst nightmare overnight if some competitor learns to utilize it better than you.

There are entire books on this subject, but here's my five-pronged approach to tie this together with everything else you are doing here:

1. Capture leads.
2. Build a relationship.
3. Interact as much as possible.
4. Offer a webinar (Web seminar).
5. Convert traffic to sales.

One of the best lessons I've learned about building a healthy database is the concept of the "shy yes" page taught by Alex Mandossian. My main home page, www.chetholmes.com, is packed with opportunities to get things for free. At the time of this writing, that site is getting 52,000 unique visits every month. These are generally people who have heard me speak, read one of my articles, or heard about me from someone else or from some marketing we've done. On every page and at the end of every article, that site offers you a subscription opportunity for a free newsletter, free mass teleconference, free event, and so on. And with all that going on, only 1 percent to 3 percent of the visitors subscribe. That's 520 to 1,560 of the 52,000.

That site has other uses besides capturing leads, like branding and acquainting new folks with my material. But imagine how highly inefficient it would be to advertise that site on the radio, for example. I'd pay thousands of dollars to drive leads and, of those, I'd drive a tiny percentage who would register to be emailed other promotions. And then those promotions might not even get opened.

So, using the concept of the "shy yes," we designed another site. Alex likens a Web site to trying to get a date. If you ask someone to marry you the first time you talk to her, you're not likely to get a yes. But if you ask her to have a cup of coffee, you might get a yes. It is hard to say no to a cup of coffee when you're in the market for romance and you kind of like the person. So it's an easier step.

Translating that to the concept of a Web site, my main page is in your face from every direction with offers and things to do. This is not a bad thing, but the direction of the relationship is now unclear. You have to decide what you want to do on my site, and I have no control over what you choose. On that site, I also offer, right on the home page, a chance to go to a webinar. Of those who go to the site, maybe one in 52,000 will actually register to attend a Web seminar.

Rather than my articles and interviews directing people to www. chetholmes.com where there are 100 choices of what they can do, we created www.howtodoublesales.com. This site only gives people one choice: give me your email address and go look at a four-minute video on how to double your sales. At this site there is a small paragraph with an audio component of my voice welcoming you to the site. To enter the site, you give just your first name and email address. There are no other choices, nothing to distract you. Get this: an astonishing 37 percent who go there opt in. This has built my database dramatically in a very short period of time. Of those who opt in, 2 percent to 6 percent opt to go to the next step, which is to participate in a webinar. So if I'm getting 10,000 unique visits, 3,700 of them give me their email address, and, of those, 74 to 222 opt to take the webinar.

So, effectively, we moved from a site where only one of 52,000 visitors went on to our recommended next step, to the shy yes site with 10,000 visits and 74 to 222 people going on to our recommended next step. With one fifth the traffic, we are getting at least 74 times the results. That's a pretty good improvement and shows that the soft yes site that offers only one choice for how to proceed is an effective tool for driving leads. Companies should have sites like this that are specifically designed to capture leads. Or on your main site you need to make the lead-capture effort your most prominent graphic or offer.

The Web Site

Web sites suffer the same problem as most brochures. They are mostly ego pieces touting your greatness. In contrast, a Web site that offers information of value to your prospects can be a community, a place where your prospects go to look at new things, to get information, to interact with you, and to get to know you better. Have free articles, free education, free sound bites, and free insights. Once prospects have registered with your shy yes page, connect them to the rest of your world with a follow-up email or with a click-through at some point after the shy yes page. Remember, the goal is to create a marketing program in which all the pieces work together like a finely tuned machine. So your Web site should look very much like your brochure and direct mail pieces, using the same graphics, headlines, and market data from your core story.

As you learned in Chapter Four, I don't care what kind of product or service you offer, there is information that can be of value to your prospects that can soup up your ability to spread your fame and advance your brand. The information on your Web site will get search engines to send you even more leads. Then once folks come to your Web site because it has information of value to them, you can then go a step further and offer Web seminars and mass teleconferences to teach folks how to be more successful in the area in which they live that intersects with your product or service. This will get you even deeper with your prospects. So think of your Web site as a community where there are benefits to your prospects when they visit.

When I was in the advertising business, I used to offer free seminars to advertisers about how to create better ads (the material in this chapter being the content). That was not so long ago, but since then the Internet has ballooned to major significance. If I were selling advertising today, I'd have that seminar online. Think of how this cuts down on your travel expenses. I used to fly all over creation to deliver those seminars. And appointments were harder to get.

The education-based marketing concept that you learned in Chapter Four works hand in glove with the ability to do things over the Internet. Here's the pitch I'd do today: "How would you like to learn to make your advertising literally 10 times more effective? And you can do it right from the comfort of your favorite office chair." It's hard to resist such an offer.

There are many examples I could give you to flesh out the model of turning your Web site into a community. The examples below are simple and some are even silly, but each shows how far this concept can go and how it helps you capture more leads and build a better brand.

If you sell water (as a mundane example), you could have a site with "Everything you wanted to know about water" or "Everything you'd better know about water." This site could then show all the things that water does for the body. It could explain why you need to drink water, how much water you should drink, what the status of water is on the planet, what the different additives are in the water we drink today, and what's happening to our tap water today. Now when you're advertising your water, you can send folks to your site to learn "The five most dangerous things everyone should know about water today." Put that little plug on every bottle of water that you sell, in every ad that you have, and so on. Then have a place right on the screen that says: "Want to make your friends healthier? Send them to this site and get a chance to win a new car." Give away one car per year, and millions will send others to your Web site where you brand like crazy—and, of course, capture emails. Now you have a free way to further your brand.

If your product is shaving cream, you can use the headline, "The five things you'd better know about shaving and how many different ways it affects your body." Plus, you can include tips on how to shave, the best ways to shave, and what every kid should know when it's time to shave. Cover topics such as the structure of various shaving creams and the impact that shaving has on your skin. You could even give the history of shaving. When did it start? How did it start? Who started it?

Get this: if you offer all this advice and plug that Web site everywhere you're already promoting your product, the site becomes an information source that folks are going to send other folks to in order to get this information. So information-based marketing accelerates your reach and increases word-of-mouth advertising. This is the Information Age, for Pete's sake, so provide as much as you can.

This can get more interesting if your product or service is more interesting, but every product or service can create a community—even bottled water or shaving cream. And I could go on with a chapter of ideas to expand on the concept, but you'll do it yourself as you start down the path. Just think of your Web site as a community. Focus on it, not on you, and look to get involved with and serve that community at every turn.

A good consumer example of a Web site that builds community is Stonyfield Farms, producer of organic dairy products (yogurt, milk, etc.). Their Web site offers terrific information on organic foods and how to help protect the Earth. They also provide recipes and a multitude of other information on wellness. One thing they could do to improve their community is to prominently promote a subscriber program. As of this writing, they have no easy-to-find newsletter or other subscription opportunity that would tie them closer to the consumer. If they sent some of their articles directly to consumers, those consumers might forward them to friends and family, thereby using the Internet as a vehicle to dramatically enhance or increase Stonyfield's word-of-mouth marketing.

There are mistakes that some folks will make, for sure. After I teach this material, I'll sometimes stumble on someone who has heard the concepts and liked them a lot but, in the execution, lost the real message. I will see students of this concept come out with "five reasons why our product is better than anyone else's." Who is that focused on? Who cares about your five reasons? What I care about is what five things I need to learn that will serve me. And then, once I'm into that education, make it a good one. And then somewhere along the line, you can use your product or service as an *example*, and that is where you get to promote your product—but always from the perspective of "what's in it for the client."

Conclusion

The key for all of these marketing weapons is that they work together. Have a meeting once per month in which you look at each of your Seven Musts of Marketing and see how you can make them all work together more effectively. Are your articles on your Web site? Do your salespeople use your articles? Does your advertising also drive leads to the Web community you've built? Are you promoting referrals at every turn? Is your sales staff offering free education? Make it all work together.

Here is the list of the Seven Musts at a glance:

1. Advertising
2. Direct mail
3. Corporate literature: brochures, promotional pieces
4. Public relations
5. Personal contact: salespeople, customer service reps
6. Market education: trade shows, speaking engagements, Chet-style marketing efforts as described in Chapter Six
7. Internet: your Web sites, email efforts, and affiliate marketing

(8)

The Eyes Have It

Attract and Close More Buyers by
Using More Compelling Visuals, Plus, the
Biggest Mistakes Everyone Makes
When Presenting

As you've learned throughout this book, building the Ultimate Sales Machine is not just about sales but about tuning up every aspect of your business to run with precision. In this chapter, you will learn how to use visual aids with tremendous effect. You will also learn how to attract more buyers, influence them more effectively, and close more sales once you are in front of those buyers.

We human beings remember 20 percent of what we hear, 30 percent of what we see, but 50 percent of what we both see and hear.[7] Obviously your communication impact nearly triples when using visual aids over not using them. Information that is visually illustrated and communicated has a dramatic and direct impact on the brain.

As a top producer, I recall being very resistant to using visual aids. "I don't need them," I said. "I'm a top producer." Then I took a high-end training program that showed not only how powerful visual aids are, but that they close more sales and close for higher rates. That's right. Take the same product and present it directly to the prospect by talking about it and then take that same product and present it using visual aids. You will find that, not only do you close a higher percentage of prospects, but they will actually pay more money for the same product. That was it. I was sold. I began using visual aids in every sales situation.

Now, as a trainer, I always use visual aids in my training programs and find that they make the programs much more effective. In a recent seminar, I was speaking in front of 1,500 CEOs using slides every few seconds to illustrate my points. I was pounding through the slides and then came to the point where I was saying how powerful visual aids were. At that moment, I blanked the screen and asked the audience, "What just happened to this communication experience?" You could feel it. Every person in that room knew that the experience had just fallen off dramatically. Right there, they decided that they, too, had to start using more visual aids to better communicate

The Eyes Have It

Eighty-five percent of the information taken into the brain enters through the eyes. The largest part of the brain is set aside just to deal with information taken in visually. In my seminars I'll ask folks, "How many images do you think the eyes can process in a single glance?" People will yell out, "Twenty!" or "Two hundred!" Then on the next slide I'll show an aerial shot of a city skyline with millions of images. Obviously, the eyes can take in a lot more than 20 images in a single glance. With the eyes playing a significant role in the communication process, you'd be crazy not to use visuals every chance you get.

If you ignore the power of incorporating a visual component into your sales and marketing process, you may as well deliver it in a closet. Fail to stimulate the eyes, and the brain tunes out. As stated in the previous chapter's section on radio advertising, the brain can take in information at 400 to 500 words per minute, yet people speak at only 125 words per minute. We can take in a lot more than we are given in a normal conversation or even a lecture *if we can stay present*. A visually rich presentation keeps the eyes busy and, therefore, keeps the brain more active and alert to learn the information you are presenting.

Color Also Helps

There are numerous studies on the impact of using color over black and white in your communication. Color attracts the eye and helps set the mood of your presentation, and each color has a different effect on the viewer. While red is the color that draws the eye the most, it may not be the color you want to use for everything. Red denotes passion, but it is also the color for danger, blood, or being "in the red" on your balance sheet. Blue says tried and true, but it also means cool and refreshing. You'll note that almost all bottled water companies use blue, as it is the color of our oceans. Orange says value. Think Howard Johnson's or Home Depot—they use orange because studies show it denotes good value. Green is the color of money, but it's also the color of fresh greens from the garden. So color has an impact. Think about what colors you want to use. And certainly, for your corporate look and feel, you want to choose the color that best suits your main message.[8]

Graphics or photos of people are particularly effective. The physical body is the most attractive shape to us because it is the most familiar. Almost any part of the body draws our attention, including the hands, shoulders, or face. Even when looking at vacation photos of beautiful landscapes, most people's eyes are drawn to the people in those photos before they consider the actual landscape.

In my presentations, I use a graphic on every single panel, and every single area I cover is what I call storyboarded. When I present the information about what the eye is drawn to, I put up a graphic of a well-developed man running on the beach. Next is a graphic of a woman in a swimming pool. Then I ask folks what was in the background. Usually they've barely noticed. But they *can* tell you what the woman was wearing and the color of the man's swimming trunks. The eye is drawn to physical images, so use the human figure wherever you can in your presentations.

Visual aids such as PowerPoint, storyboards, flip charts, and diagrams can keep your audience engaged in your presentation. Even if you are selling by telephone, it's important to incorporate something visual. Ask the prospect to draw a diagram or two as you are talking and use it to make your points. The triangle graphic we used in Chapter Four to illustrate who is in your stadium is a perfect example. If I were trying to teach you that over the telephone, I'd say: "Draw a triangle. Now draw a line through just the top 3 percent of that triangle. Next to that write down, 'Buying now,' " and so on.

Here is a graphic I used in a core story for a company that was selling to lawyers.

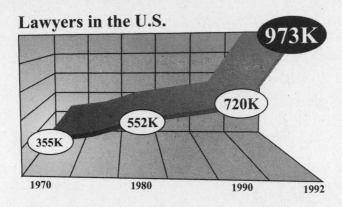

Lawyers in the U.S.

973K

720K

552K

355K

1970   1980   1990   1992

In the 10 years between 1970 and 1980, the number of lawyers in the United States grew by almost 200,000. From 1980 to 1990, we added another 168,000 lawyers. But in the *two* years from 1990 to 1992, we added another 253,000 lawyers! The United States gained more lawyers in two years than in any 10 years prior. Do you know why? Some speculate that the show *L.A. Law* made the legal profession appear a lot more glamorous than it had in the past.

Look again at the details of the graphic. Notice how the sizes of the numbers (of lawyers) get bigger as the numbers get higher. We didn't have to do that. We could have made the numbers the same size for each decade of growth. But by making the numbers bigger as well, the graphic has a lot more visual impact. Every detail can make a difference. In the actual slide, we use the color red for the biggest number, 973K. That number is surrounded by a red circle. Red draws the eye to the important information, but it also is the color of danger. For the lawyers to whom we were presenting this information, such a rapid swelling in their professional ranks was bad news. As the number of lawyers in the United States grew, the total billing for the market was only growing at its normal rate, and so as a group, lawyers were going to be making less money than ever before.

As you can see, visual aids enable you to tell more story in the same period of time. They can communicate more information, with more impact, and they make your presentation much more professional and polished. Visual aids immediately raise the expectations of your audience. If your material is well prepared, your prospect's interest level and expectations go up immediately. Think of how much closer you are to closing the deal when your prospect is in that state of mind as opposed to half asleep and wondering when your presentation will be over.

○ Exercise

Right now, think of a few of your sales points that you can communicate using visual aids. Maybe it's the performance of your product or service. Is it faster or easier than your competitors'? How would you show that? Maybe it's production or output? Can you use a bar chart or graph to show the difference between you and all your competitors? Write down five sales points you want to communicate and think through how you might show these points instead of just telling them. Can you use common shapes? If you sell by phone, can you say things like "Picture it like a triangle with the top cut off." Or can you get your audience to actually draw something? This would be a great exercise to do with your team as a workshop.

Rules for Effective Presenting

Rule 1. K.I.S.S. (Keep It Simple, Stupid)

Your presentation needs to be easy to follow and understand. Don't clutter the page with text or too many graphics. You should have no more than one big heading and only three to four bullet points per panel.

Rule 2. K.I.F.P. (Keep It Fast Paced)

Prospects will get bored if you spend too much time on one page. You should be covering two to three panels a minute. Don't just show one and stand there and talk for 10 minutes. Keep the presentation moving. There should be a new point coming up visually every 15 seconds or so. Or, if it is a panel with three bullets, have only one bullet come up at a time. If all three come up, your audience will read on ahead and you will lose control. Done properly, visual aids give you more control over the communication experience at every level. In Web seminars, it's critical to have constant images flashing across the screen. You're not in the room with them, so they can start checking email and multitasking unless you're showing so much new data or so many images every few seconds that they have no time to multitask. One of the bonuses that you receive from purchasing this book is a

$61 discount to a superbly crafted Web seminar that follows all these rules. See www.chetholmes.com/book for details.

Rule 3. Use "Wow" Facts and Statistics

You literally want your client to say, "Wow! I didn't know that." As you learned in Chapter Four ("Becoming a Brilliant Strategist"), factual information at the beginning of any presentation creates a sense of credibility that carries over even for the "sales" part of your presentation. But facts that are particularly jarring or revealing have a power beyond just establishing credibility. They keep people interested and give them something right off the bat to remember. Later that night at dinner, your prospects might tell their husband or wife. The next day, they'll tell a colleague and it will spread from there. Choosing Wow facts can also set up the buying criteria for your product or service and turn everyone who hears your presentation into a minisalesperson for you.

Here are two examples:

This is a Wow fact panel.

Breast cancer is the leading cause of death for women between ages 40 and 55.

Fifty years ago there was a 1 in 20 risk.

Today it's a 1 in 8 risk.

1940: 1 in 20 Risk

Since 1940, when the Chemical Age was dawning, breast cancer deaths have risen steadily by 1 percent per year in the United States. Similar increases have been reported in other industrial countries.

Today: 1 in 8 Risk

Breast Cancer in Women

This information was used by a client who sells supplements that improve your body's ability to fight toxins in the environment. His entire core story was filled with remarkable data that made people say, "Wow!"

Here's a Wow factor visual for men.

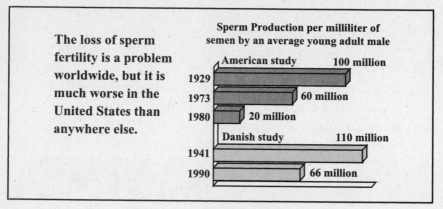

Dangerous drop in sperm count.
Are we on the verge of extinction?

According to research that was done for this client, in 1929 the average male's sperm count was 100 million per milliliter. By 1980 it was down to 20 million. Today it's only 5 million. While 5 million still sounds like a lot of sperm (it only takes one to get a woman pregnant), this information viewed in context of our past is pretty darn scary. The loss of sperm and infertility are worldwide problems, but they are much worse in the United States than anywhere else. This is market data and it's way more motivational than product data. Especially if you are selling nutritional supplements as this company is doing (www.primezyme.com). Again, to get "wows" you need to look at information over time. If I told you that we have 5 million sperm per milliliter, that's not big news. But when you see that it was 100 million, 70-some years ago, that's really powerful.

The first thing to do with any presentation is provide an overview of your industry over time. I had a client who sold to car dealerships. So the first thing we did was look at how many car dealerships there are selling how many cars. And that's a nice little fact that should be in your core story if you're presenting to car dealerships. But if you look at what's happened to them since 1950, it gets you a "Wow, I didn't know that," from the dealer. According to this client's research, in 1950, 47,000 car dealerships sold 7 million new cars per year. Now 17,000 dealerships sell 21,000 new cars per year (does not count used vehicles sold). Car dealerships are consolidating like crazy. Is this important? Not really. Does it get the dealer to say, "Wow, I didn't know that." Yes. Does it start right off establishing that you know more than the person you're presenting to? Yes. So begin every core story or presentation with Wows.

⚙ Exercise

Who is the audience for your presentation? Write down five overview facts you'd like to know about that would be interesting to *them*. Then set about finding this information over time. How many of them are there? How many were there 30 years ago? What is the failure rate of this type of company? Or if it's a consumer matter, what are the issues surrounding those consumers that are going to be of interest to them? The same information you put on your Web site can be used in your presentations.

I had a client that wanted to sell skincare products to day spas. So I asked the researcher to tell me the failure rate of day spas. I was looking for the pain point to motivate spa owners to take interest in my client's hot new service. The data came back—the failure rate was very small. However, because we asked the researchers to look at data over time, we discovered that the growth rate was unbelievable—from approximately 90 day spas in the U.S. in 1980 to 16,000 today. So instead of focusing on the failure rate, what conclusion could we draw from that data that might be bad news for day spas? Competition—major competition. When you do the research, it will give you all kinds of ideas you'd never think of for positioning the importance of your product or service.

Rule 4. Build in Opportunities for Stories

Well-told stories increase recall by another 26 percent over making a point without a story to illustrate it. People love stories. When I was selling advertising for a magazine, I tried to get to a big advertiser. I met with the director of marketing, who would not let me meet the owner of the company. But he loved my ideas, and I was sure I had the sale. After I left, he went to the owner with the information. The owner said no. The marketing director thanked me for trying and sent me on my way.

I deliberately didn't follow up with him because I knew the only thing he could say was no. In fact, I waited six full months, hoping he would forget me altogether. I then went over his head to the owner of the company and got an appointment. If I had done this right away, the marketing director would've felt slighted. How dare I go over his head? But since I waited six months, it went exactly as planned. Basically, he had forgotten all about me, and when I got there, the CEO called in the marketing director to join us. He said to me, "Hey, I know you." We shook hands and I got to present my material to the owner with this fellow in the room. He was supportive once, so I figured he'd be supportive again.

When I finished, the CEO said: "Okay. You convinced me. We'll take a page of advertising and try it out." I said, "One page is *not* the way to test advertising." The owner said, "Atta boy," impressed that I was pushing him to make a real commitment. He took three pages for his test. They sold training programs and needed to make 28 sales to break even on the ad. He pointed out: "I don't even need to make a profit on it—I'll make that on the back end. Once a client buys from us, they keep buying. So all I need to do is break even and we'll advertise again."

The first ad ran and they only got six responses. It was an awful response rate for an expensive magazine ad. I did tremendous amounts of follow-up. I went to see him and showed him letters with impressive success stories from other companies that had advertised in the magazine. I stayed in his face, my faith in my magazine unwavering. This is the opposite of what most salespeople do when things don't work. When a deal starts to go bad, most salespeople start to back off from calling the client. They're afraid to face the music.

The next ad ran and got an even worse response rate—just four responses. This was abysmal. And then the next ad ran and got only two responses. Each time, I intensified my follow-up with more and more stories of how other companies got amazing response rates. Maybe I should point out in my defense that he ran an ad that featured three different authors of his training programs, and each one had progressively less hair. The dull black-and-white ad looked more like a hair replacement ad than an ad for professional training programs. I told him his ad wasn't working and he needed one that would stand out. I presented all the information you learned in the previous chapter about how to create an ad that will stop people in their tracks and suggested, "If you really want to get attention, you need to buy a full-page spread and put an insert in the middle of it. This way the magazine will open to your ad (because the insert is a card stock material). On the insert you can put an order form for folks to order."

He listened and took a four-color, full-page spread and insert, following my advice on content and design, in the annual trade show issue. This was much more expensive than his other three ads, so this was sink or swim for me. I had built enormous credibility by not backing off in the face of failure, and the client was following my advice one last time. With that single $18,000 insert ad and spread, he sold $650,000 worth of programs. I was vindicated and the company became a regular advertiser, never to doubt me again.

This story illustrates many points. If I just said to you, "Make sure you stay in your prospect's face even more if things aren't going right," that sounds good, but telling this story dramatically makes the point. I sell training programs that teach the importance of better follow-up, so this story certainly shows the importance of that. What are you selling and what story illustrates the need for your product or service?

Rule 5. Your Presentation Should Be Curiosity Driven

Unfold the information in a way that keeps your prospects curious. Give them a fact first and follow it with an explanation. Also, continually presell the rest of the presentation throughout the presentation. Keep alluding to information yet to come. Keep them anticipating the information you are about to tell them. For example, while presenting the information about the increase in lawyers, you could say, "And this means you have some serious competition, but the news gets worse when I show you the next point." There is a righteous presell that really makes the person want to see the next slide.

Rule 6. Think of Each Headline as Valuable Real Estate

Every header should work as hard as possible. It should intrigue the prospects and sell the panels. Don't waste them by being repetitious or not thinking them through. A good rule is to summarize the most important point on the panel. I've seen a lot of people build a presentation that will use the same headline (say, "Facts about the market") on several panels in a row. That might be fine for the first panel that starts off with facts about the market, but then on the next panel (which talks about growth rate of the industry or trend), put "Staggering growth rate" or "Slowing growth rate hurting us all." Don't be lazy. Work to make every headline work hard for you.

Rule 7. Be Confident but Not Obnoxious

Develop a rapport with your audience even if it's just one person facing you. If you have a large audience, one way to do this is to stretch with them. Ask them all to stand up, put their hands over their heads, and stretch to their right. Since you are facing them, stretch to your left. That way you are stretching in the same direction as they are. This simple act creates a subconscious bond with your audience. Another way to bond is to have them talk about their problems or the things that are not working for them in their business. Misery loves company, so engaging them on problems creates an instant bond.

Rule 8. Focus on Them, Not on You

Maturity is when all of your mirrors turn into windows.

anonymous

Most people live their lives surrounded by mirrors, focusing on themselves. They see their feelings, their needs. They think about how they are coming off to other people and whether or not they will get what they want. I love the line where a famous actor says to someone: "But enough of me talking about myself. What do *you* think about me?" Everyone's favorite topic of conversation is themselves. So turn those mirrors into windows and you will be a much better presenter, salesperson, trainer, executive, or leader. The most mature person in a relationship is the one listening the most. He or she is thinking about the other person's needs and how to meet them. If you can be this person when you are presenting to your prospects and remain focused on their needs and how you can help them, you will become a top producer.

Whenever possible, I start all my training by finding out the challenges that my audience is facing. After building a little rapport in a one-on-one meeting, it's also good to ask, "So what are some of the problems you're seeing in your industry right now?" After you gather all their challenges, a great segue to your core story is to say something like "Those challenges you've mentioned come up a lot with other clients. That's one of the reasons we had some research conducted about our industry/market/profession. Our findings were so profound that we put them into an executive briefing that's quite revealing. Here. Let me show you some of this data." At that point you can open your laptop to present your core story.

The Three Modes of Communication

There are three modes of communication operating simultaneously as you present: your words, the tone of your voice, and your body language. Your prospect's subconscious is processing all of these cues at once. When I teach this live, I show how the same words said with different tonality can change, if not the meaning, then certainly the perception of your prospect. Over the telephone, your tonality is going to be far more important than the words that you use. If you are insecure, even if you're saying the perfect words, prospects hear that insecurity and their reaction will reflect that.

The most powerful thing you can do over the telephone is to speak with what I call a voice of authority. Sound important or like the issues you are about to discuss are important. That screams to the subconscious of your prospect. When I have a top studio head or the CEO of a $100 billion company on the telephone, my voice communicates that I am important and that what I have to say is important as well. Practice sounding like an investigating detective with a lot of authority in your voice. It's a very powerful tonality and grabs the attention of your prospects right away.

In person, tonality's impact is strong as well, but now your body language and facial expressions, no matter how subtle, tell your prospect a lot about what you really believe.

Everything you do from saying "um" to tucking your hair behind your ear to cracking your knuckles is communicating something to your prospect. And it may even contradict what you are actually saying. You need to be conscious of how you move and speak. Make your body, your face, and your voice work in your favor. Be confident on the inside, and your communication will show it.

For example, you can use your own body movements as well as theirs to take control of the meeting. As I just mentioned, in a large group, it's a great idea to ask people to stretch. Not only are you bonding with the audience, but you are also taking control of the meeting by telling your audience what to do. When you walk on stage and immediately tell your audience to stand up, they feel they are probably going to have a good experience because you seem so in control. This is especially useful if you are nervous in front of groups—it will give you a better sense of control.

An audience likes a speaker who appears to be in command. In a small group or one-on-one sales meeting, you also want to take control. Unless you are a yoga instructor, it would be awkward to ask one or a few people to stretch. But it's still a good idea to ask them to move. Since you never want anything between you and your prospect in any sales situation, ask them to move out from behind their desk. I've asked hundreds of CEOs to do this, and only one of them has ever said no.

I've been in situations presenting my film ideas to top movie studio executives. In one such meeting, I had a seasoned producer come with me to meet with an executive whom I asked to come around his desk so that he could better see the material I wanted to show him. The producer nearly fell over in astonishment. But, sure enough, this top studio executive came around the desk and sat next to me. That gave me far greater control, not to mention a much better opportunity to build rapport. So if you're presenting one-on-one, simply say: "You know what? I think I can show you this better if we sit side by side."

Eight Common Mistakes Presenters Make

Mistake 1: Thanking Prospects for Their Time or Apologizing for Taking It

I know other trainers say to thank prospects for their time, but I do not agree with that philosophy. This shows that you consider their time more valuable than yours. It also suggests to them that listening to you is far less important than other things they could be doing. It belittles everything you have to say. Never apologize or thank them for their time. If you do a good job, then they will thank *you*. I was traveling with a salesman who was selling to lawyers. He would start off the meeting saying: "The first thing I want to do is apologize for taking your time. I know you charge for your time, so this is valuable time for you." It was straight uphill from there. The attorneys would take the postition that their time was very valuable and everything after that was rushed. Big mistake.

Mistake 2: Presenting with Your Hands in Your Pockets

This makes you look like a slacker. Always keep your hands above your waist and out in front of your body.

Mistake 3: Presenting from a Sitting Position

People will pay more for the same product when it is presented to them from a standing position than when it is presented from a sitting position. So stand up when presenting. It's a position of greater authority. Even in one-on-one meetings, it will change the dynamic. "Do you mind if I stand while I present this? I think better on my feet." I've never had anyone say, "No, don't stand."

Mistake 4: Being Led Around by Your Nose

If the prospect asks a question in the middle of your presentation, a common mistake is to interrupt what you are saying and answer it right then and there. I've seen this 100 times. If the prospect takes control of the meeting, you will not make the sale. Don't let him lead. In any sales situation, you need to take the lead. Even if you are selling retail, you're never going to close someone if you're following him around the store. Instead, ask him what he's looking for and lead him to that item in your store. Get him to follow you and you're on your way to a close. You must lead to close even if leading means asking a lot of questions. You're still the one controlling the meeting.

Mistake 5: Letting the Materials Upstage You or Guide You

Many salespeople cling to the presentation as if that would make the sale. The presentation is never going to make the sale. You are. Visual aids are just that, aids. You are the presenter.

One thing I do when interviewing salespeople is to have them present something to me. I'll give them 10 panels of a presentation (core story) and allow them a few minutes alone to practice them. And then I'll come back in and ask them to present. If they read the bullets mindlessly, they're in for big trouble out in the field. A great presenter can make those bullets roar to life with excitement.

Mistake 6: Keeping It Totally Serious

Humor increases interest and retention. Every core story or presentation should have some humor built into the panels. A joke from a popular cartoon like *The Far Side* is great for this—you can buy the 365-day calendar and just page through it, looking for a joke that will be funny at a certain point in your delivery. When I teach this program live, for example, I introduce "Sammy Schleb, the world's worst presenter," and show how he ruins his opportunities by presenting poorly.

Mistake 7: Failing to Practice the Presentation Each and Every Time Before You Give It

The more you know the material, the more persuasive, powerful, and effective you can be. If you are glued to the presentation and have to read it, you're in trouble. The biggest mistake most presenters make is reading the presentation without practicing aloud, pretending they have a live audience. It's in the out-loud practicing that you'll develop great segues, presells for info yet to come, and perhaps even a little humor.

One of my clients hired a salesman and gave him a video training program teaching him how to present and a fantastic full-color presentation to practice. He rehearsed until he felt he was ready, and then presented to me and the CEO of the company. We listened to a painfully dull, word-by-word reading of the bullets. I retrained him immediately. We covered all the points in this module:

- Make it exciting.
- Move fast as the wind.
- Make it a dynamic and compelling experience.
- Know the material cold.
- Draw some conclusions for your audience.
- Don't read the bullets mindlessly.
- Develop the "patter between the panels" covered on the next page.

Then the sales rep went out and presented to 20 clients. He didn't get even one sale. Confounded, the CEO and I thought we'd better take a look at how he was doing the presentation. To our horror he was still reading the bullets mindlessly. He did not link the points together or relate them directly to the prospect's business. There was nothing dynamic about his delivery, no stories to illustrate his points, no humor.

I worked with him some more and then we reviewed his process two weeks later. He had developed cue cards to help him be more dynamic. No help. He was still sluggish and wooden. The moral to the story? Some people just can't present. Others are natural communicators and born to present. That said, practice can make a huge difference. And whatever you do, test this trait *before* you hire someone.

Here's another true story: In an almost identical situation, where the rep just did not know his material, the client actually took the presentation away from him. The client said, "I can read these bullets faster on my own." That's what you call dying in front of an audience.

Mistake 8: Having No Idea What Comes Next in the Presentation

You need to presell every panel if you can. Make your audience's mouths water with anticipation. "The next panel is the number one most important point I am going to show you." By knowing your material so you know what comes next, you can preframe, presell, and promise great material in the sections yet to come. This way you keep the excitement and anticipation going all through the presentation. By knowing the material cold, you can have what I call "the patter between the panels." Draw some conclusions for your prospect/audience. Have great segues. All through the earlier chapters in this book, I reference material yet to come. That's called a presell, and you may have noticed how it made you want to continue.

⚙ Exercise

Outline a quick 30-panel presentation that you could deliver to a prospect. Write a great title that makes people want to see the presentation. On panel 2, put "Areas covered." The purpose of this panel is only to sell the heck out of the material yet to come. It's not to upstage you by giving things away. So here's a boring example of areas covered:

AREAS COVERED
- State of the industry
- Five trends in our industry
- How our product helps you
- What you need to know about our product

There is no sizzle here. You're also telling them that there's going to be a sales pitch at the end. So let's try this:

AREAS COVERED
- State of the industry, how times have changed
- Five trends that could put you out of business or send you to the stars
- Some solutions everyone should know to succeed
- How you can be ahead of the pack in every way

The next part of your presentation should cover industry data—Wows that establish interest right away.

Then you can go into issues or problems that your clients are going to have. I know other trainers say: "Don't call them problems. Call them challenges." Yes, that's fine when you're referring to your "challenges" internally. But when you're presenting to clients, you can tell them that they have problems. It sounds worse and puts them in the mind-set to be open to solutions.

If you've done a great job, it will be extremely clear that your products or services will solve some of those problems. In the case of the client selling art to hospitals, obviously, his art isn't going to solve all the problems they present, but presenting a lot of problems motivates people to action. Often, some of that action will come your way—making executives want to take some action at the end of the bad news you showed them.

Finally, you should never just blatantly pitch your product. You should only use your product or service as an example. You can even have a section that says, "What to look for if you need to buy artwork." And there you can lay out the "buying criteria" that will help them make a wise decision in their purchasing. If you do a great job and they agree with the criteria, you are now well on your way to their wanting *your* product over any other. This is a science of intelligent thinking that can reward you with much higher closing rates and a vastly improved method of getting in to see prospects.

Conclusion

You will get in to see far more prospects if you offer education than you will if you just try to sell your product. Often, a great education can make people realize they need your product. When you offer just to sell them the product, they might not feel they need it, so you're not going to get in the door.

One last thing: Even though we have talked about all the things your "presentation" should do, never call it that to a prospect. A "presentation" sounds like a sales pitch. We call ours an "orientation." An even better term for some people is "an executive briefing."

9

The Nitty-Gritty of Getting the Best Buyers

Step-by-Step, Day-by-Day Tactics to Land Your Dream Clients

As you learned in Chapter Six, the Dream 100 effort is your plan of attack to penetrate your best buyers. This is the fastest way to becoming the Ultimate Sales Machine because these dream clients are the people or businesses that will buy your product or service faster, in greater quantities, and more frequently than any other buyers. Landing just a handful of these dream clients can have a seismic impact on your bottom line. The reason the nitty-gritty of getting those best buyers comes at this point in the process is because the preceding chapters provided more depth and layers about marketing and presenting to set you up for the nitty-gritty and being as effective as possible in getting your dream clients. But the chapter that follows this one also contributes significantly as it spells out specific sales skills you're going to need to turn your dream prospects into clients.

When you've identified someone who is a dream prospect or you find a dream neighborhood of your best buyers, you need an organized, consistent, and relentless program to win them over as clients for life—no matter how many times they tell you they're not interested. And that's the key: you are actually expecting and planning for these dream prospects to say no several times, and these rejections will not cause you to give up. What's the first marketing piece you send them? What's the second? What do you do if they hang up on you? How do you set it up so your staff can handle multiple rejections without taking it personally or giving up? This chapter gives you detailed instructions on how to explode every sales record your company has ever had.

I've taught the concept of the Dream 100 to individual clients, rooms full of executives, and people through my training products that sell in more than 20 countries. When I run into people who've had some of my training, I often find that one of their favorite growth strategies is the Dream 100 concept or "best-buyer strategy." Then I ask them, "What have you done in that area?" That's when I find out that the missing ingredient has been the lack of pigheaded determination and discipline. These people understand the best-buyer concept intellectually and know that it is a great strategy for growing their company. But they didn't take the time to create a detailed plan, or, if they did, they abandoned the concept too easily. When I worked for Charlie Munger, I made zero sales for four months. Nothing. But I kept at it and went on to double sales three years in a row. So this chapter spells it out step by step, inch by inch, word by word, letter by letter.

Executives and salespeople reading this book know they are not going to give up after the first rejection; in fact, they will become more determined. But most executives and salespeople are trained to try for a month or two and go away after receiving rejections from nearly 100 percent of their dream prospects. How important could your product be if you go away after a single rejection or two?

By being pigheaded, persistent, and determined, and by continually finding more clever and aggressive ways to get in front of these dream buyers, you actually earn their respect in the long haul. Everyone respects persistence in the face of resistance. I had a PR person chase me diligently for two years. I finally hired him out of respect for his diligence more than the initial belief in his talents. So if someone keeps coming after you, you begin to almost feel an obligation to reward their persistence. This strategy will show you how to win your place as the player at the top of the market where no one can compete with you.

The Perfect-World Dream 100 Sell

Here's how it works when you are determined and stick with it. The client I had that sold OEM products to manufacturers came to me in deep trouble. The company had had three years of declining revenues and it was $6 million in the red on sales of $100 million. I trained the staff on the Dream 100 strategy to help them sell their OEM products to the biggest manufacturers in their market. As I mentioned in Chapter Two, I worked with the 50-person sales team over a five-month period with astonishing results.

The first thing we did was to offer the CEOs of the largest manufacturers in their market an opportunity to learn "the five most dangerous trends facing manufacturers." That's pretty hard to resist if you're a manufacturer, especially when it's presented by a well-respected company—which this client was. The offer letter we sent to these CEOs said something like, "As you know, we rely on the manufacturers to be successful. To that end, we have commissioned a study and found that you have some serious problems. To help make certain that manufacturers are successful, we are now making this information available at no cost to you." You'll notice that I use this approach often. When you seek to serve your industry, it justifies your offering to do this for them. As previously stated, if you really want to serve your market, do some research that will be of value to them. Apparently, our letter was compelling, as it resulted in a 7 percent response rate. Most direct mail is lucky if it receives a 1 percent response rate.

Two weeks later we sent another letter offering the free education, but this time we included a Rubik's Cube with the following headline: "This Rubik's Cube has more than four billion possible combinations. Fortunately, there are only five that you need to worry about when it comes to being a successful manufacturer in the new millennium. Don't be puzzled by the dangers facing manufacturers! Get our free education today."

We followed this clever mailing with phone calls from all the salespeople. As I do with most of my clients, I role-played with the sales team every single week for an hour on a mass teleconference. I strongly urge every company to have a sales skills teleconference once per week. If your staff works in single location, you can meet live rather than use the phone.

Here's how we spent our hour a week working on the business: I would ask each of the sales reps questions on what they said, what the prospect said, how they were turned down, and why they were turned down. Then we would role-play possible responses to effectively persuade a disinterested prospect and turn him into an interested prospect. As I mentioned in Chapter Two, when I first started with this company, not one salesperson was razor sharp at persuading CEOs who said they weren't interested. That's not to slam them; it's just to say that these salespeople normally called on production people in the bowels of the factory, and here I had them calling CEOs. And they weren't selling the OEM products they were used to selling—they were now selling a free educational program (that ultimately sold the OEM product much more effectively).

All the sales reps were rough in the beginning. But thanks to constant pigheaded determination and role-playing with them every single week, each rep got better and better. In fact, the whole team got surprisingly good. By the end of the five-month period, every role play with every rep was pretty darn effective.

Back to the mailers: We continued sending their dream clients a clever mailer with a cute gift every other week for five months. We sent a flashlight with the message, "Don't be in the dark about the five biggest dangers facing manufacturers." Then we sent a compass with a note that said: "Most companies are losing direction when it comes to manufacturing in today's environment. Don't be one of them. Get our report on the five biggest dangers facing manufacturers today." Then came a tape measure: "If you want to measure up to the highest manufacturing standards, get our free report on the five most dangerous trends facing manufacturers."

It might sound expensive to send a gift to every prospect every other week. The key here is that this company was only sending them to a few hundred prospects. Since these few hundred prospects were the biggest companies this company could possibly target, if the mailers got them one client, it would pay for mailers for 20 years.

We had sent only four such mailers when a huge client told one of the salespeople: "Oh, yes, glad you called. I just have to have you come here and meet with me." The sales rep was so shocked he asked, "Why's that?" The client responded, "Because I've been getting all those little gifts of yours and I just think your marketing is super." When the sales rep arrived, the prospect had all the little gifts on his desk, where he constantly played with them. He even jokingly cursed out the sales rep because he was addicted to the Rubik's Cube. This kind of diligent and consistent marketing effort wins over just about everyone if you stick with it long enough. The point is that you stand out in the crowd with great marketing.

Within three months, we secured meetings with half of their Dream 100 prospects. The education, which was their core story, was so compelling that 100 percent of the prospects who responded and experienced the education took the offer to test my client's OEM product. And of those that tested, 100 percent bought some product and a relationship began.

This single activity took this company from being $6 million in the red to being $2 million in the black the following year. Needless to say, the client was utterly thrilled.

Six Simple Steps for Getting Down to the Nitty-Gritty

Here are six simple steps to help you get your dream clients:

1. Choose your Dream 100.
2. Choose the gifts.
3. Create your Dream 100 letters.
4. Create your Dream 100 calendar.
5. Conduct Dream 100 follow-up phone calls.
6. Present the executive briefing.

Step 1: Choose Your Dream 100

In Chapter Six you made lists of your dream clients, neighborhoods, and affiliates. Take a look at those again. This is your starting point to create your Dream 100 target list. Make sure you are clear on your criteria for your dream list. What kind of clients or neighborhood qualifies as your Dream 100? Are they successful, so they have the money to spend if they want or need to buy? If you're in healthcare, do you want to go after the biggest hospitals? If you're in real estate, you probably want to target the neighborhoods with the most expensive homes. For companies that sell business-to-business like the office supply company I used as an example, you will want to decide on criteria such as the number of employees, value of company, location, industry, or whatever else qualifies a company to buy faster, more, and more often than any other buyer. You can do this easily online. One way is to go to www.zapdata.com. Input your criteria and, in minutes, you'll find out all the companies of a given size in any industry in your area.

It is important to create a database where you can store a lot of information about your prospects. The more you know about your dream clients, the better you will be able to target them. Also, by getting your salespeople to capture great data on each client and having a database to store it, you'll have all the information you need to continue targeting them even if a salesperson leaves. If they are really big clients, it's worth the time to do a little research on them before you begin your hunt. Check out their Web site and any other promotional materials or articles on them that you can find. Every phone call you make to that prospect— even if it's merely to find out the correct address or spelling of the CEO's name—is a great learning opportunity. Another common tool used by many sales reps to get more details about their prospects is www.hoovers. com. Hoovers is a subscription service that provides up-to-date information on companies as well as industries and markets.

If you do sell business-to-business, you need to decide who at each dream company will be your ideal prospect. Here's the rule for choosing your target: approach the one who has the authority to say yes. In the case of the manufacturer, the reps sold to a line executive who only had the power to say no. If that line exec wanted to add that client's product, he had to go higher up in the company to get permission. The person who would give the permission is the one you want to target with your efforts. This also dictates the kind of information you send. In the case of the company selling art to hospitals, the information in its core story was of ultimate value to the CEOs of the hospitals. Therefore, the education-based marketing approach enabled it to get hundreds of CEOs to participate in its free education.

So who is the person who can say yes to your product or service? Is your market data targeted effectively at that person?

Step 2: Choose the Gifts

I've found that one of the best ways to get noticed by your Dream 100 is to send them small gifts every two weeks. Choose gifts like the Rubik's Cube I've already mentioned. It's just an inexpensive plastic puzzle that is slightly bigger than a cube of sugar. You want to consider many ideas for this. Just keep the gifts inexpensive. Expensive gifts come off like you're trying to bribe them. I have a client who has paid me millions and he won't let me buy him anything expensive as a thank-you present. For Christmas he has sent back the $1,000 pen I tried to give him to thank him for his business. Some executives will view expensive gifts with discomfort. So cheap is better. The prospect smiles at the gesture and doesn't feel bribed.

Another key to this is that the gifts should be useful, things that they will want to keep or play with—or take home to a child. Later in the chapter we'll provide a list of ideas along with sample headlines you could utilize to accompany the mailers. You want to make your gifts useful so the prospect will keep them and think of you often. If you send them a fake $100 bill key chain, it is likely to go right in the garbage. But if you send them a penlight, a tape measure, or even a squirt gun, the executives are likely to put it in their drawer and hang on to it.

Once when I ran a trade show, the salesperson who sold us all of our incentives—binders, bags, and so on—stopped by and gave me a flashlight pen as a thank-you gift. I put it in my jacket pocket, thinking I would give it to my kids later. That was the day of the 1989 San Francisco earthquake. I was sitting in my office on the phone with a friend in New York when the earthquake struck. Everything started shaking and the office was in a panic, with people running helter-skelter. Being new to California, I was more prepared than the folks who lived there because I actually paid attention to the "what to do in an earthquake" public service announcements. I ran to my door frame and yelled to everyone, "Get in a door frame." Since I was the voice of authority in a panic, 25 people suddenly ran to my door frame.

With my entire staff in tow, we headed to the emergency exit, descending 13 stories in a concrete-encased, windowless stairwell. The emergency lights didn't work and the stairwell was pitch-black. So here we were, feeling our way along the walls and trying to find the next landing or set of stairs. I suddenly remembered the flashlight in my pocket. I pulled it out and clicked it on. I can still see all the faces light up in the total blackness. Someone said, "You carry a flashlight in your pocket?" I wasn't just a good executive but also a good Boy Scout, prepared for all emergencies. (Not really. Just a rare case of serendipity.)

The point is, you never know when your gift is going to come in handy. And you can bet I called the salesperson the next day to tell her the story. We used that salesperson every time after that for all our incentive needs.

The goal is to stand out in the marketing crowd and to breed more brand awareness. Even if prospects do not take you up on the offers, the effort still dramatically raises your visibility and solidifies your brand.

Here's a quick list of great gift ideas—inexpensive knockoffs manufactured in China at ridiculous rates and purchased on a Web site:

- Magnifying glass, 100 for $60
- Calculator, 120 for $200
- Miniature tool kit, 120 for $120
- Paddleball, 120 for $50
- Glider, 1,000 for $70
- Rubik's Cube, 120 for $40
- Metal whistle, 120 for $100
- Plastic dinosaur, 100 for $26

Step 3: Create Your Dream 100 Letter

A letter should accompany every gift you send. The letter should be short so the prospects will read it. It should tie into the gift in some clever way. You need to offer something to which they can easily say yes. The letter must include a call to action so they know exactly what you want them to do next.

The success of your Dream 100 effort depends on what you decide to offer them. Remember what you learned in Chapter Four: strategy before tactics. If your effort is tactical, your letter might say, "We sell the best widgets known to man." This tactical approach will work eventually as well, but not as effectively as making your first offer a chance to get in front of the prospects in some way that serves them first, before you.

If you're selling to a business, what you really want is an appointment or the chance to walk it through a Web seminar (as explained in previous chapters). One strategy I use with these mailers is to make the letter vague. The letter itself is probably not going to make the sale, but the follow-up phone calls will get you what you want. We'll get to that in step 5.

Here's a letter that could accompany a stopwatch:

Dear [personalized],
  Every second that you do not get our free executive briefing, The Five Most Critical Insights in [blank industry] Today, *you are losing money.*

This is a free [your industry] community service sponsored by our firm as a way to give something back to the market. This executive briefing contains more than $3 million in research; it's boiled down to a bullet-style, fast-paced outstanding education on how to increase business in this scary period of rising competition and [fill in other pain point here]. Call for your free executive briefing today. The clock is ticking and you're losing money.

This is a very short letter. It has a clever tie-in to the stopwatch. Since the letter is so brief, it will actually get read. Remember that you are going to launch a campaign, not merely send a single letter. You are committing to breaking through the clutter and gaining brand awareness with this client. Plus, as stated, you're not going to get what you really want from a letter. Consider the letter to be like long-range bombing: it softens the prospect before you attack directly—before your salesperson calls.

⚙ Exercise

Take the list of gifts and write headlines around each gift. Focus the headline on the prospect, not on you. For example:

Tape measure: "Make sure you measure up."
Whistle: "Blow the whistle on rising costs in [your industry]."
Calculator: "Calculate how much you're losing/saving in your battle to dominate."

Naturally, you have to focus these letters on your offer. If your offer is for a free education, then I have just given you a great foundation for that. However, there may be times when you don't want to offer an education. You can use this approach in a tactical way to just directly promote your product or service by focusing the letter on the benefits your product or service brings to the prospect.

I have two approaches for using the gifts—before and after the "free education" has been presented. Right now I have a client who has been very successful at getting in front of large buyers and presenting the information. And while the information is excellent and gives my client quite an "in" to get closer to these massive prospects, several of the prospects have seen the information and not yet bought—some just putting off my client, saying, "I would be interested in this in six months," or a flat-out "Thanks for the info, but I like the providers I have now." In this case after you present and get turned down, now, the letter can and should be very tactical. Once you have presented, you've established a small beachhead in the prospect's mind. But it is only with constant and intense follow-up that prospects will be won over after they have said no. If you continue to send them the gifts with clever tie-ins to your product, eventually the prospect begins to think: "You know what, let's give some business to that company that keeps sending us those gifts. Those guys just never give up. Let's try them out." Or, it could happen, as I've seen 100 times, that you keep following up and one of their preferred providers lets them down in some way and, wham, you are the first company they think of because you never gave up. They turn to you when they need a new provider. So keep sending the mailers. And keep calling behind them.

Business-to-Consumer Strategy

A best-buyer strategy to consumers is more expensive than one that targets businesses because usually you must target a higher number of consumers in order to have an impact. Meaning, if you are going after manufacturers, you can do a major company turnaround by approaching only a few hundred massive companies. But if you are a jewelry store, a car dealership, a dentist, a chiropractor, a boat dealer, or another type of retailer, you have to target a larger number of best buyers to make a difference. Take my example of the real estate salesperson who went after an entire neighborhood of 2,200 upscale homes. She only sent a three-fold flier, but she sent it every month to the same 2,200 homes without fail. If you are a dentist and want your office packed with people who are more concerned with their health than with the money they have to spend to maintain it, then a concentrated effort must be made to target those best neighborhoods. Here's a letter to that group that you can use as a model:

Dear [personalized],

We have written to you because of who you are in the community. It is our goal to provide outstanding service to the finest families in our community. Hence we are willing to do things to win you over as our patient that we would simply not offer to anyone else. We want you to see how superbly we serve you and so we are willing to give you a cleaning and examination worth $125 at no cost to you.

This is just an example. Some states have laws that prohibit dentists from doing things like this. You are responsible for knowing the laws that govern your market or industry.

Let's say you sell boats. Let me show you how to open your market and attract more buyers. Most boating showrooms have to advertise in boating magazines and appeal to those who are already in the boating world. In my case, it had never occurred to me to own a boat and I certainly wouldn't have read a boating magazine. When a friend suggested it, I thought, "Hmm, sounds like a nice hobby." I bought a used boat to see if I liked boating and then, the following year, stepped right up to a yacht and have become an avid boater. In my case, the impetus was a friend's suggestion, but the following strategy might have lured me in just as well.

So here is the strategy for penetrating an entire group of potential buyers using the concepts in this chapter. Of course, do not limit your thinking to just boats. This strategy might apply to any upscale product or service. The first step is to write a letter to the upscale homes in your area offering them something of value to them related to your product or service. Use the following boating letter as a model for your own letter:

Dear [personalized],

We are writing to you because many people in your position in life are now discovering the beauty, peace, and fun of having a family boat. There is no escape quite so wonderful as having a boat. It's an adventure, an opportunity to bond with family and friends, and a way to get away from everything.

For a limited time, and only to people in your position, we are offering a boat day. Come and see if you love boating. We'll take your family out for a fabulous day of boating.

If you do sell boats and don't want to offer a boat day, you could offer a sunset cruise and take several couples at once. A few drinks later, as you cruise into the sunset, you will have several viable prospects for your boat business. You're not going to offer this to just anyone—just to the type of homeowner who can buy a $30,000, or even $300,000, boat. These people are worth a day of your time. Naturally, not everyone will buy, but you'd be surprised how the word can spread and how one good deed like this can bring you other buyers at other times. Think about this: part of your best-buyer strategy is to also know who are the great affiliates. Go to a Mercedes dealer and do a trade. Anyone who buys a certain price Mercedes gets a gift certificate for a sunset cruise on one of your boats.

How else can you work with affiliates? On your sunset cruise, you may want to invite a diamond dealer to have a jewelry show on your boat and maybe even give you a commission for sales made. Or go to that diamond dealer and offer to give a sunset cruise to anyone who pays cash for more than $5,000 worth of diamonds. If you are a diamond dealer, you can go to a boat showroom and offer to do a show for any clients who buy boats. Or give a coupon. The possibilities are endless. It's easy to increase sales if you use some of the concepts in this book.

⚙ Exercise

Best-buyer exercise: Write down three things you can offer your best buyers that you wouldn't offer the greater population. Choose the best one and, using the above models, write a letter that you will send to those buyers.

Affiliate exercise: Who else sells to the buyers you want to reach? What can you offer them or how can you work with them to better target your best buyers? Write down 10 ideas.

Back to Dream 100 for best neighborhoods. Remember to keep sending offers to people in this neighborhood. They will then go from never having heard of you to knowing you well. And do something special for them. They are special so treat them like it. To make sure you are not taken advantage of, set time limits on your offers. Otherwise someone can come in with 12 offers and want to collect all 12. The other thing you can do is remove folks from the free-offer list once they have taken advantage of one offer. Your offers are to get the initial contact. Once you have that, it's up to you to have an outstanding offer to keep those clients.

Step 4: Create Your Dream 100 Calendar

What are you going to do to market to your Dream 100 each and every month without fail? Actually, it should be *at least* every month. It's even better if you send them something every two weeks. Stay in their face. Not every mailing has to be a gift, but those are the ones that they will definitely look at. You might send a gift a month with newsletters or press releases in between. The more they become familiar with your name, the better your chance of gaining them as clients.

Here are some marketing tools that can be coordinated into your Dream 100 effort. Remember, as you learned in Chapter Seven ("The Seven Musts of Marketing"), each of these could highlight your core story and be consistent in the appearance and message you are sending out to your prospects and clients:

- Cards
- Letters
- Novelties
- Newsletters
- Promos
- Surveys
- PR articles and press releases

⚙ Exercise

Design a Dream 100 effort that hits your prospects every two weeks. Write down on a calendar which gift and/or offers you will send first. Next, mark on your calendar what you will send two weeks later. Will it be a newsletter or a coupon? Or will you just hammer them with gifts so you know they will at least pick up what you sent and look at the letter? Map out your first three to six months for your Dream 100 effort.

A Side Note

Many companies that sell incentives offer a discount if you buy a certain quantity. So buying all of your Dream 100 gifts at once does two things: it commits you to the process (you already have the gifts, so you'd better follow through now) and gets you the incentives at a lower price.

Step 5: Conduct Dream 100 Phone Call Follow-up

After every gift or mailing, you'll need to follow up with each Dream 100 prospect. This is easier with business-to-business sales as phone numbers are readily available. In business-to-consumer cases, numbers may not be listed or the prospects may be on the "do not call" list. So in the case of business-to-consumer your best bet is to continue to send the offers so consistently that everyone on that list gets to know who you are.

For business-to-business, the goal of this follow-up call is to schedule an appointment to get your core story in front of the prospect. The procedure is the same after each mailing to your dream list. You will call after each mailer. However, I've seen it happen where the above de-signed letters will prompt some executives to actually call *you* to get the free report that you offered. In the case of the client selling to manufac-turers, the letter referred to a "free report" but it did *not* spell out that the "report" was actually delivered live. Don't make the mistake of say-ing in a letter, "We want to come and present to you." That's a much bigger sale to make from a mere letter. From this brief letter, it's highly unlikely that your prospects will make the decision to have someone come and present to them live. So the letter offers a free report—and then when they call, your salesperson has the opportunity to go much deeper and explain that the report is delivered live.

When we sent letters like this offering to come and present to people, we received zero phone calls. When we altered the letter to offer a free report and did not specify that the report is delivered live, 7 percent of those who received the letter called to get the free report. Now a live body (your salesperson) can transition the caller to a much deeper experience.

To paraphrase, the salespeople's pitch went something like, "Oh, you thought it was a report that we'd just send over. No, it's much better than that. If we just sent you a report with hundreds of pages of raw data, you'd probably never read it. So to go the extra mile, we actually hired a graphics firm and had the data converted into a riveting full-color orien-tation that we present live right in your office. It's packed with great in-formation and graphics to illustrate points, including bar charts, graphs, and photos. It's a great experience. And everyone we've shown it to is impressed. Most of your competitors have either already seen it or are on our list to show it to them. It takes only 38 minutes to see and we have speakers who are going around the country right now presenting it. You don't even have to travel. You view it right in the comfort of your own office. You can even have it as a lunch and learn. Are you familiar with that term? It's very popular in business today. You have to eat lunch any-way, so here's a chance to learn while you eat. We underwrite every-thing. It costs us plenty, but it won't cost you a penny. Why do we do this? It's a PR effort on our part—a way to form more relationships in the manufacturing community and to share information to help us all be more successful. We like to meet folks like you and even learn things from you as we share the data with you. Do you have your calendar handy?"

Note that the salesperson said that a "speaker" would come in and present to you. Again, being a strategist means that you maximize everything including the words you use. The right title for your salespeople can be very strategic. As stated, no one likes to be sold to, so develop non-sales-sounding titles that position the rep better in the prospect's mind. And besides, who's to say that your salespeople can't also be speakers? They can certainly have another function in your company.

For those prospects who do not call you to request the report, you are going to call them. One of the hardest tasks today is to get around the gatekeeper whose job is to guard top executives. Let's do some training on that right now.

How to Get Around the Gatekeeper and Get Anyone on the Phone

If you're selling business-to-business, how much is it worth to you to talk your way into a meeting with the most powerful CEOs on the planet? Imagine sitting in front of your dream prospect, who just happens to have the ability to hand over a seven-figure check before you leave his office.

I've been able to get around gatekeepers and reach the following executives on the telephone (some are not in these positions anymore, but they were when I got to them):

Michael Eisner at Disney
George Zimmer of the Men's Wearhouse
David Pottruck, CEO of Charles Schwab
Phil Purcell, CEO of Morgan Stanley
Carl Reichardt, chairman of Wells Fargo Bank
Alan Horn, COO of Warner Bros.

The biggest tip is that your voice has to sound like you're important. The dead giveaway that you are selling something is when you try to be charming to the assistant. Do not ask her, "How are you today?" That's the biggest giveaway that you are a salesperson. As I've already mentioned, I got the chairman of Wells Fargo Bank on the telephone by calling with a very authoritative voice and saying: "Hi. This is Chet Holmes. Is Carl in?" To my utter delight, he called me back.

Who calls CEOs of the largest companies in the world? Very important people. So if your voice has that tone of authority and you tell the assistant what to do—not ask them—you are very likely to get right through.

The other secret to getting that top executive on the telephone is to send the gatekeeper back as many times as you can, each time giving very little information. Let me show you the difference.

Here's a weak salesperson:

YOU: Hi. How are you today?
ASSISTANT: Good.
YOU: Is Mr. Smith in?
ASSISTANT: Who's calling?
YOU: This is Bill Johnston.
ASSISTANT: May I ask what this call is in reference to?
YOU: I'm calling to talk about my product.
ASSISTANT: I see. Let me take a message.

First question: Who was leading this conversation? The assistant. As long as the assistant is leading, you lose. You must lead the conversation at all times. Let me stress one key thing: never lie. Never give false information. That doesn't mean you tell the whole truth. You just don't lie. Ever.

Observe the subtleties here as I show you how to send the gatekeeper back so many times that the CEO finally gets fed up and tells her to put the call through. In fact, have a contest. Let's see how many times you can send that gatekeeper back to that CEO.

YOU: Hi. This is Bill Johnston. I'm calling for Carl. Is he in?

[Notice that the assistant can't ask my name, I've given it. Important people give their names. And I didn't ask, "How are you today?"]

ASSISTANT: Can I ask what this call is in reference to?
YOU: Just tell him it's Bill Johnston.

[The assistant goes to Carl and tells him it's Bill Johnston. The boss says, "What's it about?" The assistant says: "He didn't say. It sounded like he knew you." The boss tells the assistant to get more information.]

ASSISTANT: I'm sorry. Can you tell me what this is in reference to?
YOU: Did you tell him it's Bill Johnston?
ASSISTANT: Yes. He didn't seem to know you.
YOU: Hmm. Just tell him I'm from XYZ Company. That might jog his memory.

Remember to keep a tone of authority. That keeps assistants off-guard. They don't know if they have any power over you yet. The minute you start sounding like a salesperson, you give them that power and they will wield it well. You must keep them off-balance.

The assistant now goes to the boss again, expecting that he might know you. You didn't say he would. You said that the name of your company might jog his memory. Ideally, you will have sent a letter in advance with very little information. Even if it gets thrown out, it still gives you the liberty to act like he might remember you, your company name, or the purpose of your call.

The boss says he doesn't know the name and sends the assistant back to you once again.

ASSISTANT: I'm sorry, Mr. Johnston, but the company name didn't ring any bells. Can you please tell me what this is in reference to?
YOU: Who am I speaking to?

[You take control of the conversation.]

ASSISTANT: This is his assistant.
YOU: Are you his regular assistant?
ASSISTANT: Yes.
YOU: What's your name?
ASSISTANT: Shirley.

We want to get as much info as possible from every call. Not only are you taking control, but you are just beginning to work on this dream client and want to keep impeccable records and gain more info from every call that you make.

YOU [tone of authority]: Shirley, if you'll tell Carl that I'm following up on some correspondence sent to him, that should be enough.

Be clear that a top executive is surely not afraid to take your call. And most are rescuers. They will rescue the assistant and just say: "Put him through. I'll handle this." By now, often the CEO comes to the phone just to have the assistant stop coming back to him. He will be gruff, a little impatient. That means that the first words out of your mouth have to be sharp and to the point and sound important. Whatever you do, don't now turn into a salesperson and ask him, "How are you today?" Salesperson! Maintain your authority. And have a fantastic two-minute opening worked out (like the script ideas provided in this chapter on the educational approach). Be clever, be confident (that's key), and know that your tone of voice has five times more impact on their perception than the actual words that you use.

Step 6: Present the Executive Briefing

This step has been thoroughly covered in Chapter Four on strategy and Chapter Eight on effective presentations, but here's a review of the key points to remember about building your core story:

- Use market data, not product data.
- Set the buying criteria in your favor.
- Find the "smoking gun," the one thing that undeniably positions you over everyone else.
- Make sure you hit their pain points.
- Include your own pitch for your product or service *only after you have covered the education thoroughly*.

The biggest mistake I see salespeople make is pitching themselves too early in their free education. You promised an education, so you need to deliver. The beautiful thing about the core story sales approach is that you give them a lot of great, usable information and then the presentation funnels down to where you've built rapport and trust. You can then say, "I have a little two-minute section about our company. Would you like to hear it?" If you did a good job with the first part of your presentation, no one will refuse.

I've helped companies use the core story/free education strategy a number of ways. Here are some options:

1. All your salespeople are trained as "speakers" and each one of them can take these education-based sales tools into the field, get their own appointments, and present. Just make darn sure that they can present and that they don't die out there. Test every single salesperson. You might even want to have a contest for "best presenter" and put some money on the table that a few of the presenters can win. This makes everyone practice the material, plus it forces everyone to watch each other's presentations in which they'll learn many different approaches that their colleagues may have developed.

2. Your sales rep can just sell the appointment and you can use only your absolute best presenters to present the material. I worked with a company in Norway that perfected this method. It found that one of its presenters was closing three or four times more sales than anyone else. So we worked out a small override for her, and the sales reps all sold clients into her webinars. The sales reps then would follow up on their own clients to close the sale.

3. Naturally, this can be done in person if the sale is big enough and worth the investment to send live bodies to prospects. If it's possible, the rep who made that appointment should attend the meeting and then should also be the person responsible for following up after the appointment and closing the sale. Naturally, it's better if this is all done in one meeting. The speaker does the presentation with a call to action at the end, like a free assessment or audit of their current methods. Right there on the spot, the rep sets this up if possible.

Important note: only one person can present to any client any time. If the rep goes with the speaker—a person clearly great at presenting data and keeping the attention of the prospect—then that rep's job in that room is to support the efforts of the speaker. I was once in a meeting where the rep started doodling. He had seen the info so many times that he was bored, so he acted that way. How do you think that made the prospect feel about the information? I felt like reaching over and slapping the pen out of the rep's hand. So make sure that the rep is utterly riveted by the amazing data presented. I've also seen cases where two people presented and basically competed for the attention of the client. The client's head looked like he was center court watching a tennis match—his head bobbing back and forth between the two opponents.

The Web now makes it so that you can use both options: the rep can present over the Web or the rep can make the sale for the prospect to attend the Web seminar, and the company's best presenter can be the one to do the actual orientation or executive briefing. Check out www. gotomeeting.com, or www.livemeeting.com, or www.vlinklive.com— providers that enable you to present images over the Web while you are also on the phone with the prospect. This is a very cool way to sell. No one has to travel and sometimes it's easier to get an appointment with prospects if they don't have to commit to having you in their office. On the other hand, it's also a lot easier for them to not show up.

So if you take the Web seminar route, you must build excellent follow-up pieces that keep the prospect hot on the idea. If my salespeople talk to the prospect on a Monday and set up an appointment for two days later, the prospect will get three communication pieces from us. One comes immediately to confirm the appointment and sell the heck out of the content that they're going to see. The next day the prospect will get a brief one-page letter from another executive who has seen the material and is raving about how valuable it was. Then the day of the appointment, the prospect will get a second letter raving about how good the content is. Recently, we developed a worksheet that requires prospects to fill in the blanks. The prospects look at the blanks and their brains says: "Wow, I want to know the answer to that question." For example, our worksheet has things like "[blank] is the single most important trait shared by entrepreneurs who grow their company to $100 million per year and beyond." The worksheet has two pages of teasers like that. When we started offering this worksheet, our show-up rate to the Web seminar increased by 20 percent.

Conclusion

An education-based Dream 100 strategy has worked again and again to help many companies penetrate impenetrable accounts or to attract those best buyers in the best neighborhoods. The biggest weakness I notice when I see companies utilize this strategy is that either they are too inconsistent or they give up too quickly. Remember that getting the best buyers is a process—not a single event. It's a campaign to stay in their face forever. This might not replace what you're doing now, but it should at least be an additional effort that you police really well through your organization. So while you are doing everything else you're doing, make sure you have a consistent and constant additional effort to go after those best buyers. And then make sure you treat them like they are special once they get into your realm. To build the Ultimate Sales Machine, you must devote machinelike precision to chase and tackle those dream prospects.

(10)

Sales Skills

The Deeper You Go,
the More You Will Sell

Most companies leave far too much of the sales process up to individual salespeople. Yet, to create the Ultimate Sales Machine you must work as a team, utilizing everyone's brainpower to drill down, perfect, and procedurize each aspect of the sales process. In this chapter we combine workshop training with the perfect sales process for any company that wants to slaughter the competition and be king of the jungle. Star salespeople will improve on everything you give them, but at least if you set standards, you know the minimum performance of each person on your team. Without this kind of training, the interaction with the buyer can vary enormously depending on the mood, skills, attitude, and training of that salesperson. If you could be a fly on the wall during a sales call with your salespeople, you might be horrified to hear some of the things they are saying.

Sales is a science that has been studied and well defined. This chapter gives you a simple blueprint for creating sales activities that work. As the top producer in every sales job I've ever had, I have dedicated myself to understanding the science of sales. This is not some abstract theory. It is the result of in-depth experience in the trenches on the front lines of capitalism, as a top producer and then as a line executive who increased performance of every sales team I've ever worked with. If you don't understand sales and you haven't defined it, you can't improve it.

This chapter outlines the seven steps that every salesperson should go through in influencing a buying decision. The key for any company is to create the policies and procedures you learn here and work with your sales team to consistently follow them. As I've mentioned, I give spot quizzes, ensuring that my sales team can define every inch of the sales process. All sales reps and managers should be able to answer specific questions, like, "What are the five steps to gaining deeper rapport with every prospect?" and "What are the six questions to ask every prospect and the reasons we ask them?"

Whether you are a dentist who needs to persuade people to spend $2,000 on a new bridge, a purchasing agent who needs to persuade your vendor to give you a better price, a customer service person who needs to calm down an irate customer, or a salesperson in the trenches or on the telephone who needs that prospect to buy that product or service, this chapter outlines the seven steps to any sale that will turbocharge your bottom line.

Levels of Learning

If you've ever been part of a highly trained team, you know the sense of confidence that comes with that. The secret to building an excellent sales force (or team of any kind) is in repeating core training on basic sales skills again and again.

The lowest level of learning is memorization. It is easy to memorize the seven steps to every sale, but that does not mean that you can apply them. However, it is an excellent starting point. The highest level of learning is known as "synthesis" or "subconscious competence." This means that you have learned the material so well that you can synthesize it into your own style and method of doing things. Synthesis requires a lot of repetition and practice.

To achieve synthesis in your sales team, begin by having them commit the seven steps to memory, then set procedures, and polish each skill area until your people are masters of each.

Sales Step 1: Establish Rapport

When I ran a magazine for Charlie Munger, we took it from number 15 in the market to number one in a single year. The biggest player in the market was four times our size. When it saw our success in our market niche, it started a magazine to compete directly with us.

When this magazine launched, the publisher made offers to my clients that they knew I would never match—offers like "Buy two advertising pages and get two pages for free." Since my clients trusted me entirely, many of them even asked me what I thought of this new publication. If I had immediately attacked the new magazine, I would've lost credibility. Instead, I would casually say: "You know what? My philosophy is this: let them get successful, and once they've proven themselves, then put your money in there. I would not let them build their success by experimenting with your money."

The magazine struggled for six months, unable to land many advertisers. And when I'd see an advertiser in there, I'd get on a plane and go take that client out for lunch. Somewhere along the line, we'd get around to talking about the competitor and I'd make my little speech. Here's the key: All my clients were also my friends. To advertise in a directly competitive magazine was almost a violation of our relationship—especially if my clients discussed this with me (and I made sure they did) and we (the client and I) mutually decided to wait and see if the magazine became successful. With everyone waiting, no one advertised in the magazine and it closed its doors in six months flat. Gone.

If you are friends with your clients, it is very hard for another salesperson to take them away from you. That needs to be part of your sales process. Most companies leave this up to the individual salespeople. In my companies, we built in opportunities—parties, events, boat trips, you name it—to become friends with our clients. This might not be practical for every company, but the more you create a sense of community and friendship with your clients, the stronger the grip you will have on your market.

Practically every client I've had has become a friend. Most have dined at my home or I at theirs. Some have even stayed at my house, been on my boat, talked into the wee hours. Those bonds aren't easily breakable. In my case, I have to say that this is part of my nature anyway. I'd rather be a friend, and I'm a devoted friend, so I work at these relationships and seek out occasions to connect. But not every salesperson is built this way, so set up procedures or opportunities to build relationships and have fun with the client.

Think of your favorite client relationships right now. If you're business-to-business, answer these questions: How many children do they have? What are their ages and names? Have you been to their home or vice versa? What are their hobbies? Do you know what will make them more successful? Do you know their goals in life? Where are they from? What is their history? That's real rapport. If you sell business-to-consumer, you need to know what small rapport-building opportunities you can put into place—especially if they are your "better buyers."

A restaurant, a bookstore, a supermarket, a copy center: I don't care what kind of business you're in, you need to make "client rapport" part of the process and every person working for you needs training on this. Role-play this and have a constant focus on client rapport so they'll know that part of their job is to win people over, to create a bond wherever possible. When you meet someone new, you need to look that person in the eye and be overtly friendly. Ask them how they are. If you sell retail, ask them if they've been in your store before. Look at Home Depot. You can ask any clerk where something is and instead of just saying, "Aisle five," the clerk will take you right to the item you're looking for—even if she has to walk across the entire store. Wait staff, receptionists, customer service people, and, yes, especially salespeople all need to understand that building rapport is a standard job requirement.

You will find that you close a much higher percentage of sales if you have good, solid rapport with your prospects. According to the Encarta *World English Dictionary*, *rapport* is "an emotional bond or friendly relationship between people based on mutual liking, trust, and a sense that they understand and share each other's concerns." So how do you achieve this mutual liking, trust, and sense that you share their concerns?

Let's break it down. One thing you can do to establish trust is to make your prospects feel that they are working with an expert. As you learned in Chapter Four, selling breaks rapport (no one wants to feel like you're selling them), while educating builds it. That is why I have every single company that I work with design a core story packed with data of great value to your prospects. As said, even if your salespeople never actually present the information as a cohesive whole, knowing it and offering it at appropriate times can elevate their status in the eyes of a buyer.

So one of the best ways for establishing rapport is for your sales staff to be more knowledgeable than any other sales staff they could possibly run into. When the salesperson is highly knowledgeable, it translates to "influence." Here's a simple example: I was looking for a good book to read for a trip I was taking. The clerk in the bookstore was extremely knowledgeable and well read. I bought three books, all based upon his recommendation. On a broader scale, if you develop a core story and create an orientation to offer your prospects a "community education to business owners to help them succeed," you are going above and beyond the call of duty and you will be a champion in your market.

Providing information that helps your client succeed helps you build trust and respect. Your clients and prospects will be happy to hear from you. Even better, they'll start to call *you* to get your input on decisions they're making for their business. Here are some other ways to help establish rapport:

- *Ask great questions.* Establish rapport-building questions that your sales team will ask every prospect. Teach your salespeople to use those questions to make a connection, to find common interests. Also, "get personal." As fast as you can, get into the person's world. You can start with questions that seem like business questions, but they are personal questions: How long have you been doing this? Oh, really, how do you like it? What got you into it? What did you do before this? These kinds of questions help you create a deeper bond. Remember, everyone's favorite person to talk about is themselves. Can you go deeper? Ask these: What do you do for fun? What do you do to be creative? What are your hobbies? Naturally, you have to build up to some of these.

  In consumer situations such as in a restaurant or retail environment, you can ask, "Are you familiar with our store/restaurant/company?" This gives you the opportunity to do a strategic pitch as you learned in Chapter Four, but it can also lead to more personal questions, such as, "Are you from the area?" These are harmless questions, but they connect you to the person in a way that goes beyond just making the sale.

- *Have a sense of humor.* Have fun together. My stockbroker calls me with the "joke of the week" and they're actually funny. Now the Internet makes it easy to forward a good joke, but don't be one of those people who sends every little joke. My clients know that if I send them something, it's going to be really funny. Therefore my emails get opened and answered. When I sold advertising, I would go out of my way, scouring hundreds of jokes to find a great one. I'd sit there and handwrite personalized notes to 30 to 50 big clients and send the joke with the note. Each client probably thought he or she was the only one receiving this because it came with a handwritten note. Again, don't do this too often; it's just another rapport-building opportunity.

- *Commiserate.* Misery loves company. If the client wants to complain about anything from business to personal life, be a good supportive ear. You'll escalate the bonding process.

- *Be empathetic and care about them.* Be more interested in them than anyone else has ever been. There's a saying, "If you want to be interesting, be interested. If you want to be fascinating, be fascinated."

- *Find the common ground.* I had a terrible time bonding with one client until we discovered that we both liked the same band. In fact, we grew up listening to the same album. It was like a magic key to unlocking a bond that we share to this day. Find the common ground. Hunt for the things that you can relate to.

- *Mirror.* If you match your body language and tonality to what your prospects are doing and sounding like, they'll make the subconscious connection that you are like them. For example, if the client leans forward, you lean forward. If the client tilts her head slightly, you can tilt yours the same way.

Exercise

Workshop rapport skills with your salespeople. Ask each person to suggest three ways to establish deeper levels of rapport with your prospects and clients. Naturally, you will get some obvious answers, such as, "Ask good questions" and "Be interested in them." But, for most companies, this will be the first time you've drilled them on what establishes good rapport, and that's the first step in making rapport building a standard procedure in every sales interaction. You will also find that your best salespeople are doing things that no one else is doing. They're asking better and more in-depth questions. They're specifically looking for things they have in common with every prospect.

When you have five or six great methods to establish rapport, do a workshop on each one of them and turn them into procedures so that every salesperson can do them every time.

Revisit this material regularly, drilling your salespeople: How long have they (the client) worked there? How many kids do they have? Some companies keep all this information in a client database, so even a new person can gain all kinds of insights on the client. Other companies have contests to see who can learn the most about their clients.

The bottom line is that rapport can make you bulletproof, increase referrals, boost your closing ratio, and help you become more and more sought out by your clients. Work on this regularly.

Sales Step 2: Qualify the Buyer (Find the Need)

Qualifying buyers means finding out what they are looking for in your product or service and what factors will influence them to buy. In this step you need to learn everything you can about their existing buying criteria, but the key to developing your Ultimate Sales Machine is to reset that buying criteria so that your product or service becomes the most logical choice. To reset a customer's buying criteria in favor of your product or service, you must begin by gaining a complete understanding of his or her current buying criteria. Develop the six to 10 questions that you would like to know about every prospect. Drill these questions into your salespeople until every one of them can recite them by heart.

When I sold advertising, for example, asking the following questions was mandatory:

1. How do your customers find out about you right now?
2. What's the most effective way you have for gaining new clients?
3. What's the amount of your average sale? (This enabled us to cost-justify. Meaning, if their product cost $400 and the ad cost $4,000, then they only needed 10 sales to justify the cost of the advertising.)
4. What are the three biggest problems you're having in [your area of business]? (Get their pain and help solve it.)
5. How long have you worked here?
6. How'd you get started?
7. What are your goals for your company?
8. What are your goals for yourself?
9. What are your criteria for making a decision about buying a product or service like ours?

This last question is quite direct, so you need to find a subtle way to ask it that fits into your conversation. For example, with advertising we would ask, "What are the factors that make you choose one advertising vehicle over another?" Additionally, when you understand their personal and business goals and their needs, you will be able to show them how your product or service can help them achieve their goals and fulfill those needs. Our sales staff was drilled on these questions, given spot quizzes, and then assigned role-play exercises to make sure they understood what they were looking for each time.

Think of every question your salesperson should ask in order to thoroughly understand the client's needs. For example, in all my years of buying suits, I've never had a rep ask me what I do for a living or what I have in my current wardrobe. Would knowing the answers to these questions help you establish deeper rapport and get deeper into my world while helping me to buy more suits? I worked with a large retail men's clothing chain in an attempt to get them to be much more effective at this. I even designed a program called "Dressed for Success," where the salesperson would have a presentation binder in the store to show people how to dress for success. The salesperson was even supposed to offer a "wardrobe analysis," getting deep into the prospect's wardrobe to help flesh it out, round it off, and make sure that the client had appropriate attire for every occasion.

On their own, most companies just don't go this deep. Yet if you study their best producers, you'll find variations on all these rapport-developing techniques. Your job is to set up systems, procedures, and training that create a machine where every salesperson gets deep with your prospects. In the words of Jay Abraham, "If you truly believe that what you have is useful and valuable to your clients, then you have a moral obligation to try to serve them in every way possible." I believe this. I practice it. And when I work with companies, I work very hard to make sure they go at this from every angle possible.

The best method of selling I've ever seen is when you can guide your prospects through a series of questions and they sell themselves on your product or service.

For example, someone will call in from our radio ad and we will have a conversation that goes something like this.

REP: What was it about the spot that made you call us?
THEM: I liked the idea of getting all my dream clients
REP: What is a dream client for you?

THEM: Heck, Microsoft would be a dream client.

REP: What would a client like that mean to your business?

THEM: Millions?

REP: And how many clients like that are there out there for you?

THEM: One hundred sounds like a good number.

REP: So if our program worked for you, it could be worth $100 million?

THEM: Well, if it worked, yes.

REP: Would you be willing to spend $199 to find out if it would work, especially if you only paid after you saw it and only if you thought it would work? Does that sound fair?

THEM: I'm not sure.

Of course you need to have a "close," but to speed this up a bit, here are a series of questions all designed so that the callers close themselves.

- What's it costing if you're not getting those dream clients? Are you the type of person who likes to learn new things if they're going to give you a breakthrough? Let me explain a breakthrough. It's when you find a method of doing something that dramatically accelerates your ability to accomplish your goals. So let me ask again, are you the type of person who likes to learn breakthroughs?
- What if you could learn the breakthrough and then decide if it was worth the money? Would that seem fair to you?
- (Here's the close.) Let's take a look at some dates for you to attend one of our Web seminars. Do you have your calendar handy?

⚙ Exercise

First, is there a way to guide your prospect through a series of questions in which your product or service becomes more and more valuable to her, from her perspective? What would those questions be and what could you do with that information to target that prospect better?

Next, have a workshop to establish the 6 to 10 questions your salespeople will ask all your prospects to qualify them and find out their buying criteria. Drill your salespeople with role-play exercises and pop quizzes to make sure these are so engrained in them that they never forget to ask them.

Sales Step 3: Build Value

After you have assessed your customers' buying criteria, you must begin to build value around your product or service. You've already built rapport. You've asked a lot of questions. Now you ask them, "How much do you know about us, by the way?" This is the time that you've got your little one- to two-minute pitch that builds value and lets them know your reputation in the marketplace.

An even more powerful way to do this, as you have learned, is to present your core story/executive briefing. This orientation should be targeted to the buyer, not to your product or service.

As mentioned, I worked with a prominent Canadian retail chain called The Shoe Company. The CEO, Alan Simpson, is one of the better CEOs I've worked with. They also own Town Shoes, a more upscale line of shoes. They have the best education you will ever see in a shoe store. I've described the data they had on feet, fashion, and footwear, but did you know there's a thing called "the threshold effect"? This study shows that when you walk into a room, people make 11 different assumptions about you (such as your level of education and economic bracket), strictly based on your appearance. Your clothes and, yes, your shoes add to or detract from the impression you make. If a shoe store salesperson can show you all this information, do you think it builds value in that store and that salesperson?

How you introduce the education to your clients is as important as the education itself. You need to presell everything you are about to tell them. For a clothing store you might say:

> Our company has commissioned research on dressing for success. Surveys show that 90 percent of people who wear suits don't know the perfect combinations of styles and the impressions your clothes make on others. Let me take you through some of this data.

Shoe store salespeople could say:

> Most people think the way in which shoes are made is unimportant. But did you know that there are 23 different decisions a shoemaker makes when creating a cheap shoe or a good shoe? Here. Let me show you this. [The salesperson pulls out the binder and flips through some of the data.]

In business-to-business situations, often your core story is the reason you are in front of them in the first place, as you saw in the examples of the newspaper company and the company that sold art to hospitals. It's easy to introduce market education as long as it serves the prospect: "Whether you ever do business with us or not, you should know some of this data we've gathered on being successful in your marketplace."

○ Exercise

Do a workshop on building value. Ask your team what builds great value around your product or service. How and where and what will you say to introduce your market education? To be the Ultimate Sales Machine you need to define and perfect every single step of the sales process. In this exercise you are perfecting a precise way in which you will introduce market education to your prospects.

Sales Step 4: Create Desire

Now it is time to make your client want your product or service and want it right now. There are a lot of things you can do to increase this desire. As I've mentioned, two powerful techniques are:

1. Lead them through a series of questions in which you intensify their need from their perspective.
2. Present killer data that truly motivates your buyer to take action now.

Be clear on this important point: Your buyers will be a lot more motivated if their current situation becomes unacceptable. To create desire, you must motivate your buyers using a combination of problems and solutions, even if you are the one pointing out the problems that they haven't really considered. Market data and your core story can do this well.

Market data can show your prospects that their market is fierce with competition and can spotlight the high failure rate of businesses. Do the research to find out this information.

If your prospects are comfortable with the current situation, they are not motivated to change. So make them feel uncomfortable. People will act faster to solve a problem than they will to gain an unrealized benefit. People naturally move away from problems and discomfort to solutions. Once you have shown them the problems, paint the picture of their wonderful future with your products or service and you will create desire. Just be sure you are painting a picture of *their future* and not just *your products*. Remember that *features tell, benefits sell*. Don't tell them what it is, but rather why they need it.

⚙ Exercise

Do a workshop asking all of your salespeople, "What are some pain points that would motivate your prospects to buy?" Write down four of them. Then write down the four benefits of your product or service that directly address those pain points. Check yourself: have you just written down features or benefits? Your prospect doesn't care that your product is faster or more energy efficient. Tell them why that matters to *them*. How will it make their lives or jobs better?

Sales Step 5: Overcome Objections

What are the most common reasons that you lose a sale? And how many different ways have you developed to eliminate barriers to buying? The toughest objections are the ones you don't know. A talented salesperson establishes need and finds out the objections early in the sales process. But often, when you go into the close, the hidden objections arise. Certainly, you can ask your client outright, "What's stopping you from making this decision?" Using a standard set of questions, top salespeople will qualify buyers' buying criteria right down to their toes, before they even begin to sell. The better you qualify them, the fewer obstacles you'll have as you come into the close. Do another workshop with the broad question, "How do we create desire in our clients to have our product or service?"

As I already mentioned, the best close of all is when the buyers make their own decision to buy because it's the most logical conclusion they can draw from the information you've given them. Again, the core story should work really well to reset the buying criteria and bring the sale to a logical close as explained in Chapter Four. You can also ask questions that show them the cost or downfall of not moving forward with your product or service. My salespeople ask questions such as:

• What is your biggest marketing challenge?
• What would it be worth to you if this challenge could be fixed forever?
• What does it cost you to not fix this problem?

When prospects thinks of it like that and learn that working with us can fix that challenge forever, they close the sale themselves.

However, even with great questions early in the sales process, an objection can still surface when it is time to close the sale. But if you remember that *an objection is an opportunity to close*, you will always be happy to hear one. For example, the client states this objection: "I'd love to buy it, but I just can't afford it right now." You should agree that the objection is valid. Always agree with an objection. The clients will drop their guard. You might say, "Well, that's certainly a good reason not to invest in this today. [meaningful pause] But let me ask you a question: Is money the only thing standing between you and the purchase of this product?" At this point, if there are more objections, they will surface. If not, the client will say, "No, if I could afford it, I'd buy it."

This is called *isolating the objection*. It's standard sales stuff that is taught in every major sales training program, and yet every day I see salespeople make the mistake of not isolating the objection. I suppose the real lesson with any type of sales training comes down to the main lesson in this book: you must work on each of these strategies with pig-headed determination and discipline. That's the only way you're ever going to fully integrate any of this so that it becomes synthesized into the way people think and operate.

So when someone throws you an objection, if you isolate the objection you have just moved a huge step closer to closing the sale. Now it's up to you to lock down the sale. You say, "So if I can find a way for you to afford this product, you will buy it?" If the client says yes, you have just closed the sale. You will now need to be more creative in the financing of the product or service or help create more desire, showing how not buying it will cost them a lot more in the long run.

Sales Step 6: Close the Sale

Although the goal is to set up such logical buying criteria that the prospect and the salesperson walk to the close together, it should also be stated that most people need help in making decisions. I had one client who spent two years deciding whether to hire me to help grow his business. I finally said to him: "Look, you don't need any more information. You already know as much as you're ever going to know. You just need to make a decision. Do you have what it takes to make the decision? Because that's where you're at right now." That's a hard-core close, but without it he might have continued wasting his time struggling over the decision when he could have been working with me to improve his business. He said: "You're right. I do know. I want it." And he bought.

I faced another prospect who had the same problem. He just couldn't make the decision, so I took him through a series of questions:

ME: Do you believe that I will help you go to the next level?
CLIENT: Yes.
ME: Do you honestly feel that my help will earn you far more than you will ever spend on my services?
CLIENT: Yes, I know you'll be worth a lot more than I'll spend.
ME: Do you see that the problems I've laid out for you are going to cost you far more in the long run?
CLIENT: Yes.
ME: What do you think is the main result you're going to get from working with me and how valuable is that to you?

It went on like this, as I asked about 10 of these questions until the client finally agreed, in a fervor of decisiveness: "Yes. Let's do it."

You may need to help prospects make the decision. It's okay to make them feel a little pressure. If you believe that what you have is good for them, close already!

Another tried-and-true sales method is to *assume the sale*, saying things like, "Do you want that today?" or "Where do we ship that?" I was a young man of only 19 the first time I saw a master salesperson assume the sale. It was my first day working at a furniture store, and the sales manager said to me, "Watch this." He grabbed a clipboard with an order form on it and walked over to an elderly couple looking at recliners. They tried two or three and decided which one they liked. He then said, "Where do you live?" They told him and he replied: "We deliver there on Tuesday or Thursday. Which day would be best for you?" The couple looked at each other and decided that Thursday would be best. He then said, as he put his pen to the order form, "How do you spell your last name?" They started spelling and he had closed the sale.

That was an interesting experience for me. Besides showing the technique of assuming the sale, it demonstrated how a salesperson has a huge impact on whether or not, or even when, the buyer will buy.

When I worked as a real estate salesperson, I was asked to go out with another salesperson in our office, one who was having trouble closing sales. So we go out with a young couple looking to buy their first home. Seven houses later we find the one they like. They start saying all the right things: the living room is perfect, the garage is great, the yard is large, and so on. If they were my customers, I would've casually said: "Well, let's get an offer in to take the house off the market. You can't imagine how many times I've seen a house taken right out from under you. Best to get an offer in that keeps other buyers away."

A typical objection from this type of couple is, "Well, my dad is putting up the down payment for us, so we want him to see it." To which I would answer: "Great. We'll make that a contingency. If he doesn't like it, you don't have to buy it. How does that sound?" Closing.

But they weren't my clients, so I just observed. Here this couple is ready to go. A little push and we'd be filling out that binder. Suddenly, the salesperson says: "Now don't rush into anything. Buying a house is the biggest decision you'll ever make, so you want to take your time."

Slowly, my head turns to look at this salesperson in complete disbelief. I had to stop myself from reaching over, putting my hand over her mouth, and saying: "She's running a fever. Ignore her. Let's get that binder filled out." The salesperson had not only not closed, she talked them right out of making a decision.

Important lesson. This comes from "weak ego strength," as explained in Chapter Five. Inside, this salesperson was afraid to make the sale, do the close, or apply any pressure whatsoever, because the fear of rejection was making her weak. That's why most salespeople don't close well: weak ego strength and fear of rejection.

So let me help everyone with this problem right now with the words taught to me by John J., the sales manager at that furniture store where I got my first sales training:

> You see, these people come in here who've been looking for a living room set for, like, four months. They've been to a dozen stores. Know what that is? That's weak salespeople who don't know their job. Your job is to take those folks out of their misery. Ever see someone who's been looking for six months and then the day they make that final decision to buy, they can't wait to get that set in their home. Jeez, they'd take it the same day if they could get it. People don't regret when they buy, unless they buy a lemon. Most people are thrilled when they buy. Your job, Chet, is to help people make that decision to buy. That is the greatest weakness in folks—they're not good at making decisions. If you truly believe that your prospect should benefit from your product or service, it's your moral obligation to help them make a decision and get on with their lives.

Great speech. Stuck with me ever since. If you don't believe in your product or service, then by all means, don't close. But if what you sell is truly going to serve that prospect, then go at him every which way until he buys.

Other ways to induce people to buy faster and with greater enthusiasm include risk reversal and offering a free product or service with the sale. Can you add on something that motivates them to buy right now? Or can you reverse the risk (a concept that Jay Abraham teaches) so all of their objections are neutralized?

My company sells a comprehensive training program and then we add on a few thousand dollars' worth of bonuses. Here's our risk reversal (paraphrased): "We're so sure that this program is going to help you, we're going to give you $2,000 in bonus products. Take this program and use it. If you feel it is not more than 1,000 times worth the investment, send it back and get a complete refund. And for your trouble, you can keep the $2,000 in bonus products."

When we did this, our sales doubled. And yes, you have that 1 out of 10 who might buy it just to get the bonuses, but you still had nine more sales you would not have gotten if you didn't make the offer in the first place. A money-back guarantee is a great way to take away objections, but the idea of offering a bonus that they can keep soups it up quite a bit.

⚙ Exercise

Write down eight things you can do to close more sales. What can you add that would encourage people to buy right now? How can you use risk reversal? What gifts could you give away with purchases that would motivate your buyers to buy? What product or service can you get for free that would be of great value to your prospect?

And then do workshops with your staff on overcoming objections and closing techniques. There is nothing that increases sales skills like role playing. Some people hate it, and I don't care. They have to do it if they work with me. I will be gentle at first, but I will get every salesperson role-playing. I worked with a group of industrial technicians who had to get used to selling a new product that was highly technical. When I started working with them, not one of them was very good at any of the techniques I was introducing and not one of them liked to role-play. I role-played with them for six months, one-on-one with everyone else listening. By the end of the six months every one of those technicians could do a decent job of every aspect of selling the product. It was impressive to watch the progress, even though, in the beginning, I'm sure they all hated me.

Sales Step 7: Follow Up

The process after the sale is so important that the entire next chapter is devoted to it.

Conclusion

These seven steps are core sales skills and procedures. Just as basketball coaches must constantly train their players on lay-up shots and blocking, sales managers must constantly train their reps on polishing every angle of the seven steps to every sale. Smart companies build tools, policies, and procedures that support these seven steps. The more standards you set, the higher the performance you can expect from every level of talent. Only constant practice and repetition will create master-level salespeople.

11

Follow-up and Client Bonding Skills

How to Keep Clients Forever and Dramatically Increase Your Profits

If you look at most companies and their efforts to grow their business, the majority of their focus is on the first six steps of the sales process to get new clients. They think their job is finished once the sale is closed. Yet it costs six times more to get a new client than to sell something additional to a current client. If you want to build the Ultimate Sales Machine, you need to have highly procedurized follow-up and follow-through.

The hardest thing we do is to get the attention of the client in the first place. Everywhere you go, there is a commercial message in one form or another. As the number of messages grows, people's memories shrink. This is called the clutter factor. It means that if you touch down with someone and get her attention, you need to do it again and again and again as fast as you can or she will cool off and forget about you. Once you've made the sale, you may have achieved top-of-mind awareness, but if you are out of sight, you are very quickly out of mind. You need to have excellent follow-up procedures to stay at the top of your client's mind.

Follow-up—the seventh step to every sale—is so important that it gets this entire chapter to itself. This chapter will give you the tools to evaluate and improve the follow-up and client bonding procedures you already have. It will also show you how to devise and implement new, more creative and cutting-edge procedures to take your current client relationships to a whole new and much more profitable level.

When I worked for Charlie Munger, I had a sales rep who was fantastic at getting in the door and terrific at closing sales. However, it was not in his nature to bond with people. He just made the sale and moved on. I started putting the three Ps into place to set policies for bonding permanently with clients. I created mass opportunities for bonding such as trade show parties and award ceremonies (which you learned about in Chapter Seven), but I also had one-on-one trainings and even role-play exercises to teach the salespeople how to ask the kinds of questions that got them involved in the prospect's or client's life (as covered in the previous chapter).

In that example we were selling business-to-business where each client can be worth a lot of revenue; hence, entertaining on a grand scale is a wise investment at every turn. For business-to-consumer selling, you need to implement bonding opportunities on a smaller scale. For example, if you own a restaurant, spa, hair salon, or boutique, you need to have procedures in place to make sure your people establish relationships with clients and make them feel special.

Example

Here's an example of client-bonding mastery. One time I took 18 people to Spago when it was the hottest restaurant in the country. There was a trade show in town, so all my advertisers were there from all over the country—Lincoln, Nebraska; Pine Bush, New York; Albany, New York; Pittsburgh, Pennsylvania; Miami, Florida; you name it. Most of them otherwise might have never had a chance to go to Spago. I had to set the reservations a month in advance: table for 18.

There were three movie stars within 10 feet of our table, which was thrilling for my clients. It gave them something to talk about when they went home and another opportunity for me to bond with my key advertisers. Suddenly, a few waiters and Wolfgang Puck himself (owner and celebrity chef) came over to our table with free samples of hors d'oeuvres. Wolfgang walked over to me, using my name and telling me how wonderful it was to see me. He didn't say "again," but it was implied that he knew me, even though he didn't. What he *did* do, quite effectively, was make me feel very special. After all, how many people bring 18 guests to Spago?

Additionally, the sight of Wolfgang shaking my hand and telling me how nice it was to see me impressed my clients. It impressed *me* so much I'm mentioning it almost 20 years later. In the best restaurants, the owner or manager will go table to table introducing him- or herself and seeing that everything is excellent.

Believe me—if you don't have procedures for this, this will never happen by accident. What are your client bonding procedures to make sure you are keeping clients happy? How many do you have?

The Cool-Off Factor

Enthusiasm is contagious. When you are with a prospect, your enthusiasm rubs off. The second you leave, the prospect begins to cool off. But your job is to keep the prospect hot on two things: you and the sale.

They need to stay hot on you, not just on what you're selling. If you made a good impression, you have to "keep those cards and letters coming." If you didn't bond very well during the first six steps of the sales process, follow-up is even more important. Remember the story of the company that advertised with me three times to utter failure. Because I followed up so heavily in the face of failure, I gained enough trust to get it to spend even more money—resulting in a dramatic success.

Remember, trust and respect are the largest part of the sale. Every minute that a prospect doesn't hear from you after you leave their office, his respect falls off. Out of sight, out of mind.

The real success formula for selling:
Trust and respect = Influence = Potential for control =
More market share at every mutually beneficial opportunity

You are a major part of why they buy, which means that you must reiterate your connection in your follow-up correspondence (examples coming up). But you also want them to stay hot on your product or service. If you used the techniques you've learned in this book and presented the clients with a ton of useful information from your core story, they stand a better chance of remembering why they bought your product. An excellent brochure or "leave-behind" helps as well.

The more you remind them, the less chance they will ever forget why they bought. Putting the hot buttons, the pain points that made them want to buy in the first place, in your follow-up letters and phone conversations is one way to reduce the cool-off factor. If you come away from a meeting or phone call without knowing those hot buttons, you are in trouble.

As you learned in the previous chapter, successful companies know every aspect of a client's criteria for making a purchase. The deeper your understanding of your clients, the better the opportunity to help them and the more market share you will acquire. Your goal is to become such a bright spot in your clients' day that they actually look forward to your calls, letters, and emails. Keep things exciting and interesting. You must become part of your clients' lives in order to stay in their top-of-mind awareness. This requires massive, diligent, and entertaining follow-up.

Make the relationship fun and entertaining by incorporating into your follow-up such things as cards, letters, games, jokes, and gifts. For business-to-consumer companies, you need to have a constant touch system to keep the relationship strong. This may mean a VIP card that your clients can use to get express service or special benefits. It may be personalized invitations to come to a special VIP sale preview event or to remind your clients of their next scheduled appointment. With the Internet, this can be inexpensive or even free. Again, it should be stressed that "education-based marketing" is an excellent method of staying in touch. No matter what you sell, you can find valuable information that your client will appreciate receiving.

Every company today should have a major initiative to build email databases and relationships with its buyers. Drive as many folks to your Web site as you can, as often as you can, and for every reason you can think of.

Let's look at a practical example: At the time of this writing, I went to the official Web sites of Disney, Warner Bros., and Universal Studios. Looking around, I could not easily find anywhere to subscribe to be on an email list to receive promotions. If I owned a studio, the most prominent graphic on the Web site would be an offer that would capture data to begin a relationship with every fan coming to the site. One of my goals would be to collect millions of fan emails. This would hedge my investment, giving me an opportunity to promote my movies in advance and build an even stronger brand with moviegoers. The home page should give ethical bribes to fans to get their email: "Enter your email address and win a chance to have dinner with a star." Surely, you could create dozens of juicy opportunities that would make folks want to give you their email addresses. As you learned in Chapter Seven, create a "community," a great place to visit and get involved. Imagine the power of giving fans the possibility of tracking a movie for months and building excitement to see it on that critical opening weekend. All free over the Web. No media costs.

No matter what you sell, you can create a better relationship with your buyers using the Internet. But the main point is to have constant follow-up efforts with buyers—especially with those who did not buy.

Set Yourself Up for Great Follow-up

Rule: Your follow-up is only as good as your first six steps and you should be considering your follow-up during every step of the sales process.

Here are the goals and questions that should guide you throughout each step of the process:

- *Create rapport.* What professional goals did you note during the meeting? How can you help prospects achieve those goals? What personal tidbit, common interest, or funny story can you refer to later to remind them of your bond?
- *Qualify and establish need.* Do you understand prospects' needs and objectives? What are their most pressing problems and how can you help solve them?
- *Build value.* What do they consider valuable? What benefits or add-ons would appeal to them and build the value around your product or service?
- *Create desire.* What are their hot buttons that can increase their desire? What is the pain point that you can use to remind them of why they bought and why they will want to keep buying from you? Remember that people naturally gravitate away from problems and toward solutions.
- *Overcome objections.* What are their objections and how can you put them to rest?
- *Close.* What closed them?

The more effective you were and the more information you gathered in steps 1 through 6, the more penetrating your follow-up will be.

When I owned an advertising agency, one of my clients was a magazine. In order to research for this client, we had the salespeople come in from competing magazines and do a pitch so we could see what our client was up against. Here's what they did for their pitches:

Competitor I talked about their magazine.
Competitor II talked about their magazine.
Competitor III talked about their magazine.
Competitor IV talked about their magazine.

This was astonishing to me. I literally could not believe that not one of these magazines asked me any questions. This is weak selling at best.

When all you do is talk about the product or service you're selling, what is the only thing you can focus on in your follow-up? There's not much else to say in your letter but "Thank you for the meeting and, by the way, did I tell you our product is great?" There's no opportunity for quality follow-up because you didn't find out anything about me or my problems or my buying criteria. The follow-up letter becomes no more interesting to the client than a direct mail piece from a total stranger. Needless to say, I trained and role-played and quizzed our sales staff to ask a lot of questions with the goal of learning the client's entire decision-making criteria and quite a few professional and personal tidbits about the client. By the time they were in the follow-up phase, my sales staff had plenty of information.

10 Steps to Great Follow-up

Follow-up Step 1: Send the First Follow-up Letter

If you sell business-to-business, get a letter off to your client within an hour or two of your meeting. When I went on sales calls, I would call from my car, dictate a letter to my assistant, and have it faxed off. Do you think it would impress the client to get a follow-up letter within an hour when she knew I wasn't even back at the office yet? Here's a good letter structure:

1. Start with something personal that you remember from the meeting.
   Example: "That was a great story you told about your daughter. In our next meeting, I have a similar story to tell you."

2. Include a compliment.

Example: "You certainly seem to have a great grasp on how to make your company succeed. They are lucky to have you."

3. Push their hot buttons and stay focused on the benefits your product or service offers to them.

Example: "With the challenge you face, it seems clear that six of our machines are exactly what you need. You will reduce costs, speed up productivity, and, most important, relieve a lot of stress for quite a few people. I'm checking on how fast we can move on this one."

4. Use a personal close.

Example: "Once again, it was great meeting you. I have a few ideas about some other productivity issues that I know you will like."

Here's a bad follow-up letter:

Dear Joe,

Thank you for your time. I know how busy you are. Our machines are great. With our strength, we have become great. We're great. I really want your business, and I'm willing to work hard to get it.

You won't regret buying from us. I will call you soon to sell you some more.

Sincerely,
Bernie

Of course, this is an exaggeration, but many sales letters can be boiled down to exactly this. They begin with an opening that is not personal and, in fact, belittles the salesperson. As stated, never apologize for taking their time. You must feel that your time is also valuable and they are lucky to be meeting with you because you are bringing them important insights and solutions. However, don't put all the emphasis on you and your products or services as this type of letter does.

Second, this letter is focused on the sale, not the customer. You can tell prospects all day long how great you are, but unless you know why they buy, you aren't going to make the sale. Focus on *them* and the benefits your product or service would have for them.

Third, there is nothing in here to endear you to this client. Get personal. Great follow-up letters have more than a little personal touch. Remind the prospect of a laugh you shared with him or something he said that really stuck with you.

I once pulled off the miracle of catching the senior vice president of Xerox on the telephone during his lunch hour. We talked for an hour and my boss at the time kept coming in and giving me the hard stare, thinking I was on a personal call. It sounded like a personal call. Laughing and talking about life. My boss became hotter and hotter, especially when I waved him away like "Stop bothering me." When he heard me get off the phone, he called me into his office and said: "Who the hell was that? You were on the phone for an hour!" To which, I responded proudly, "That was the senior vice president of Xerox." He continued, "What in the world do you have to say that would keep you on the phone for an hour!" And here I was amazed that I got deep enough rapport that this executive *wanted* to stay on the phone with me for an hour.

I then wrote a follow-up letter filled with personal stuff about the conversation. This same boss snatched the letter from me and said it was unprofessional to go into all this personal information. He then rewrote my letter, taking out all the personal references, and made it similar to the example of a bad follow-up letter I just gave you. Later, when he went home for the day, I used my original letter and sneaked to fax it off to the client.

I had many a battle with this particular boss. That is, until Xerox came in as the biggest sale in the history of the company. After I brought in many more large sales like this, the boss finally let me do things my way. But in the entire time I worked at that company, no one ever asked me how I was bringing in so many large advertisers. If this company had organized the workshops described in Chapter Three, everyone would've learned all my insights. You'll find that top producers are eager to share. I certainly was.

If you sell business-to-consumer, you may not have the personal interaction that you would in a business-to-business play. But you still need a personalized follow-up letter. Email makes this quite easy. I bought two suits a few days ago. The salesperson didn't ask me a lot of questions, but I mentioned that I'm a public speaker, so he asked me for my card. When I got home later that evening, to my shock and surprise there was an email from him. Unfortunately, it was almost word for word the bad follow-up example given, but hey, I was impressed nevertheless.

That's an example of retail selling where follow-up can be instituted. I'm not sure if this is the policy of the store, but it impressed me. If there is a salesperson involved, as in the suit example, use the structure I've provided. The sales rep should have asked me a lot more questions. Then his follow-up could have capitalized on my answers, beginning with some personal note. Make clients feel good about themselves. Let's say he had asked me what I speak about. He then could've said something like, "I loved hearing about the topics you cover in your lectures. It must be exciting to be able to share such great information with business owners." He then could've added value, saying, "I'm sure those suits will make you look great on stage."

Now imagine if this suit store had a club membership or, even better, a "wardrobe analysis" or "dress for success" program. Then every email that followed could provide information of value to me, keeping me updated with the latest fashion insights. This is applicable for practically any type of retail situation, outside of mass marketers. If you sell cars, you could send updates on driving tips, safety tips, or maintenance insights on how to preserve the mechanical integrity of your vehicle. Create a relationship with the buyer. If you sell jewelry, you could send information on keeping it clean, what types of jewelry increase in value with age, the latest fashion, and insights on what to wear with what. Be an expert in your area and offer excellent insights to your buyers.

Let's say you have a cosmetics counter at a fine department store where they do makeovers and have a wonderful opportunity to bond with clients. If you've ever had a makeup session at, say, Nordstrom, have you received a follow-up from them? Have you ever received makeup tips from these companies? Have they tried to make you brand-loyal so that you only want a specific brand of makeup?

If you sell boats, how about boating tips, safety tips, and suggestions on places to take your boat—all valuable stuff. There's no area of business where you can't build a far stronger bond with your client with outstanding follow-up.

Even mass merchandisers like Wal-Mart could go a step further, bringing news and insights about products, consumer alerts, and things of value—not just selling, but offering something that the client will value. For example, as of this writing, Wal-Mart is on a big initiative to offer more organic foods. Why not send emails offering insights on organic foods? There are probably many studies on this that would be of interest and value to buyers. And every cashier at every register could give an ethical bribe to get email addresses: "If you give us your email address, we will send you a gift certificate (through email) for $5 good in any Wal-Mart." Surely it would be worth $5 to reach every Wal-Mart buyer via email. Plus customers might make a special trip to use the coupon before it expires and then spend more money buying something they might not have bought in the first place.

Think of the cost savings of reaching folks over the Internet instead of through fliers, mailers, television, or radio. Imagine the power of having 100 million email addresses. But rather than just using them to send sales notices, send things that get opened—things of value. And then, you can also mention a great sale. Wal-Mart goes to great pains to offer lower prices than anyone else. Imagine getting an email that reads, "How we negotiated with Sony to get you this amazing offer." Then the email is like an article showing how Wal-Mart negotiates on behalf of the consumer to keep prices low. Such emails could blend items of interest with sales information.

No matter what you sell and to whom, great follow-up is something every company can do a heck of a lot better. This is a new world we're in and so many companies are missing these opportunities.

⚙ Exercise

Create a follow-up letter that is a model for your product or service. If you're a mass-oriented company, do a workshop on education-based marketing ideas to get those emails opened. If you are business-to-business, use the format provided to compose a template for your first follow-up email. If you are more salesperson-to-client direct (like retail suits or jewelry), create a template to guide your sales reps in doing their follow-up.

The following steps are especially for direct sales efforts, where a salesperson is trying to build a long-term relationship with a buyer, but many of the concepts may stimulate ideas for a mass audience as well.

Follow-up Step 2: Make the First Follow-up Call

The follow-up call should come right after the letter. It should offer something of value, something that doesn't necessarily have to benefit your company directly. You're trying to bond with your client, so this follow-up call does not have to be selling them anything. This is absolutely critical if you sell business-to-business. You may call and say: "Hey, Jim. I thought more about your challenges, and I think I may have a great idea for you." For business-to-consumer, it may be a reminder call or offering further education or a chance to bring a friend to a special event.

If you're business-to-business and you had a good meeting, you should now be working your way into your client's staff as someone bringing enough value that they let you into their world. This is how I became top producer at every company. I became such a valued contributor it was like I was on my clients' staffs. I helped them find talent, design more effective ads, do better at trade shows, hook up with other companies that can help them, and so on. They'd say, "Let's call Chet and get his input on this one." I had total control of my accounts and never lost one to a competitor. On the other hand, if you had a bad meeting, monster follow-up is your only hope.

For business-to-consumer, your best follow-up call offer may be something educational. If you sell bedding, what are five tips to better sleeping? If you sell furniture, can you offer decorating tips? The business-to-consumer examples may not require a telephone call, but by continually establishing yourself as the expert, you will become part of your client's decision-making process in your arena. Your clients may call you for advice on whether they should buy a new suit from your suit store or what they should order from your catering business to serve at their next dinner party. Also, think of the increase in referrals. I've never had a relationship with a suit salesperson, but there are suit salespeople who are such experts, they are constantly recommended by their clients to others. Experts will get three times more referrals than "salespeople."

⚙ Exercise

What is going to be your standard second follow-up after the buyer buys? What script will you use for a phone call? Write down some ideas. What can you offer that's valuable to the client?

Follow-up Step 3: Share Something Amusing or of Personal Interest

As you learned in Chapter Ten, you are establishing rapport throughout the sales process so you can use similar approaches. As mentioned in that section, send an amusing cartoon or article that you know will be of interest to them. Even if it does nothing else but make them smile and laugh, it's building that bond and keeping that top-of-mind status. So send something of interest to them every month. Don't sell; just schmooze.

⚙ **Exercise**

What is going to be your standard third follow-up after the buyer buys or after that first meeting? Think of your top clients. What can you send them that would amuse or interest them? Write a note that you could send with it that would keep you in their top-of-mind.

Follow-up Step 4: Throw a Party, Share a Meal, and Bond Like Crazy

If you're business-to-business or business-to-consumer, throwing parties is one of the best ways to bond. Refer back to Chapter Seven to see exactly how to do this.

Sharing a meal with your clients is another great way to bond. Here's the scale of bonding effectiveness:

Breakfast: Good rapport
Lunch: Good rapport
Dinner: *Great* rapport

You must ease into their lives. Don't be too pushy. You must judge what the appropriate invitation is for your situation. One way to do this is to offer a bonus. Here's a script you can use: "I did some research about your industry and learned some interesting things. If we can get together for a breakfast or lunch, I'll take you through some of this information."

⚙ **Exercise**

What is going to be your standard fourth follow-up after the buyer buys? If it's going to be a meal, how will you invite her? Write your phone script now. If you're business-to-consumer, what else could you offer your clients? An accountant or financial planner may offer a quarterly breakfast to educate clients on great strategies to keep and grow their wealth. What can you offer that's valuable to your clients?

Follow-up Step 5: Send Another Fax/Email/Letter/Card

If you get top-of-mind awareness, you need to never let it go. With unceasing follow-up you'll never lose a client to a competitor. If you've just had a meal with your client or she's attended a party or event you've sponsored, follow up immediately with another letter. Here's an example:

Dear Gail:

You make a great lunch guest. I wish all my clients had your sense of humor.

I was intrigued by your thoughts on direct mail, so I've asked for some further research. I'll let you know when it comes in. Meanwhile, stay away from those anchovies.

Regards,
Kevin

These letters are short and interesting. Be personal and complimentary, and tell them what the next step will be in your relationship. Kevin's letter to Gail tells her that he'll take the next step by doing some extra research for her and let her know when it comes in. At that point, he has set himself up to share another meal with her so he can present that information to her.

⚙ Exercise

What is going to be your standard fifth follow-up after the buyer buys? Write a letter that would be the perfect follow-up to a meal, party, or gathering.

Follow-up Step 6: Plan Something Fun That Can Include the Family

If you're business-to-business and your clients are big enough to warrant it, you can invite your clients to join you in fun activities such as boating, tennis, hot air ballooning, or scuba diving. I have done all of these and more. The more memorable the experience, the cooler it can be, the more likely the client will not only go, but will talk about it to others. You're becoming part of their lives. At a convention in Hawaii, we rented a catamaran and took 30 clients out for a cruise with drinks and food. It was an awesome bonding experience. I had five salespeople with me and we bought wild-looking cardboard sunglasses that had palm trees coming out of them. Then we took photos of all our clients wearing them and passed them around at the trade show.

At another trade show (where clients are all in one place), we had a gambling night and made paper money with a photo of a different client on each bill. They got such a charge out of those fake dollars that they took them home to show their families.

You could take clients to see a play or have a picnic. If you're business-to-consumer you could throw mass parties or buy blocks of tickets to a comedy club, sporting event, or concert. The goal is to become part of clients' lives. Look for something exciting that you can do together. It might be your nature to do these things, but if it's not or if you have salespeople, you need to build them into procedures.

⚙ Exercise

What is going to be your standard sixth follow-up? List 10 fun events you could do with your clients and their families. Write a letter or phone script you could use to invite your clients to these events.

Follow-up Step 7: Offer Something to Help Their Business

Can you be the king or queen of networking? Great companies are always finding ways to help their clients succeed. Can you hook up two clients to form a referral network? When we sold advertising, we would take up-and-coming companies and get them together with much larger companies. This often resulted in relationships that were of value to both players. For that reason, my clients always took my calls—always. Since they never knew what cool new thing I was going to offer, they always welcomed, and even looked forward to my calls. Be a resource.

Can you provide an idea to help your client succeed? Put helping the client above all else. Perhaps you can sell more product or services in the process.

⚙ **Exercise**

What is going to be your standard seventh follow-up? Think of your top clients. What could you do for them to help them improve their businesses? Are there ways that you could connect two or more of them that would be beneficial for everyone?

Follow-up Step 8: Send Another Fax/Email/Letter/Card

Your client needs to hear from you often so that you become permanently bonded. Keep sending follow-up notes and jokes. If you become best friends with your clients, it will be natural to keep doing these things.

⚙ **Exercise**

What is going to be your standard eighth follow-up? Write another letter that you could send after you've helped them improve their business in some way.

Follow-up Step 9: Offer More Help to Succeed

What else can you do to help your clients succeed? Perhaps you could take them to a seminar or give a seminar at their location. You could give them a training course on some topic they are having trouble with or that would help their business. You could help them find new personnel or alert them to important trends in their market. We are working with a restaurant chain that is offering business owners lunch and learns as a way to bond better with companies in their area. This gives them an excuse to call business owners and invite them to something cool. If you feel that sales training, marketing training, or management training would be valuable to your client, and you can get a good group together or even offer something over the Web, you will find many training companies willing to provide you with their content as a way to gain more exposure. (Mine certainly can.)

By this ninth follow-up step, you are becoming a valuable asset and trusted confidant to your clients. This breeds remarkable customer loyalty so that customers will feel like they are engaging in a personal betrayal if they buy from a competitor. Loyalty gives you unequaled control over market share and the inside track on everything your customer is thinking. Since it's so expensive to gain new clients today, what can you do to establish an unbreakable bond?

⚙ Exercise

What's your ninth follow-up procedure? Write down the types of seminars or training courses that you could give them. What could you do that would lock you in as a valuable asset and trusted confidant?

Follow-up Step 10: The Ultimate Follow-Up; Invite Them to Your Home or Be Invited to Theirs

When you have them in your home or they have you in theirs, you know you have done fantastic follow-up. Here are some revealing quotes from top producers on the importance of this step:

"Every important client I have has dined in my home."
"Half the people at my wedding were my clients."
"From their dreams to their hobbies, to their children's hobbies, I know everything about my top clients."

⚙ Exercise

What is going to be your standard 10th follow-up procedure? How will you invite clients to your home? What can you do at your home that sounds too irresistible to refuse? Can you put on an art show and get a local gallery to come and put its artwork all over your house? Can you challenge a local restaurant to prepare a gourmet feast for your private dinner party? Write a letter or a phone script that would be appropriate for your top client.

Conclusion

Bonding is everything. Your ultimate goal is that all of your biggest clients also become your best friends. Become involved in their lives and in the success of their businesses. Make it your personal mission to help them succeed. The bottom line is that you need to do follow-up or you will be mediocre. With a fantastic, structured follow-up, you will propel yourself so far above your competitors that they won't be able to touch you or your clients.

(12)

All Systems Go

Setting Goals, Measuring Effectiveness, and
Activating Your Master Plan

Goal setting and measuring effectiveness is the 12th core skill area of the Ultimate Sales Machine, and it's designed to soup up all 11 that come before it. According to the Ultimate Sales Machine mind-set, setting goals is not simply about writing them down periodically, although that is a part of it, but about mastering your focus so that achieving those goals happens quickly and automatically. This chapter will help you to not only improve your business but live a healthier and happier life.

As you've learned throughout this book, mastering anything is not about doing 4,000 new things, but doing 12 things 4,000 times. To master your business, you will no doubt go through each of the competencies in this book again and again, each time seeing more and more improvement and growth in your business. You can't be a master at all of these skills instantly, but setting periodic goals will speed the process. The latter half of this chapter will give you detailed processes for tracking all your major initiatives, especially your Dream 100 effort.

What if in addition to all the steps, tools, workshops, and insights you have learned in this book, you had one more added advantage—a computer programmed to exclusively focus on seeking out opportunities and generating success for you even while you sleep? This computer does nothing else all day but look at the world around you, searching for anything and everything that will create more success in every aspect of your life. Sound good?

In fact, you do have exactly that kind of computer in your brain. It's called the reticular activating system (RAS), and the problem is that most of us have unknowingly set it to seek out things we *don't* want instead of achieving the amazing results we dream about.

In this chapter you will learn what the RAS is and how to harness its power to create success in every area of your business and your life. You will also understand exactly how to set goals and measure effectiveness to put you on the fast track to growth. Finally, you will get a detailed look of the best example I've ever seen of a company using pigheaded discipline and determination to master and execute the 12 competencies you've learned in this book so it could become the Ultimate Sales Machine.

What We Think Defines Who We Are

The reticular activating system is that awesome computer in the brain that most of us never use on purpose.[9] Every day we have thousands of thoughts that seem to leap in and out of our minds. The truth is that those thoughts affect every cell in our body. Our cells are completely reactive to the environment in which they dwell, and thought is one of the most powerful sources for creating that environment. Some now say that if you're angry, fearful, or anxious when you eat or drink, you literally poison the food you're putting into you're body (see the 2004 documentary film *What the #$*! Do We Know?!* for more on this). But when you keep your thoughts focused on all the positive things in your life and the positive things you want to happen in your life, you awaken and purposefully focus your subconscious to create outstanding improvements on every front.

Take a minute and think about the kinds of thoughts you've had today. What has been the predominant tone and character of those thoughts? If you're like most people, your thoughts are dominated by problems and self-criticism. People tend to dwell on what's not working in their lives and, as mentioned before, people bond easily over shared unhappiness, sorrow, or complaints.

Listen to the people around you. It's amazing how many times you will hear things like "I hate when that happens" or "I'm so out of shape" or "I can't do that." The reticular activating system is the attitude programmer of the brain, and its power lies in the fact that the subconscious accepts all you feed it as reality. So if you're telling it you *can't* do something, guess what? You won't be able to do it. The subconscious cannot make judgments about the thought and say: "Oh, she doesn't mean it. Let's do it better this time." It cannot distinguish between a real perception and an imaginary one. So if you perceive you can't do something, you'll probably fail. Worrying has the same impact. If you worry about a problem, your subconscious thinks the problem is what's important to you and it won't help you find solutions. To find solutions, you have to change your thinking from worrying about the problem to demanding solutions. I've done it 100 times in seemingly impossible situations.

I have even applied this information to how I raise my children. When either of them says anything like "I can't" or "I'm no good at that," I say, "What's that called?" They moan, "Failure reinforcement." One day when my son was learning tennis, he said, "I just can't get the hang of that serve." Then he looked at me and caught himself. "But I'm getting better every day." They may have moaned and groaned, but in no time they were both seeing the fantastic results that come when you focus your RAS on what you want in your life instead of what you don't.

Have you ever heard the saying "Fake it till you make it"? The reason this works is that by adjusting your attitude (or faking it) as if you had already reached the goal you are trying to achieve, you are tricking your subconscious into creating that success or skill level as a reality. Whatever you tell it over and over again is what it believes and what it will bring more of into your life. Have the attitude that you already have the success you want, and your subconscious will work to bring about more success in your life.

Attitude is the only thing we can control in life, yet it's also the most powerful. You can't control your spouse, your kids, the weather, your co-workers, or the economy. You can try to better understand each of them, but you can't control them. All you can control is your perception and your attitude. The good news is that perception and attitude are all you need to control to achieve your goals and dreams in life and business.

How It Works

Let's say you're walking through an airport terminal, looking for your gate. You've got two hours until your flight so you're not in a hurry. You're not expecting any calls or anything—just walking along, looking for the gate. There are 1,000 things going on around you—conversations at various volumes, announcements over the loudspeaker, kids running around and getting yelled at by their parents. You're not paying attention, so you're not hearing any of it. Then suddenly, "Joe Smith, pick up the white phone!" And you go, "Hey, that's me!"

That's your reticular activating system screening out everything that won't interest you and then waking you up to something that will interest you. In a crowded airport with thousands of commercial messages and announcements and other distractions, your RAS will tune out everything. Imagine what it would be like walking along or sitting in a restaurant if you couldn't tune out those things that didn't matter to you. You wouldn't even be able to have a conversation or focus on anything.

Another example is when you buy a new car. You never noticed that car before and suddenly you start to see it everywhere. Now that this specific car has become of interest to you, your RAS will pick it out of thousands of cars you see every day.

Here's another example: my screenplay has caught the interest of quite a few actresses and recording stars. I would never have even heard of some of these women had they not been interested in making this film. When LeAnn Rimes was reading my script to play the lead role, suddenly I couldn't open a magazine or turn on the television without seeing her. Had she not been interested in the film, I would have only noted that she had a hit song or two. But once she was on my radar and my RAS was informed that I was interested in her, I noticed her in hundreds of places.

A very efficient machine, the RAS zeros in on any area of interest. This is whatever is occupying your thoughts: your car, your hobbies, your goals, your success, your limitations, your failures, and so on. If you are constantly thinking about failure, problems, and concerns, your RAS will continually hone in on and bring you more of what you're most interested in. Whether it's failure or success, your RAS will direct the full force of your brain to sort through the clutter and carefully select and guide you to the reality that is consistent with your thoughts. You could be walking down the street, thinking that business is bad all over. You look around and see a GOING OUT OF BUSINESS sign and think, "See, business really is bad." But right next door there is this huge expansion project with lots of new businesses, yet you don't even see it because that's not what you're thinking about. The RAS is a powerful device that most of us don't consciously use.

Harnessing the Power of the RAS

When I go in to help a company that's in trouble, the most powerful thing I do is to get them focused on solutions and setting goals for improving the situation. This shift in focus shows up in the results the company is getting. With everyone devoting at least an hour a week to focusing their RAS on finding solutions and improving the business, solutions begin to appear and the business begins to improve. One way to harness the power of the RAS is to do proactive workshops to get everyone focused on solving the problems instead of focusing on the problems.

Strings into Steel

The truth is that RAS is already fully functioning in your life, helping to create a reality that is in line with your thoughts. Any statement you make to yourself begins in the subconscious as a thread of an idea. Each time you make a statement, the thread gets thicker. Say it to yourself a few more times and the thread turns to string, then rope, then bands of steel that absolutely obey the reality you create.

We all have programmed beliefs about our own limitations. We tell people things like "I can't remember names," "I'm a klutz," "I can't cook," "I can't dance," or "I always mess these things up." When we first said them, they were just a tiny thread, but now that we've said them to ourselves and others hundreds or even thousands of times, imagine how ingrained they've become. We've focused our subconscious on fulfilling our programmed reality of forgetting names, tripping up the stairs or over our dance partner, burning dinner, and messing things up. But what if you believed that you were great at names, extremely coordinated, and a great cook and dancer—and that success came easily to you? If that were your belief system, what activity would your subconscious be working on right now? Creating your success!

A Shortcut

Keeping your mind focused on your success may be difficult at first, but here's a shortcut to help you make the transition. Your mind is more receptive when it is less busy. Right before you go to bed and right when you wake up, you are at your most receptive. That's the best time to really focus your RAS on all the positive things you want in your life. If you picture yourself succeeding or overcoming something at those times, your brain will grab hold of that much easier. If you're about to have a big meeting, picture it exactly as you want it to go. This visualization will stick with you as you enter that meeting and help create the results you want.

It's important to keep your brain working in the present. Tell yourself, "It's a great day today," rather than "I will have a great day today." Or "Success comes to me easily" rather than "Success will come to me easily." This is called autosuggestion. Phrase your goals and desires as if they already exist because then your brain will work on fulfilling them faster for you. If you say you will be a billionaire, the brain says: "Oh, okay. I *will* do it. That means I don't have to do it right now." Instead say, "I *am* a billionaire." Then your brain says: "Oh, wow, I have to make that happen."

Have you ever gone to sleep saying to yourself, "I have to wake up on time tomorrow," and the next morning you wake up right before the alarm goes off? How did your brain know? Think about that. In addition to the billions of calculations per second that our brain makes, it also has a clock that can tell you exactly when to wake up. Or have you ever said to yourself, "I better not oversleep tomorrow," but then you did? Note the difference in the way you say things. With "I have to wake up on time tomorrow," all your brain hears is "Wake up on time tomorrow." Say, "I'd better not oversleep tomorrow," and all your brain hears is "Oversleep tomorrow." So phrasing is important to the subconscious mind. You must state things as if they are already in existence. Tell your RAS exactly what you want and focus on the positive.

Thomas Edison, who invented the lightbulb, the movie camera, and dozens of other ingenious things, said, "Never go to sleep without a request to your subconscious." You can actually pose something to your subconscious as you go to sleep and wake up with the solution in mind. Napoleon Hill wrote that you should "demand" that your subconscious give you the solutions or answers that you desire.

One way to put your subconscious mind to work for you is to create a recording of your own voice that you listen to every night before you go to bed, feeding proactive affirmations into your subconscious. For 12 years, I listened to a tape of my own voice every single night before I went to sleep. I was talking directly to my subconscious and I played the tape when my mind was most receptive. My income doubled for three years in a row.

⚙ Exercise

Create an RAS recording of your own voice using whatever technology you have—cassette, digital recorder, and so on. First, use your favorite relaxing background music to play as you record. Then, talk yourself through some relaxation exercises. Tell yourself to close your eyes and imagine you are in a calm place like a peaceful lake or in a hammock on a sunny day—whatever is a calm image is for you. Tell yourself to relax into that scene and breathe deeply. Count back from 10 to 1, feeling each number relaxing you more and more. This puts your brain into a less active beta mode. This also helps you sleep and close down your mind. Next, state a series of affirmations about yourself and your life. These are all positive beliefs about yourself, who you are, and what you want in your life. Just make sure you state them as if they are already a reality so your brain starts to work on them subconsciously. Here are a few great affirmations for anyone:

- I attract success.
- Success comes to me easily.
- Abundance and prosperity flow to me from every direction.
- It's easy to be successful.
- I only think positive thoughts.
- I'm in perfect health.

Sales Affirmations

In each of my weekly sales meetings, I make every salesperson repeat after me as I give them various affirmations. One of my favorites for salespeople is "I *love* to cold-call in the morning." When I was a sales rep, I wrote those words on a sheet of paper and put it up on the wall in front of me. I would then say them out loud and with great fun in my voice. If you are in sales or run a sales team, there simply is no better affirmation. Cold calling is the toughest activity for most salespeople. Me, I *love* to cold-call in the morning. I suppose it's from years of repeating that affirmation.

Record 10 affirmations that are perfect for you. Remember to keep them positive and in the present. Restate them again and again until the tape ends. I have to say that this is the most powerful thing I've done to climb out of my blue-collar upbringing. Once you've created this recording, listen to it just before you go to sleep every night. Yes, my wife made me put on headphones so she wouldn't have to listen, too.

Using Your RAS in Goal Setting

Goals focus your attention and enforce your brain to attract what you want. Most people spend more time planning a vacation than they do planning a life. But setting goals in every aspect of your life and business puts your RAS to work (on purpose) at attracting great things. This is because the minute you write your goals, you have focused your subconscious on your success and it immediately begins creating that reality. That's why just the act of writing down your goals can make you feel like you have direction in your life. This becomes even more effective when you post them somewhere so you see them and even say them every morning and every night.

I have 27 lifetime goals that are posted on the inside door of my medicine cabinet so I see them every time I reach for the toothpaste. One day I realized how to put five of them together and accomplish all five with just one action. Had I not looked at that list daily, I never would have connected those dots that way. My subconscious was constantly looking for ways to realize those goals as easily as possible.

To get the most out of goal setting, make sure you set incremental goals as well as long-term goals. Your incremental goals should be things that are challenging but that you know you can achieve. This way you make it easier on yourself to stay focused on your success. If you make outrageous goals and never achieve them, then you reinforce your own failure.

Goal-Writing Workshop

Write down the following:

- Five lifetime goals
- Five annual goals

- Desired annual income for the next five years
- Three things you will do each month to improve your life
- Three things you will do each month to improve your company or department
- Three things you will do each month to improve your performance

Post each of these lists in an appropriate location so that you will see them every day. State them as if they already exist: "I make five sales every day." "My business grows by X percent every year."

Answer these questions to create more goals and focus your attention on creating success:

- What three obtainable things do you want from your business/job? Write them as if you already have them.
- What three things will you do with your staff every month to make them more effective?
- What three things will you do to make yourself happier and healthier? How often and when will you do them?

Measuring Effectiveness: Keys to Increasing Performance

Another way to achieve goals quickly is to measure effectiveness every step of the way. If you are constantly measuring effectiveness, then you will be able to quickly and easily adjust when something is not bringing about your desired result.

People *re*spect what you *in*spect. So when I work with companies, we put all kinds of measurement systems into place. Here is a tool that you can duplicate and adapt to specific areas of business where you want to measure the effectiveness of your procedures. This is a sales performance worksheet for a salesperson selling employee benefits and insurance packages to companies.

First I'll show you the pieces of the report broken down and then I'll show you how all of this information fits on a single sheet of paper.

Month/Day	1/21	1/22	1/23	1/24	Totals
Dials	41	27	77	69	214
Presentations:					
CEO/president	8	4	9	5	26
CFO	3	1	3	3	10
Controller	1	0		2	3
Human resources	10	5	10	4	29
Voice mail invites	24	19	43	32	118
Orientations scheduled				4	4
Interested, call back	7	6	10	12	35
Hung up/not int./happy	5	2	6	5	18
Gatekeeper	3	3	3	3	12
Actively looking					
Just changed broker	2	1	3	2	8
Insurance meeting				4	4
Subsidiary	4	3	7	3	17

Across the top it shows how many calls this salesperson made each day—in this case, it was a four-day week. Because he was selling these insurance plans to entire companies, his target contacts were CEOs, CFOs, controllers, and human resources people. As you can see, he got eight CEOs on the telephone the first day and 26 during the week. He also got 10 CFOs, three controllers, and 29 human resources people on the telephone.

But if you look down at the next section of the worksheet, you see he only got four orientations or appointments scheduled out of 214 calls he made. It doesn't sound like much, but this form tracked his Dream 100 effort, so each of the four appointments set were huge companies. Therefore, this was actually a highly successful week.

Notice that he got 35 people who wanted him to call them back, while 21 people hung up on him or told him flat out that they weren't interested. Then there were 12 times that he couldn't get through the gatekeeper at these huge companies. I included "actively looking" as a category because every now and then you get someone who is looking for whatever you sell. This salesperson didn't find any of those this week, but when you do it's a great day. "Just changed broker" is another important and motivating category to track because those are the ones that you might have gotten if you had called just a few months earlier.

Getting appointments wasn't the only objective for this salesperson to achieve with each phone call. Here's the next part of the call report.

Sales Force Updates					
Direct phone number	22	14	19	13	68
Email address	11	4	18	5	38
Fax number	8	3			11
CEO email address	19	8	32	24	83
CFO email address	7	4	9	6	26
Controller email address	3	1	2	3	9
HR director email address	15	14	25	19	73
Insurance meeting		1		4	5
2nd appointment					
3rd appointment					
Summary					
Renewal date	6	2	8	7	23
Broker relationship	9	5	10	9	33

As long as you're going to be on the phone with someone and do all this work, you should capture important data to help target this company even better at every turn. So this salesperson asked questions and collected direct-dial telephone numbers, email addresses, and direct fax numbers as he went, putting more and more information into the database on his dream clients.

As you saw in the first section of the worksheet, this salesperson only got four appointments, but he wasn't going to just give up on everyone who said no or whom he couldn't reach. The next section of the worksheet tracks his follow-up activities.

Follow-up Actions					
Email confirm orient.	2			4	6
Fax confirm orient.					
Fax not interested					
Fax call back			2	1	3
Fax hung up					
Fax John Smith					
Fax delegated					
Email promotion	3	3	2	1	9
Fax promotion	2	1		1	4

For every single call he made there should have been a follow-up action. So, for example, we designed a fax to send when someone hung up on him. Remember that breaking through the clutter, even to get hung up on, now gives you a tiny filament of contact. If.you immediately fax a note, you've strengthened the filament. So a fax should go off immediately that says: "You just hung up on me, but I don't think you understood the significance of my call or you would not have done so. Consider this: [pitch again what they'll learn from the "orientation"]. The second largest expense in your company is the cost of employee benefits. I teach nine different ways to reduce those costs, something I'm sure you would find quite valuable. I will contact you again to give you another opportunity to gain this valuable information."

Have you ever received a note like that when you hung up on someone? It's things like this that make a salesperson stand out in the crowd. And if you keep contacting the people who hung up on you, you will eventually win their respect. After all, you can't possibly respect someone who goes away after the first rejection.

Why a Fax and Not an Email?

Email is too easy to delete. A fax has to be touched and looked at to decide if you want to throw it away. If the fax is short, they'll read it. So keep those faxes short and powerful.

There was also a fax for anyone who asked him to call them back. It basically said:

Dear Kathy,

As you requested when we spoke on the phone today, I will call you back on Friday at 3 PM. At that time we will discuss five important ways you can save money on your insurance while still offering your employees the best in healthcare coverage.

Sincerely,
Tim

Remember that the hardest part of sales is getting their attention in the first place, so once you have it, you need to follow up so well they don't have a chance to forget you. Make sure you include follow-up in your tracking efforts.

Note the other follow-up categories on the worksheet:

- **Fax John Smith**: This means to fax an endorsement letter from John Smith. This endorsement letter says how great your information is that you want to present.

- **Fax delegated**: You got the CEO on the phone and he bunted you to the CFO or HR executive. Send a note saying: "Great speaking to you about the five ways to save money on your company's largest expense, employee benefits. You said you wanted me to talk to Kimberly Bird, so I will contact her immediately."

  Why would you send a letter like this? If you did an even halfway decent job of selling your offer, the CEO will now pass your note on to Kimberly and he may even say, "Kimberly, this sounded interesting." Now you know that Kimberly is going to pay attention when you call.

- **Fax promotion:** This is your standard promotional piece that sells the heck out of the education you want to offer this executive.

- **Fax confirmation of orientation:** How many times have you set a meeting only to have the prospect cool off and cancel or not show? The way to make sure that this doesn't happen is a complete "warm-up program" to keep that executive interested in the meeting. So first, fax a confirmation that is full of sizzle about how great the meeting's information is going to be. Then, a day later, fax (or email at this point) an endorsement letter from someone else who saw the information you're going to show them. As mentioned, the fill-in-the-blank "Worksheet for our meeting" document is a great piece to send. Executives look at the teaser and, if you've done a great job, they'll want to know what they're going to write in those blanks.

This single sales performance document is not just a measuring tool but a management tool. You'll note that this particular salesperson didn't do all the follow-up he should have for the effort he made at the top of the document. So when I received this call sheet, I was able to train and improve the rep's skills based upon the data reported. In many companies, you have sales management software that can make assembling these reports easy. But for small companies without such software, this single sheet can track a week's worth of activity with no trouble at all. Five minutes per day is all reps need to record their activity.

Here's what the entire sheet looks like:

Sales Performance Worksheet

Month/Day	1/21	1/22	1/23	1/24	Totals
Dials	41	27	77	69	214
Contacts:					
CEO/president	8	4	9	5	26
CFO	3	1	3	3	10
Controller	1	0		2	3
Human resources	10	5	10	4	29
Voice mail invites	24	19	43	32	118
Orientations scheduled				4	4
Interested, call back	7	6	10	12	35
Hung up/not int./happy	5	2	6	5	18
Gatekeeper	3	3	3	3	12
Actively looking					
Just changed broker	2	1	3	2	8
Insurance meeting				4	4
Subsidiary	4	3	7	3	17
Sales Force Updates:					
Direct phone number	22	14	19	13	68
Email address	11	4	18	5	38
Fax number	8	3			11
CEO email address	19	8	32	24	83
CFO email address	7	4	9	6	26
Controller email address	3	1	2	3	9
HR director email address	15	14	25	19	73
Insurance meeting		1		4	5
2nd appointment					
3rd appointment					
Summary:					
Renewal date	6	2	8	7	23
Broker relationship	9	5	10	9	33

Follow-up Actions:					
Email confirm orient.	2			4	6
Fax confirm orient.					
Fax not interested					
Fax call back			2	1	3
Fax hung up					
Fax John Smith					
Fax delegated					
Email promotion	3	3	2	1	9
Fax promotion	2	1		1	4

Contests

Another way to measure and increase effectiveness in sales or any other areas of your business is to use contests. My client who has a picture framing business noticed that his best framer was doing two or three times what the other framers were doing. So we took the number that the top framer was doing and added one and then challenged the rest of the framers to beat his performance. We told them that anybody who hits that number in a day with no damage to any of the products gets a bonus for that day. It immediately increased the performance of all of the framers.

This could be applied to anything. Take your top performers and analyze what they are doing. Then procedurize it as much as you can and put a contest in place to give everyone the incentive they need to step up their performance.

Henry Ford used a similar tactic, but he didn't even need to create a reward for the increase in productivity. As Napoleon Hill mentioned in *Think and Grow Rich*, Ford went onto the factory floor with a can of paint and put a large number 6 in the middle of the floor. When the night workers asked what it meant, he told them that it was the number of cars the day crew built. The next morning he came in and learned the night crew had built seven cars. He then painted a 7 over the 6 that had been there. When the day crew asked about it, he told them that that was how many cars the night crew had built. Just by playing the day crew off the night crew, he was able to substantially increase productivity for his factory.

I am using this same method with a sales team I am working with on cold calling. Every two hours we post in the sales room the number of calls each person has made. Every two hours everyone looks up and sees where they stand in terms of productivity and who is ahead or behind them. This creates a natural competitiveness that is also fun. In one week this simple act of posting the numbers has tripled the amount of cold calls this team is making. This company even has a software program that gives them this data at the push of a few keystrokes.

If you're not measuring effectiveness, your organization's productivity is lower than it could be and your goals are further away than they need to be. So create performance worksheets, institute contests, and put the numbers up. Then see what happens in your company or department.

Firing on All Eight Cylinders

As you have learned, the key to success is not about doing 4,000 things but mastering just 12. This book has taken you through the 12 core skill areas that will put you at the top of the market as long as you continue to perfect and systematize those skills with pigheaded focus. With these steps and your determination, there isn't any problem that you cannot overcome. To illustrate this point, here's an example of an impossible situation that was turned around just by doing the 12 things you have learned in this book. I've told small parts of this story already, but it is the ultimate example of everything you have learned about working together to create amazing results.

Billionaire Charlie Munger first hired me to sell advertising for a magazine called *California Lawyer*. At the time, it was the highest-circulating publication for lawyers in that state. But it had only 2 percent of national advertising market share out of 45 competitors, which meant it was all the way down in the number 15 slot. The national lawyer magazines holding the first four slots had so much of the market that everyone else just got scraps.

There were two major challenges I faced in getting national advertisers to advertise with us: First, we were a vertical market publication, meaning we reached only one profession, lawyers. Companies like Xerox, which was front and center in my Dream 100, typically followed a strategy of horizontal marketing. They advertised in magazines like *Business Week* that had a national circulation reaching businesspeople in all fields. They were already reaching doctors, lawyers, dentists, and zookeepers all over the country, so why would they want to spend a lot of money to go into a vertical market publication?

The second biggest challenge was that we were a regional publication. Large companies don't buy advertising in regional vertical publications. Some of those big companies might spend a small part of their budget on vertical markets (doctors, lawyers, architects, etc.), but they surely weren't going to buy into those vertical markets state-by-state when one or two national vertical publications reach lawyers or doctors in all 50 states. From a strategy standpoint, it was a sale that simply couldn't be made.

In fact, many of these big companies had already decided that specific vertical markets were not worth the trouble. An advertiser that had already decided it was not interested in the lawyer vertical market was definitely not interested in *California Lawyer*, no matter what our unique selling proposition was. I could tell them over and over again that we were the highest-circulating magazine for lawyers in California, but was I going to get them to advertise? Never.

Clearly, our unique selling proposition would get us nowhere, so I focused all of my efforts on establishing our other *ultimate strategic position (USP)*. Using each of the 12 core skills you've learned in this book, this is how we outthought the pants off the competition.

First, we went totally generic and offered a presentation called "How to Succeed in the Legal Market" based on all the core story research we had done. The research was amazing. According to the U.S. Census Bureau, lawyers are the largest daily producers of words. They put out more data every day than any other business or profession. This, and their high income and profits, made them an excellent target for technology companies. So the first part of the sale was not to sell our magazine at all, but rather to educate companies on why they need to be interested in the legal market.

But now, even if I were to make the first sale—that of getting large companies to take an interest in the legal field as a fertile vertical market—my regional publication was not a viable place to advertise. If they went in California alone, what kind of thinking would that be?

So the next part of the sale had to give brilliant justification: it had to set the buying criteria. We had all this data on California as "the state that leads the nation." At the time, the average state had 18,000 lawyers, while California had 143,000 lawyers (today California has more than 200,000 lawyers). Huge difference. California led the nation in cutting-edge legal initiatives and thinking. In fact, more precedent-setting law comes out of California than any other state. One third of all the nation's largest corporations house their corporate counsel in California. The data went on and on, effectively showing that if you really want to make it in the legal market, first, you must have a stronger position in California than anywhere else, and next, you could test the legal market in one state before spending larger dollars to go national.

So let's break this down into steps:

- **Step 1:** What is your best possible strategic position? In our case, we established our position as part of a market that was superworthy for them to go after.

- **Step 2:** Next we established our position at the top of that market so they knew that of all the choices they could make to penetrate this market, advertising in our magazine was the most potent.

- **Step 3:** We put all this into an "educational orientation" and made that our first offer to every advertiser.

- **Step 4:** We mounted a Dream 100 effort, where we started hitting the biggest possible advertisers so hard, so frequently, and with so many approaches and offers that they got to know exactly who we were in a very short period of time.

- **Step 5:** I rehearsed the sales staff on that presentation again and again and again. Still, there were those who didn't get the strategy: "Wait. Why would I do all this when all I really want to do is sell advertising?" I took these more tactical executives by the hand, brought them to client meetings, and showed them the awesome power of using market data as a motivator. They caught on pretty quickly at that point.

- **Step 6:** I worked through the time management procedures daily, constantly demanding to-do lists from the staff.

- **Step 7:** I trained the staff on the "Seven Steps to Every Sale" in great detail. I gave spot quizzes, did workshops on every step, and hot-seated the reps on specific accounts and their activities related to the seven steps.

- **Step 8:** I worked the heck out of the follow-up procedures, putting into place more and more opportunities for bonding and building valuable relationships.

- **Step 9:** We worked the trade shows like champions, always being the life of every party and throwing the best parties. Eventually, we started our own trade show for all the advertisers in the industry to come and learn how to market better to attorneys. We designed an award ceremony that celebrated the top executives in the industry and brought them all to a black-tie affair in which we controlled every inch of the experience.

- **Step 10:** We offered many other additional services that gave us unbreakable bonds with our clients. We had a free placement service to help marketing executives get jobs with other advertisers. We gave the entire market the industrywide calendar that every company used for its trade show planning. We designed ads for all our advertisers.

- **Step 11:** We set goals for every area of performance.

- **Step 12:** We measured and tracked every activity and had regular contests and rewards for our top performers.

I use this as a case study even though it was 15 years ago. I don't think my mark remains on this magazine or any of the programs I put into place. It is simply an example of what you can do with a difficult and challenging situation and it's one in which I personally had the freedom to swing the bat and make all these things happen.

It was the Ultimate Sales Machine. We outsold, outmanaged, outstrategized, and outsmarted our competition at every turn. Within one year we doubled sales. Then we doubled that figure again the second year and doubled the already twice-doubled sales figure in the third year. For this, as I explained in Chapter Six, I was called into Charlie Munger's office to hear these words: "Now, Chet, are you sure we're not lying, cheating, and stealing? In all my years, I've never seen anybody double sales three years in a row."

I laughed out loud. "No, Charlie, we're just marketing and selling way better than all our competitors."

And the best part is this: None of it was that hard. The key ingredient, my friends, is pigheaded discipline and determination. If you want to have the Ultimate Sales Machine, you merely focus consistently on the 12 skill areas in the 12 chapters of this book. Here's my promise to you: if you make this book your sales, marketing, and management bible and study it again and again, you'll never need to know anything else to rule your market. That and pigheaded determination.

Notes

1. Knell, Eric. "7 Corporate Red Flags." *Business Finance Magazine*, August 2002. http://www.businessfinancemag.com/magazine/archives/article.html?articleID=13891.

2. www.entrepreneur.com.

3. Tzu, Sun. *The Art of War*. Available from http://classics.mit.edu/Tzu/artwar.html.

4. Finklestein, Ron. *What Successful Businesses Have in Common* (ezine). Entrepreneur.com (cited April 14, 2006). Available from http://www.entrepreneur.com/management/leadership/article83764.html.

5. "Attorney at Law," Wikipedia. Available from http://en.wikipedia.org/w/index.php?title=Attorney_at_law&oldid= 93103058 (accessed December 22, 2006).

6. Nichols, Ralph G. "What Can Be Done About Listening?" *The Supervisor's Notebook*, vol. 22, no. 1 (Spring 1960). http://www.dartmouth.edu/~acskills/docs/10_bad_listening_habits.doc (accessed December 23, 2006).

7. Wiman, R. Y., and W. C. Mierhenry. "Dales Learning Cone of Experience." *Educational Media*, Charles Merrill, 1969.

8. Morton, Jill. *Colors That Sell: Tried and Tested Color Schemes*. Available from http://www.colorvoodoo.com/cvoodoo9_colorsthatsell.html.

9. Waitley, Denis. *Seeds of Greatness: The Ten Best-Kept Secrets of Total Success*. New York: Pocket Books, 1984, pp. 123–25.

Index